D0947279

Deterrence and the Revolution
in Soviet Military Doctrine

Deterrence and the Revolution in Soviet Military Doctrine

RAYMOND L. GARTHOFF

The Brookings Institution | Washington, D. C.

Copyright © 1990 by
THE BROOKINGS INSTITUTION
1775 Massachusetts Avenue, N.W., Washington, D.C. 20036

Library of Congress Cataloging-in-Publication Data
Garthoff, Raymond L.
Deterrence and the revolution in Soviet military doctrine /
Raymond L. Garthoff
p.   cm.
Includes bibliographical references and index.
ISBN 0-8157-3056-X (alk. paper). — ISBN 0-8157-3055-1
(pbk. : alk. paper)
1. Soviet Union—Military policy. 2. Deterrence (Strategy)
3. Nuclear warfare. 4. United States—Military policy. I. Title.
UA770.G28   1990
355.02'17—dc20   90-42576
                                                                      CIP

9 8 7 6 5 4 3 2 1

The paper used in this publication meets the minimum requirements
of the American National Standard for Information Sciences—Per-
manence of Paper for Printed Library Materials, ANSI Z39.48-1984

Typeset in Linotype Walbaum
Composition by World Composition Services
Sterling, Virginia
Printing by R.R. Donnelley and Sons, Co.
Harrisonburg, Virginia

Foreword

THE DRAMATIC CHANGES under way in the Soviet Union and the world compel a reassessment of policies. During the cold war, Western policy was directed at two preeminent objectives: the containment of Soviet expansion and the prevention of war. Nuclear deterrence was seen as the chief means to achieve those objectives. Preventing nuclear war was also a central concern of the Soviet leadership, but deterrence was regarded as only one means to that end. There were important similarities, but also important differences, between the American and Soviet positions.

The first purpose of this book is to examine and explain Soviet thinking on deterrence and the prevention of war from 1945 to 1985. The second objective is to analyze the important "new thinking" in the Soviet Union on these matters in the Gorbachev era and the emerging post-cold-war world from 1985 to 1990. This new thinking is, of course, a moving target, but it provides an important and timely dimension to the book. Finally, the study helps to lay the foundation for rethinking American policy in this new era.

Raymond L. Garthoff, a senior fellow in the Brookings Foreign Policy Studies program, has studied Soviet military and political developments for many years; his pioneering volume on *Soviet Military Doctrine* was published in 1953. He wishes to express his appreciation to those who have in one or more ways contributed to this study, particularly, John D. Steinbruner for his support of the enterprise and his colleagues Richard K. Betts, Bruce G. Blair, and Michael MccGwire for their advice and comments. He also wishes to thank Louise Skillings for typing the manuscript; Vernon Kelley, Todd L. Quinn, and Amy Waychoff for verifying the source references; and Jeanette Morrison for editing the study.

Brookings gratefully acknowledges the financial support of the

Carnegie Corporation of New York, the John D. and Catherine T. MacArthur Foundation, and the Andrew W. Mellon Foundation.

The views expressed are solely those of the author and should not be ascribed to the persons whose assistance is acknowledged above, to the sources of funding support, or to the trustees, officers, or other staff members of the Brookings Institution.

BRUCE K. MACLAURY
President

July 1990
Washington, D.C.

Contents

ix

Deterrence and the Revolution
in Soviet Military Doctrine

Introduction

NO U.S. ADMINISTRATION, and no Soviet leader, has ever wanted a nuclear war or planned to start one. Yet suspicions and fears have made that judgment with respect to the adversary conditional at best and sometimes seriously doubted in both countries. Moreover, many ideological, foreign policy, and military doctrinal statements, and political and military programs and actions, have caused serious concerns about the designs and intentions of the other side. Soviet pursuit of world communist domination, and imperialist determination to stamp out communism, may never have been the actual driving elements of Soviet and U.S. policy, but they did in fact exist at least as aspirations if not as concrete policy goals, and they certainly were taken seriously by the other side, directly affecting policy decisions and actions.

Ideological, geopolitical, and political causes of the confrontation of the two global powers, and their expression by leading exponents of the two socio-political systems in the era since World War II, were quite enough to create a cold war. The intensity and danger of that confrontation, on the one hand, and at the same time the fact that it never moved beyond being a cold war, were both due in large measure to the existence of nuclear and thermonuclear weapons and the development of mutual deterrence.

It is routinely said that the world has been preserved from nuclear war and devastation by nuclear deterrence. That may be true in the sense that limited conventional conflicts could more readily have broken out, and been waged, if nuclear weapons had never existed. But it is doubtful that the world has been, or is today, more secure because nuclear weapons exist. Without them, the ultimate threat of nuclear destruction obviously would not have arisen. Once nuclear weapons existed, on both sides, no doubt the possession of such

1

weapons by the adversary exercised a restraining, deterring, effect. But it remains highly probable that neither the United States nor the Soviet Union would have attacked the other, and less certain but also probable that neither would have taken other military actions so provocative as to have precipitated general war between the two powers and their alliances (assuming such alliances would have come to exist).

If war was unlikely even in the absence of nuclear weapons, and is further deterred by their existence, what is the problem? Why the fear of war, and the perceived need for major military and political efforts to prevent nuclear war?

It is at this point that the perceptions and policies of the United States and the Soviet Union diverge. The United States has focused its attention on military-technical requirements for assuring a military deterrent to dissuade any Soviet leader from seeing potential gain from launching a nuclear attack on the United States or any attack on its allies. A Soviet inclination to attack, unless deterred by countervailing U.S. military power, has often been ascribed, especially at the height of the cold war, but it is also an integral, implicit assumption of the underlying conception of deterrence.

The Soviet leaders, on the other hand, while determined to maintain parity in nuclear retaliatory capability as a deterrent, have framed the security problem more broadly and focused their attention primarily on preventing nuclear war. Dissuasion of U.S. leaders from a deliberate attack, while a necessary cornerstone, has been seen as effectively ensured by maintaining a Soviet nuclear retaliatory capability. Insofar as military factors contribute to the danger of nuclear war the problem is seen in the dynamics of escalation (including accidental or incidental triggering of nuclear war), rather than deliberate decision based on a calculus of advantage. But even this is not the crux of the matter. The problem is seen as essentially political, concerning the motivating causes of war, rather than a fine-tuning of the strategic balance.

In other words, the United States has addressed the problem of preventing war almost exclusively in terms of military capabilities, while the Soviet Union has addressed it primarily in terms of political motivations and intentions. This difference in conception has had important effects on the military doctrines and forces of the two powers. It also has complicated, although it has not prevented, agreements on arms control and reduction. It has clouded mutual perceptions. More fundamentally, the divergence in conceptions of the problem of preventing war has contributed to profound differences in foreign and military policy and complicated efforts to find common ground in dealing with the issue.

Examining these differences in understanding and addressing the problems of nuclear deterrence and the prevention of nuclear war by elucidating the Soviet view is the first objective of this book. The second is to identify important new developments in Soviet security policy and military doctrine stemming from new thinking on the problem of preventing war and measures to address that problem.

The new Soviet thinking on security embraces a reevaluation of the role of military power, recognition that security cannot rest on military deterrence or defense, and acceptance that security must be mutual, that is, must be assured for all (at least all major powers). Security cannot be achieved by any one power at the expense of the security of others. Under present circumstances military forces remain necessary, but a new emphasis on reasonable defense sufficiency reflects a desire not only to minimize the allocation of resources to this task, but also to move beyond deterrence and defense to a system of world security built on a much broader basis.

Soviet military doctrine has been redefined to include pursuing the objective of preventing war, as well as the traditional aim of preparing to wage war. The Soviet Union now seeks parity with the United States at reduced—even "minimum deterrence"—levels, has adopted a defensive military strategy and doctrine, and is reducing and restructuring its force posture to be less threatening to the West and China. Finally, the Soviet strategic concept is being refashioned to facilitate conflict termination, rather than military victory, as the operative objective in case of hostilities.

Awareness of these new developments in Soviet thinking about security and in Soviet military doctrine is important not only for better understanding Soviet policy, but also because of important implications for American policy, discussed in the concluding chapter.

A Note on Sources

The principal sources for this study are statements of Soviet political and military leaders, analysts, and commentators addressing Soviet audiences. In addition to publications and speeches of Soviet leaders and spokesmen, the record of Soviet policy actions and military programs is also an important corroborative source.

For this study, I have had access to some informative and heretofore unavailable authoritative Soviet source materials on military doctrine. In particular, a full file of the General Staff journal *Military Thought (Voyennaya mysl')* was available for the first time in the West. From March 1947 until April 1989, this journal was treated as confidential and given restricted circulation. Each issue carried the imprint "Only for Generals, Admirals, and Officers of the Soviet Army and Navy." Western scholars have had an incomplete file in translation for the years 1963–69 and 1971–73 released by the U.S. government, and a few scattered more recent issues. Since April 1989 the journal has been unrestricted, and since January 1990 open for subscription abroad, but back issues were of course written on the assumption of confidentiality and have not yet been generally released. As will be evident from the frequent citations of this source throughout the book, there has been no discrepancy between what is written in the open and confidential sources. The closed writings, such as *Military Thought*, have often been more fully elaborated, have sometimes been more frank, and have occasionally disclosed important additional data. Mainly, however, the confidential writings validate and expand on the similar statements appearing in openly published military literature. Some other secret military writings, and the secret course materials of the two-year curriculum of the General Staff Academy in the years 1973–75, also used in this study, further elaborate and corroborate open publications on doctrine.

Several additional points need to be made. First, individual statements or even extensive documentation for any particular point take on added significance when they are seen as part of a greater whole. Soviet discussion of "deterrence," "reasonable sufficiency," and "defensive doctrine" can only be fully understood in the wider context of Soviet thinking on security and military doctrine. Second, increasingly since the mid-1980s the greater freedom for individual experience under *glasnost'* (openness) means that particular statements even in authoritative journals do not necessarily reflect official positions or decisions taken. This makes Soviet political and analytical commentary much more interesting than before, and more frank, but also often less easy to evaluate. Third, there nonetheless remains a need to propagate and to explain official thinking and positions. In particular, it is necessary for military doctrine to be authoritatively set forth for guidance of the Soviet military establishment. Finally, the proliferation of official and unofficial contacts and availability of many and sometimes senior officers and officials provide a new source of background for better understanding written sources and other developments. The reliability of such oral statements (and their comprehension and transmittal), however, varies greatly. It is an important new category of source material, but one that requires careful use for many reasons other than the popularly exaggerated concern over deliberate deception.

One small example may illustrate several of these points. In December 1988 Mikhail Gorbachev announced a unilateral reduction of half a million men from the Soviet armed forces. The announcement came as a great surprise to most people in the West, including many professional analysts. Prior to that announcement, such analysts had the following data to go on in assessing the possibility of such a decision: (1) several civilian, academic writers in the Soviet Union had more or less openly advocated a unilateral reduction; (2) several senior military leaders had emphatically rejected the idea of unilateral cuts and taken the civilian commentators to task. Most Western analysts assumed the strongly expressed military objections were more authoritative and outweighed the civilian advocacy. On the other hand, some of us had been told by Soviet counterparts that serious studies of possible unilateral reductions had been commissioned and were under way. The outcome of course made clear, after the fact, what would not have been predictable by those accustomed to credit only published statements by authoritative figures.

In the final analysis, source materials are an essential ingredient but not alone sufficient; they must be interpreted and understood with due attention to historical perspective and political culture, in the present case the overall outlook and objectives of the Soviet leadership.

Chapter One

Deterrence and Prevention of War: American and Soviet Perspectives

---

THROUGHOUT HISTORY, leaders have sought to prevent actual or potential enemies from attacking their countries. This objective has been pursued in a variety of ways. Sometimes leaders have sought to propitiate a political attacker by various forms of appeasement or conciliation. Sometimes they have sought alliances with possible protectors or other potential victims of attack. Sometimes they themselves have engaged in preemptive attack. But one of the most enduring means has been an effort to dissuade a potential attacker by building countervailing strength that would make an attempt to defeat one too costly or uncertain to warrant undertaking. *Si vis pacem, para bellum:* If one wishes peace, prepare for war. This course of action was *deterrence,* no matter that for centuries it existed without benefit of that name or its theoretical elaboration. The nuclear age, however, created an unparalleled danger and unprecedented premium on deterrence of possible attack.

Deterrence, American Style

Deterrence was first articulated by Western leaders in the late 1940s and developed along two lines: a rather simple and basic understanding by most Western political leaders and publics, and a more elaborate, sophisticated—and, for reasons I shall elucidate, questionable—theory. The United States' initial monopoly, and later for some years clear superiority, in nuclear weapons and means of delivery facilitated the acceptance of the idea not only of deterrence, but specifically of nuclear deterrence—in the late 1940s, nuclear deterrence of *non*nuclear attack on friends and allies, the only possible immediate threat of which the Soviet Union was then capable.

6

Nuclear deterrence started as an idea for preventing an attack and thus for preventing war. The U.S. monopoly and then superiority in nuclear weapons, however, soon led policymakers to develop deterrence into a much broader concept. If nuclear weapons could restrain the Soviet Union from direct attack on the United States, could they not also restrain the Soviet Union from attacking other countries? Could not a nuclear deterrent indeed restrain the Soviet Union from undertaking a range of actions short of direct attack on anyone? Deterrence came to signify imposed restraint, including but also broader than prevention of attack and war. Deterrence became a strategy not only for preventing war, but also for enforcing a policy of containment.

"Containment" sought to block Soviet indirect as well as direct aggrandizement, to prevent expansion of Soviet dominion by political, subversive, and other means as well as by military power. The Truman Doctrine placed direct American assistance, and the shadow of the American nuclear deterrent, as a defensive shield to protect Greece and Turkey in 1947. The Marshall Plan relied on economic revitalization of Western Europe. In Korea the United States had to resort to conventional military forces to turn back the North Korean invasion of the south. But containment was also the heart of overall United States policy toward the Soviet Union. And contrary to partisan sniping that it was "merely defensive," containment was defined in the fundamental U.S. national security policy document of the cold war, NSC-68, as a policy designed not only to "block further expansion of Soviet power," but also ("by all means short of war") to "induce a *retraction* of the Kremlin's control and influence . . . to check *and to roll back* the Kremlin's drive for world domination."[1]

As elaborated, American deterrence theory makes a distinction between "deterrence" and "compellence," the former a defensive and the latter an offensive or coercive use of military power, the difference residing not in the forces but in the aim.[2] A Soviet threat to attack the United States, or, in "extended deterrence," its North

1. NSC-68, "United States Objectives and Programs for National Security," in *Foreign Relations of the United States 1950*, vol. 1: *National Security Affairs, Foreign Economic Policy* (Washington: Department of State, 1977), pp. 252–53, 283–84; emphasis added. (Hereafter *FRUS 1950*, vol. 1.)

2. The classical elaboration of deterrence, and distinction from compellence, are found in Thomas C. Schelling, *Arms and Influence* (Yale University Press, 1966), pp. 69–91. For the seminal development of gradations of extended deterrence, see Herman Kahn, *On Thermonuclear War* (Princeton University Press, 1960).

Atlantic Treaty Organization (NATO) allies, would be warded off by deterrence; a use of the same military power, for example, to force Soviet withdrawal from Eastern Europe would be compellence. Deterrence theory thus rests on a difference in one's intentions, not capabilities.

One of the inherent shortcomings of classical deterrence theory is that deterrence depends upon perceptions of the putative aggressor, yet these perceptions must relate to intentions, while military planning theory and threat assessment rely on capabilities more than intentions.

Although archetypal illustrations of a distinction between deterrence and compellence are easy, in the real world one side's efforts at what it regards as defensive deterrence are often perceived by the other as attempts at coercive compellence. Nor, for that matter, has the distinction always been clear in United States policy. NSC-68 even defined containment as "a policy of calculated and gradual coercion," and the aims of U.S. policy on which the 1950 "security programs and strategic plans" were based included as first priority not simply to prevent an attack and war, but "to *reduce* the power and influence of the USSR to limits which no longer constitute a threat to the peace" and "to create situations which will *compel* the Soviet Government to recognize the practical undesirability of acting on the basis of its present concepts."[3] The essence of the containment doctrine was not just to hold a line, as often popularly construed, but as repeatedly stated in NSC-68 to "frustrate the Kremlin design" for "world domination," both by preventing expansionist thrusts *and* by weakening Soviet power in the USSR as well, to "foster the seeds of destruction within the Soviet system."[4]

In sum, while deterrence originated in American thinking as an idea of preventing hostile attack and war, given the American perception of the adversary, and the clout of the American nuclear monopoly and superiority, it became a strategy for containment with coercive overtones. It also became, in time, a concept for crisis management and even management of foreign policy—the basis for alliances, and then for alliance strategy. Finally, it became a source of guidance for military requirements, for example, ensuring survivability of retaliatory strategic forces. Unfortunately, it also became a

3. *FRUS 1950*, vol. 1, pp. 253, 289–90; emphasis added.
4. Ibid., pp. 290, 252.

justification for almost any desired military program, as virtually any increment in military strength could loosely be claimed to "enhance deterrence."

Deterrence also came to affect military requirements and programs in several critical but little appreciated ways. First, it tended to displace identification of *the objective* as the key starting point for military plans and programs, subtly replacing it with a statement of *the threat* and moreover a threat denominated in terms of the military capabilities of the putative enemy. This switch distorted the relationship between objectives and means by positing a predetermined assumed objective. Paradoxically, it thus reversed the logical basis for deterrence by basing military requirements to meet (deter) the threat on military capabilities rather than political intentions. Moreover, to meet military planning requirements, maximal or worst-case existing and future capabilities have been posited, and the uncertainties and unprovabilities of intentions similarly reduced to worst-case possibilities.[5]

A related effect of deterrence dominating military strategy is the replacement of political-military analysis with a fixation on technical military capabilities for deterrence. Instead of relating military means to political objectives, and thinking in terms of concrete political-military situations, deterrence-dominated "strategic" analysis has reduced military requirements to meeting technical criteria for, essentially, a war of machines rather than political adversaries. Prudent consideration of such criteria as survivability of retaliatory forces have become laden with unrealistic "scenarios" of intricate reciprocal nuclear counterforce campaigns, while peoples and political leaders are passive observers and ultimate victims. Keying military force to such scenarios with a single-minded dedication to ensuring the credibility of deterrence produces incredible results. For example, a large and varied arsenal to destroy reinforced, high-priority targets ("prompt hard-target kill capability") may strengthen doubts in a potential attacker that he could survive retaliation. But that same force may persuade an adversary that its purpose is not to deter him from an attack (particularly if he is not contemplating making such an attack), but to deprive him of a retaliatory deterrent, that is, to neutralize *his* deterrent. Conceivably, it could even lead him to make

5. See Raymond L. Garthoff, "Worst-Case Assumptions: Uses, Abuses and Consequences," in Gwyn Prins, ed., *The Nuclear Crisis Reader* (Vintage Books, 1984), pp. 98–108.

an attack that he had not otherwise intended—thus undermining deterrence of an attack rather than reinforcing it, and causing war rather than preventing it.

Deterrence theory also came to rely basically on game theory, abstracted from political-military realities and assuming "rational actor" adversaries bent on maximizing (optimizing) power in a zero-sum game in which gains for one side are at the expense of the other, and in which decisions on war and peace are ultimately mathematical rather than political. In a given scenario, the roles of the deterrence game required attack (or surrender) unless a deterrent "balance" were maintained. Thus if one permitted a military balance in strategic nuclear forces to become technically "threatening" to the other side, the latter would be induced to strike first rather than lose by waiting for a (putative) attack. There is a role for technical gaming in military planning, and in some cases in military force programming, but not as the central element in political-military strategy. War is not a game, nor is politics.[6]

Deterrence began to supplant and absorb strategy. To be sure, particularly in the strategic nuclear field, with the attainment of substantial nuclear forces by both the United States and the Soviet Union in the 1960s (even before parity was established in the 1970s), strategy—the application of military force to achieve political aims—became even less relevant. That perhaps encouraged analysts and policymakers to substitute deterrence theory for strategy. But it did not justify it. Deterrence theory originally ensured retribution to an attacker as a means of dissuading him from attack. Later theorists broadened it to deny a potential attacker the capability to succeed in an attack—posing much more demanding requirements, and thus "justifying" much larger and more capable military forces. "Deterrence by denial," indeed, called for a superior war-fighting capability, while "deterrence by punishment" required only an assured retaliation capability.[7] Moreover, the choice was not presented as a matter of preference. Since deterrence was essentially a political and psychological matter, if an adversary believed in deterrence by denial

6. For a thoughtful argument along these lines, see Michael MccGwire, "Deterrence: The Problem–Not the Solution," in *International Affairs*, vol. 62 (Winter 1985–86), pp. 55–70; reprinted in Roman Kolkowicz, ed., *Dilemmas of Nuclear Strategy* (London: Frank Kass, 1987), pp. 25–42.

7. For an early discussion of deterrence by denial vs. punishment, see Glenn Herald Snyder, *Deterrence and Defense: Toward a Theory of National Defense* (Princeton University Press, 1961).

and sought a war-fighting capability, he could only be deterred by one's own possession of a war-waging and war-winning capability. And American advocates of such a capability asserted that the Soviet Union held such a view and pursued such a strategy, so that the United States must possess such a capability in the interests of "deterrence."

Deterrence also, to a surprising degree, has supplanted foreign policy. Military strategic and deterrence considerations have led the United States in many cases to give priority to military basing and alliance relationships over other policy objectives: support of democracy, protection of human rights, nuclear nonproliferation, and others. "Extended deterrence" not only concerns protection of our key allies in NATO, Japan, South Korea, and other areas, but also has come to be interpreted as justifying American involvement in support of anticommunist insurgencies in Afghanistan, Angola, Nicaragua, and elsewhere. Deterrence is "extended" not only geographically to protect allies from attack, but also politically to deter so-called proxy attacks, and to "deter" support for insurgencies in other countries and even internal consolidation of communist control within such countries. In short, the American policy of containment on the periphery of the "Sino-Soviet bloc" in the 1950s and 1960s, and again under the Reagan Doctrine "roll-back" on the periphery of Soviet political influence in the 1980s, was couched in terms of deterring not only Soviet third-world efforts to expand its influence, but also presumed Soviet proxy (for example, Chinese, North Korean, Cuban, Nicaraguan, Angolan, Ethiopian, and Vietnamese) direct and indirect "expansion" and even consolidation.

The heart of deterrence, however, remains nuclear deterrence of nuclear war. The strongest argument in its favor to many is the contention that deterrence has kept the peace (between the United States and the Soviet Union, and in Europe) for nearly fifty years. This is, however, an unverifiable proposition. While there obviously has been no nuclear or direct East-West war, whether or to what extent that outcome is the product of deterrence is undeterminable. It is, nonetheless, widely believed. It is also probably not true. A deterrent provides a disincentive, but deliberate attack requires a strong incentive that probably neither side has had. While many in the West believed in the late 1940s and 1950s that the Soviet Union was disposed to attack the West unless deterred by American nuclear weapons, few believe that is the case today, and many who look back on the history of the cold war now believe it not to have been true at any time.

To whatever extent a temptation to attack was countered, peace has almost certainly been due to the fear of nuclear war rather than of the particular nuclear deterrent forces of the other side. An "existential deterrence," as argued by McGeorge Bundy and some others, has sufficed without the calculated triads of nuclear forces capable of "prevailing" in second or third nuclear "exchanges" built up in accordance with deterrence theory. In short, "minimum deterrent" nuclear capabilities on both sides have sustained any disincentives to deliberate attack that may have been needed. This proposition is not, of course, provable. It is, however, supported by what one can glean from the closest moments in history, such as the American leaders' calculations in the Cuban missile crisis. President John F. Kennedy decided to refrain from actions in Cuba far, far less risky or problematic than launching an attack on the Soviet Union, notwithstanding the enormous U.S. nuclear superiority, simply because of the possibility that a chain of events might lead to a nuclear war in which even a few nuclear weapons would strike American cities. He was "deterred" from exploiting U.S. superiority, which, in accordance with deterrence theory, he should have done, by the prospect of *any* nuclear war.[8]

American grand strategy has nonetheless been defined, refined, and redefined in terms of deterrence. "Massive retaliation" in the 1950s gave way to "flexible response" (graduated deterrence) in the 1960s (and then to variants of the latter, in "realistic deterrence" in the 1970s, and an abortive attempt to articulate "discriminate deterrence" in the 1980s).

The next strongest argument for a deterrence strategy is that even if probably not needed, it is useful (or essential) insurance for whatever slight risk of enemy attack exists. This argument may well justify maintenance of a moderate-sized survivable nuclear retaliatory capability beyond a truly minimum deterrent—say, a few hundred to a few thousand warheads. It can of course be used to justify and build up larger forces—and indeed has been used to justify well

<hr/>

8. See McGeorge Bundy, *Danger and Survival: Choices about the Bomb in the First Fifty Years* (Random House, 1988), pp. 445–53; Robert S. McNamara, *Blundering into Disaster: Surviving the First Century of the Nuclear Age* (Pantheon Books, 1986), pp. 44–45; and Raymond L. Garthoff, *Reflections on the Cuban Missile Crisis*, rev. ed. (Brookings, 1989), pp. 186–88.

above ten thousand warheads. But the essence of the matter is not quantitative, but qualitative.

Nuclear deterrence was conceived, and is still generally regarded, as the answer to the problem of preventing nuclear war by dissuading a potential attacker from striking. Under some circumstances, it may do that. But it is by no means a free insurance policy. And the costs at least of a "maximum deterrent" strategy such as the one the United States has followed may not only be great, but may include an *increase* in the danger of nuclear war, rather than a greater assurance of its prevention.

Since the mid-1950s, when the ephemeral American monopoly on strategic nuclear weapons ended, nuclear deterrence has been mutual. A situation of mutual deterrence in theory is basically stable, that is, both sides gain by deterring possible deliberate enemy attacks. But in practice maintaining a mutual deterrent balance tends to engender instabilities. First, it encourages a continuing arms race, especially if one or both sides are not satisfied to accept mutual deterrence, but even if both do. The continuing advances of military technology stimulate weapons and other military system improvements, and each side seeks to hedge, to meet and anticipate new steps by the other, as well as to get advantage. Thus it is not an unalloyed benefit.

Second, deterrence focuses on dissuasion from deliberate attack, while the main problem may not be one of adding disincentives to a choice to attack; certainly that is not the *only* danger. For example, a crisis situation posing a threat and perception of unavoidable war is probably the most crucial danger, yet it can be adversely prejudiced by excessive attention to deterrence requirements. If either side ever believed the other to be imminently and irrevocably about to launch an attack, the choice between a preemptive strike and maximum readiness for prompt retaliation would be made by a judgment about the certainty of the indicators. Deterrence-generated calculations of whether there would be a net gain from a deliberate choice of attack would be completely irrelevant. The incentive to attack preemptively, whether acted on or not, would exist regardless of assured retaliation or of relative capabilities or even relative expected outcomes.

Third, deterrence as the dominant strategic factor in programming the procurement of military force negatively affects tension and the risk of war. Pursuit of "deterrent" capabilities (beyond a minimum deterrent retaliatory force) often adversely affects the other side's assessment of one's intentions. All military capabilities acquired for deterrent effect also have compellent potential, and virtually all make putative contributions to a first-strike capability—including active and even passive defense (for example, SDI and civil defense), because to whatever extent they are effective they can mitigate the impact of the other side's retaliation after the launch of a first strike. Indeed they are bound to be relatively more effective in that circumstance than in a defensive retaliatory scenario (even if real effectiveness remains low for both), and tend therefore to be seen by the adversary as reflecting an aggressive intent.

Fourth, extended deterrence and especially associated strategies of "escalation dominance" engender perceptions of an offensive or compellent threat and thus stimulate the arms competition and raise tension. Counterforce and limited war-waging force postures and doctrines, even if intended to bolster deterrence, arouse deep fear and suspicion of a desire to wage a limited nuclear war—for example, the Soviet reaction to the Schlesinger Doctrine, the Carter administration's Presidential Directive 59 (PD-59), and the Reagan military buildup along similar lines. Adoption of the pursuit of a war-waging and implicitly war-winning strategy and force posture, justified as a stronger deterrent, thus ensures continuing military competition and may even undercut deterrence.

Finally, a fixation on military deterrence and priority to it as the chosen strategy prejudices and often forecloses other means of reducing the risk of war and preventing war either as alternatives or supplements to deterrence. (This effect is, of course, recognized as negative only if these other means to prevent war are themselves recognized.) Deterrence theory by its very nature, irrespective of the actual threat, focuses on worst-case threats. It thus cultivates and perpetuates an adversary relationship and makes it harder to move toward preferable, less-threatening relationships.

Ultimately, the value of a deterrence policy and strategy depends upon four variables: the existence and nature of a threat of potential attack, the ability to maintain an effective retaliatory capability as a credible deterrent to attack, the balance of risks between a deliberate attack and other ways in which war could come about, and the balance between measures intended to deter deliberate attack and other measures to prevent war. The American debate over deterrence has focused almost entirely on the second point, retaliatory capability, with greater intensity when the threat seemed high but with little change in dedication to deterrence even when the threat was perceived to have declined, since the "capabilities threat" (to both sides) has never diminished. Professionals in national security circles have recognized that war could arise from other than deliberate attack and have given some attention to measures to reduce such possibilities. The United States and the Soviet Union have even negotiated some measures (the Hot Line and Risk Reduction Centers; efforts at nuclear nonproliferation). There has not, however, been adequate recognition of the interrelation between desired deterrent effects and undesirable tension and arms competition effects of measures pursued in the name of deterrence. And above all, there has been virtually no serious recognition of the need to maintain a balance of measures designed to deter an attack and those needed to prevent war from causes other than calculated gain.

While Western concepts of deterrence were not unreasonably (if not soundly) based on a perceived threat of attack by Stalin's Russia in the late 1940s and early 1950s, deterrence has been accepted ever since with little real reevaluation of the threat of attack; instead, it has become an unchallenged end in itself. One reason is that it has provided a widely accepted consensus rationale for political-military alliance and military planning programs. As noted, almost any program can be "justified" as a "contribution to deterrence." Another reason, as noted, is that the elasticity of the concept tempts policymakers to apply it to dissuade not just direct attack on one's self or one's allies, but also other undesired behavior. Finally, much that is done in the name of *deterrence* of a potential adversary is really done to provide *reassurance* to our allies and ourselves.[9]

While deterrence may insure against even an unlikely threat of attack, and reassure allies, it may also provide grounds for an adversary to see himself not as "deterred" from actions he may in any event not have planned or even contemplated, but as threatened by intimidation, coercion, and even attack. This has been the Soviet reaction to Western deterrence and containment strategies. But before examining Soviet perceptions of and reactions to Western deter-

9. Michael Howard first drew the attention of a wide audience to this phenomenon in a celebrated article in 1982. See Michael Howard, "Reassurance and Deterrence: Western Defense in the 1980s," *Foreign Affairs*, vol. 61 (Winter 1982–83), pp. 309–24.

rence doctrine, it is useful to look at Soviet concepts of deterrence and the prevention of war.

Prevention of War, Soviet Style

In contrast to the American focus on deterrence as the essence of strategy and policy, successive Soviet leaders have reacted to the nuclear age by adjustments of strategy, policy, and even ideology to give highest priority to preventing war. Deterrence is part of the war prevention strategy but by no means equated with it, nor dominating all other considerations. Nuclear deterrence has been seen as a means rather than an end, and not the ideal or most effective means. Soviet leaders regard it as necessary for the present, but not a preferable or even satisfactory long-term solution to the problem of preventing nuclear war. And that is the objective.

History spared the Soviet Union a choice of nuclear deterrence in the first decade of the nuclear, postwar, cold war world. While the first Soviet nuclear weapons test occurred in August 1949, four years after the first American use of the weapon, it was not until 1954 that the first nuclear weapons were available to the Soviet armed forces, and no real delivery capability or stockpile of weapons existed for several more years. In short, for some years the Soviet Union simply could not rely on nuclear deterrence because it had no nuclear weapons. But the United States did.

The Soviet strategy for averting war was mainly political. First, assessments of the threat were basically political. Stalin and other Soviet leaders considered the Americans and British adversaries but not bent on military conquest as Hitler had been. Soviet foreign policy involved a continuing series of probes to see how far other Soviet objectives could be pursued safely, without provoking a risk of war. Stalin made a few miscalculations, notably in letting the North Koreans move to pick up the south when the United States had apparently written it off, and in believing the Western powers would under pressure leave West Berlin. But he always left room for retreat, as over Berlin. He consolidated his control where he could in Eastern Europe but did not press elsewhere.[10]

10. Stalin tested Western resolve in the northern Iran case in 1946, and in attempting to pressure Turkey for concessions in the same year, but at the same time he withdrew promptly from northern Norway, Bornholm Island, and Manchuria. He

Stalin also probably believed that his actions would be seen as nonprovocative. Not one Soviet soldier moved *forward* from positions of presence at the end of the war. While the Soviets froze the Western powers out in Eastern Europe, they were at the same time frozen out by the Western powers in Japan and Italy. And the massive Red Army of 1945 was largely demobilized by 1948, though the ground forces not so precipitously or completely as those of the United States.[11]

The Soviet leaders—in the key postwar years this means above all Stalin—did share the traditional view that military power tends to deter military attack, though with the painful lesson of 1941 that it is not always a reliable instrument. In the early postwar period the Soviet Union had to rely on a nonnuclear military posture. They may have believed that if war came they could seize Western Europe, but this is not certain.[12] The idea that this capability was an interim

tested the waters and succeeded without direct intervention in Czechoslovakia in 1948, but drew back when a similar intended coup in Finland was aborted that same year. He did not support the Greek communists actively, and refused to support Tito's demands for Trieste. He gave no support to the wave of communist guerrilla wars in the late 1940s in southeast Asia, all of which (Malaya, Indonesia, Burma, the Philippines) except Vietnam failed. China of course was also a communist victory in an indigenous civil war.

11. Contrary to the common assumption, at peak wartime strength the Soviet Union had fewer personnel in uniform than did the United States. The Soviet armed forces in mid-1945 numbered some 11,365,000—as compared with some 12,123,000 for the United States. By 1947–48 the Soviet armed forces were down to 2,874,000 and the U.S. armed forces to 1,446,000. "Report of Comrade N. S. Khrushchev at the Session of the Supreme Soviet of the USSR," *Pravda*, January 15, 1960, p. 3; and Office of Assistant Secretary of Defense (Comptroller), *National Defense Budget Estimates for FY 1988–89* (Washington: Department of Defense, May 1987), p. 126.

12. The only Soviet operational war plan from this period that has been declassified, one for the Soviet occupation forces in East Germany in 1946–48, provided for defensive operations on East German territory. While the declassified plan, published in the *Journal of Military History* of the Ministry of Defense in February 1989, conceivably may have been fabricated, that does not appear to be the case. It is also conceivable that it was accompanied by an alternative *offensive* plan, not declassified. On balance, however, it is more likely that the only Soviet war plan for central Europe in the latter 1940s would have been defensive. The plan, dated November 5, 1946, to take effect on January 1, 1947, was in a folder dated August 1948, implying its effectiveness at least until that time.

The "Operational Plan for Actions of the Group of Soviet Occupation Forces in Germany" was said to have been prepared in conjunction with an overall defensive "Plan for Active Defense of the Territory of the Soviet Union" prepared in late 1946 and early 1947. That plan has not been declassified, but a summary of its coverage indicates defensive missions for the Soviet navy and air forces, as well as ground forces. Although the text has not been released, it is highly likely that any Soviet

Soviet counterpart to the American nuclear deterrent is an American projection. While an occupation of Western Europe probably was the Soviet contingent strategy for war in Europe, it was probably not a calculated deterrence strategy.[13] Stalin did not believe war was likely in the near run, and was determined to manage Soviet foreign policy so that war would not occur. Soviet military policy also made a premium of secrecy, partly to contribute to deterrence, although largely to conceal weaknesses rather than strengths. Stalin of course pressed to obtain nuclear weapons as soon as possible, accelerating an existing Soviet program in 1945; the first test of an atomic bomb

---

general war plan in the late 1940s would have been defensive if only because of the near absence of long-range, offensive air and naval power.

See "The Secret Stamp Removed—Whence the Threat," *Voyenno-istoricheskii zhurnal* (Journal of Military History), no. 2 (February 1989), pp. 24–30. The original plan was classified "Top Secret–Special Importance," and has only recently been declassified by the General Staff.

13. No Soviet war plans from the period after 1948 have been declassified or even described. The only relevant discussion of which I am aware was a statement in the confidential General Staff journal *Military Thought* in 1950 that sought to reassure Soviet officers. The author, Major General V. Khlopov, said that despite American strategic striking power and plans for its use against the Soviet Union, there was a fatal flaw in the assumptions underlying such plans: that the NATO "coalition army" in Europe could "in the initial period of the war successfully hold enemy [Soviet] troops and gain time for the transfer of forces and material across the ocean." General Khlopov said under "real conditions" the Soviet forces would have greater air capabilities "to disrupt and destroy the transfer and concentration of troops," and ground forces capable of deploying "powerful offensive operations on a large scale and with a high tempo of advance," so that "the bridgehead on which the American militarists count to concentrate and deploy their forces for land engagements will be liquidated, and their plans for [winning] the war will be buried with it." See Maj. Gen. V. Khlopov, "On the Character of the Military Doctrine of American Imperialism," *Voyennaya mysl'* (Military Thought), no. 6 (June 1950), pp. 75–76. This unique discussion of a Soviet strategic concept for sweeping over NATO on the central front before American reinforcement could arrive was not a description of a deterrent, indeed it was thought by the author *not* to be serving as a deterrent, but was depicted as a defensive counter by offensive operations if an American-led NATO attack occurred.

To my knowledge, no Soviet source has ascribed a deterrent role to Soviet military deployments in Europe. The one statement that has sometimes been considered in U.S. government circles to support that interpretation does not seem to me to do so. In June 1965 Marshal of the Tank Troops Pavel Rotmistrov told an American military attaché in conversation at a diplomatic reception in Moscow that the Soviets were gradually acquiring a nuclear deterrent to match the American one, and would continue to maintain a capability to overrun Europe in sixty to ninety days in either a nuclear or nonnuclear war because the Soviet Union was a continental power. That statement, which I have closely paraphrased from a declassified excerpt of the attaché's report, suggests to me that Rotmistrov was saying not that a Soviet offensive westward had been an interim deterrent, but rather that it had been and remained a Soviet strategic concept for action in the event of war.

took place on August 29, 1949. By the time of Stalin's death in March 1953, however, nuclear weapons were not yet integrated into Soviet forces or Soviet military doctrine (see chapter 3).

Nuclear deterrence came into its own in Soviet policy consideration only with Stalin's successors, from the mid-1950s in theory, the mid-1960s in interim real capability, and the early or mid-1970s in terms of rough parity. Paradoxically, the only period in which the Soviets claimed superiority and brandished their nuclear weaponry for political pressure was at the time of greatest relative weakness, in the late 1950s and early 1960s. With his penchant for political bluff, Khrushchev concealed real weakness by deceptively exaggerating Soviet missile strength. From Suez in November 1956 to the Cuban missile crisis in October 1962, the Soviets sought to parlay an impression of nuclear missile capability into a deterrent and even a political compellent. This policy had some success from late 1957, after the Soviet lead in testing ICBMs was confirmed by launch of the first artificial earth satellite (*sputnik*), until late 1961, when the United States punctured the fictitious "missile gap" cultivated by Khrushchev and abetted by American fears.[14] After the collapse of the Soviet efforts of 1958–62 to compel a Western withdrawal from West Berlin, and the Soviet failure in its attempt to emplace intermediate-range missiles in Cuba in 1962, the Soviets abandoned efforts to derive political dividends from marginal nuclear capability. Even as they built up real nuclear forces in the 1960s and 1970s and maintained parity in the 1980s buttressing nuclear deterrence, they never again attempted to flourish their nuclear power for compellent political purposes (some misguided Western concerns over possible political intimidation by the SS-20 notwithstanding).[15] The Soviet

14. See Arnold L. Horelick and Myron Rush, *Strategic Power and Soviet Foreign Policy* (University of Chicago Press, 1965), pp. 35–156.

15. See Raymond L. Garthoff, *Détente and Confrontation: American–Soviet Relations from Nixon to Reagan* (Brookings, 1985), pp. 870–86.

The Soviet SS-20 force replaced obsolete intermediate-range missile systems deployed in the late 1950s and early 1960s, and was intended primarily to deter NATO escalation of any hostilities to the level of theater nuclear weapons, and if such escalation nonetheless occurred to overmatch it militarily. If the Soviet leaders had intended to use this capability politically to "decouple" Europe from its U.S. nuclear deterrent, they would not have consistently and vehemently insisted that any use of nuclear weapons could not remain limited. The Soviets opposed decoupling. They were not seeking to free their own hands for limited nuclear war or political threats of such war; rather, their interest was to dissuade the United States and NATO from believing the West could wage such war. See the discussion in chapter 3.

Union, never having enjoyed the luxury of nuclear superiority, was less inclined than the United States to be tempted by the prospect of expanding nuclear deterrence into compellence. Even Khrushchev's posturing was not a real exception, and its failure did not encourage further attempts.

The Soviets expected (or at least hoped) their nuclear deterrent would stretch to extended deterrence protection of the contiguous countries of the Warsaw Pact in Europe, but not beyond. The one Soviet attempt to expand its nuclear deterrent to Cuba, not by accepting Cuba into the Pact but by deploying Soviet missiles in Cuba, suffered so sharp a rebuff as to discourage any repetition.[16] Indeed, in the wake of the Cuban missile crisis the Soviets redefined their implied commitment by revising a passage in the volume *Military Strategy* edited by Marshal Sokolovsky that had said that "in the event the imperialists unleash war against the USSR or any other socialist state such a war *will inevitably* assume the nature of a world war," to state only that "such a war *might* assume" the nature of a world war, that is, involve the Soviet Union and the United States directly.[17]

In the 1970s the Soviet leadership did harbor expectations that as a consequence of Soviet attainment of nuclear parity the United States would be more restrained from using its conventional military power in the third world. This expectation was vaguely reflected in political and military pronouncements as the "external role" of Soviet military force—not a direct or interventionary role, as misinterpreted by some Western observers, but a generally passive and existentially "counterdeterrent" role in neutralizing American intervention.[18]

The defense minister, Marshal Andrei Grechko, made the most authoritative statement on this subject in a 1975 revision of his principal book written only a year earlier. To a brief discussion of

16. Khrushchev's attempt to deploy missiles in Cuba exposed the Soviet need for an interim bolster to the Soviet deterrent, substituting forward-based intermediate-range missiles for lacking ICBMs, and its failure not only denied this deterrent but bore impressive witness to the American superiority that compelled the capitulation. See Garthoff, *Reflections on the Cuban Missile Crisis*, for a full discussion of the crisis.

17. Marshal V. D. Sokolovsky, ed., *Voyennaya strategiya* (Military Strategy), 1st ed. (Moscow: Voyenizdat, to press May 24, 1962), p. 237; and 2d ed. (to press August 30, 1963), p. 258; emphasis added.

18. See Garthoff, *Détente and Confrontation*, pp. 683–87.

the "external function" of the Soviet armed forces was added a sentence declaring their direct and extended deterrent function: "The combat strength of the armed forces of the fraternal socialist states deters reactionary circles of imperialism from unleashing a new world war and new local military conflicts."[19] But when the United States did not act accordingly, the Soviets simply lowered their expectations and dropped the rhetorical reflections of them.[20] Thus, for example, Grechko's successor, Marshal Dmitry Ustinov, wrote in 1977 that the Soviet and other socialist armed forces merely "deter the aggressive aspirations of imperialist circles, hinder their attempts to turn back the wheel of history." And even that passage was revised by 1979 in a reprinting of the article to make it applicable only to direct deterrence of attack on the Soviet Union, speaking only of the function of the Soviet armed forces "to defend the socialist homeland from imperialist aggressors."[21]

It is significant that statements about Soviet nuclear deterrence

19. Marshal A. A. Grechko, *Vooruzhennyye sily Sovetskogo gosudarstva* (The Armed Forces of the Soviet State) (Moscow: Voyenizdat), 1st ed. (1974), p. 120; and 2d ed. (1975), pp. 127–28.

20. The one exception in Soviet behavior, in the eyes of some in the West, really was not: the frantic Soviet efforts in the October 1973 war to get the United States to help bring Israel into conformity with the accepted ceasefire in the Sinai. Although the United States for its own purposes chose to escalate the issue into a global nuclear alert, the Soviet Union limited its "nuclear signaling" to a noncommittal deterrent warning not to the United States, but to Israel, whose own unacknowledged nuclear capability was appreciated by the Soviet leaders. It was not in the interests of any of the powers involved to draw attention to this element in the complex diplomatic interplay of the crisis, and it has not yet been publicly discussed. See Garthoff, *Détente and Confrontation*, pp. 368–85.

The Soviet nuclear "signal" was the passage of a Soviet ship with readily detectable radiating material, presumably nuclear weapons, on board through the Turkish straits on October 22. The United States, and no doubt Israel, quickly became aware of this as the Soviets undoubtedly anticipated. (If they had wished to transport nuclear warheads to Egypt secretly, they could have sent them by transport aircraft.) See Yona Bandmann and Yishai Cordova, "The Soviet Nuclear Threat towards the Close of the Yom Kippur War," *Jerusalem Journal of International Relations*, vol. 5, no. 1 (1980), pp. 94–110. While interpreted as a veiled threat to provide nuclear warheads for Egyptian SCUD missiles as a deterrent to an Israeli advance on Cairo, this action may also have been intended as a Soviet deterrent to any Israeli use of its own nuclear weapons, which the United States—and undoubtedly the Soviet Union—were aware had been dispersed from their Dimona storage facility to operating air bases in an unprecedented action.

21. Marshal D. F. Ustinov, "On Guard over Peaceful Labor, Bulwark of Universal Peace," *Kommunist*, no. 3 (February 1977), p. 13; and Marshal D. F. Ustinov, *Izbrannyye rechi i stat'i* (Selected Speeches and Articles) (Moscow: Politizdat, 1979), p. 314.

by political and military leaders throughout the whole period since the mid-1950s have all referred to the effect of Soviet nuclear military power in "deterring" Western (imperialist, American) *attack*, or inclinations or designs to attack. Deterrence (*sderzhivaniye*) is seen as dissuading an enemy from a decision to attack as a result of one's acquisition of a capability to retaliate with devastating effect. The term used to describe this capability is, literally, "factor of deterrence," or more simply "deterrent" (*sderzhivayushchii faktor*).

Deterrence is not, however, described or treated as a political-military doctrine or strategy, as it is in the West. Soviet military writings contrast Soviet and American concepts of defense (including deterrence). Major General Stepan Tyushkevich, writing in *Military Thought* in 1989, noted: "Our conception of defense does not coincide with the views of American political and military figures. It is related to the defense of the territory and sovereignty of the Soviet Union and its [Warsaw Pact] allies, and has nothing in common with pretensions to world hegemony or obtaining unilateral advantages. The notions of the Americans are essentially different: for them, defense of the United States is not only protection of the territory of the country, but also of their interests in various regions of the globe, often thousands of kilometers from the border of the United States."[22] To some extent this may reflect the fact that the Soviet Union does not have far-flung interests and strategic assets. Nonetheless, instead of avowing parity in rights to such global interests, as was done in the 1970s, General Tyushkevich is arguing that retrenchment of military presence (and by implication state interests) is appropriate to the new guiding principle of "reasonable sufficiency for defense," as it has been adopted by the Soviet Union under Gorbachev.

Deterrence is not made the be-all and end-all of military doctrine or strategy. Deterrence is essentially a *condition*, created by building a military capability for retaliation, contributing to the prevention of war under some circumstances. It may be essential under some circumstances, but it is not equated with preventing war. In the first place, it only prevents a decision based on rational calculation of gain from an attack. In addition, it is not guaranteed or always reliable, and the consequences of failure could be fatal. Finally, like

---

22. Maj. Gen. (Ret.) S. A. Tyushkevich, "Reasonable Sufficiency for Defense: Parameters and Criteria," *Voyennaya mysl'*, no. 5 (May 1989), p. 56.

some medicines, even while alleviating one dangerous condition it may have harmful or even fatal side-effects. Deterrence, at least as practiced for several decades, generates an arms competition and requires a continuing military counterposition.

General Secretary Leonid Brezhnev, who presided over the buildup that gave the Soviet Union parity, had proudly announced the attainment of a real deterrent in 1970. He stated: "We have created strategic forces that are a reliable means of deterrence [*sderzhivaniye*] of any aggressor." And although he endorsed the aim of restraining the strategic arms race and the existence of "preliminary contacts" with the United States in the recently begun Strategic Arms Limitation Talks (SALT), he also described a policy of matching any buildup by the United States. "And to any attempts from any quarter to gain military superiority over the USSR we shall respond by the necessary increase in military might, guaranteeing our defense."[23] SALT proceeded, but even more so did the strategic arms race.

In recent years, particularly since Gorbachev's new thinking on security was unveiled at the Twenty-seventh Party Congress in 1986, deterrence as an imposed restraint against aggression and war has begun to be criticized. Gorbachev, at the Party Congress, for the first time declared that "security cannot indefinitely be built on fear of retaliation, that is on doctrines of deterrence [*sderzhivaniye*]." Moreover, he said, deterrence "encourages the arms race, which sooner or later can get out of control."[24] And in his speech to the European Parliament in 1989, in arguing for the elimination of all nuclear weapons, he asked, "Does the strategy of nuclear deterrence [*sderzhivaniye*] strengthen or undermine stability?" His answer was that it undermines stability.[25] Nonetheless, Gorbachev understands the concept of nuclear deterrence through maintaining a capability for retaliation, and is prepared to discuss ways to diminish the role of nuclear deterrence without abandoning it, so long as that remains the U.S. position.

23. L. I. Brezhnev, *O vneshnei politike KPSS i Sovetskogo gosudarstva: Rechi i stat'i* (On the Foreign Policy of the CPSU and the Soviet State: Speeches and Articles), 3d ed. (Moscow: Politizdat, 1978), p. 105. The speech was given on April 14, 1970.

24. For a fuller quotation, reference, and further discussion, see chapter 4, where recent Soviet thinking on deterrence is discussed more fully.

25. See "The All-European Process Goes Forward: Speech of M. S. Gorbachev," *Pravda*, July 7, 1989, p. 2.

Reciprocal Misperceptions about Deterrence

The historical-cultural differences between the United States (and generally the West) and the Soviet Union are enough to generate some misperceptions. Ideological hostilities and geopolitical rivalries make such misperceptions almost inevitable. And reciprocal capacities for nuclear annihilation make reciprocal misperceptions deeper and potentially more consequential. Finally, the very concept of deterrence aggravates the matter: deterrence, at its core, presumes the aggressive intent of an adversary. A deterrence mindset inherently tends to prejudice attempts to dispel misconceptions and, even more important, to prejudice efforts to reduce tensions and to resolve real conflicts of interest.

The misperceptions of the two superpowers about deterrence are not mirror images; indeed they differ considerably. They are not "mutual," but for different reasons they are in general reciprocated. In the United States, the usual argument has been whether the Soviet Union is prepared to accept deterrence, as we do benignly in our self-image, or whether its leaders are driven to seek military capabilities and courses of political and military action going beyond defensive "deterrence." In the Soviet Union, the very concept of deterrence ascribed to the United States is not benign and defensive, but offensive: compellence or intimidation of the Soviet Union.

There is, of course, a common root to these perceptions (which I regard as basically misperceptions on both sides). Mistrust of intentions, and fear of the adversary, are powerful generators of protective shields warding off disconfirming evidence. Moreover, less than purely defensive purposes of some actions by each side have magnified "confirming" evidence. Secrecy, lack of information, and acceptance of misinformation have further compounded those misperceptions.

Soviet discussions of *Western* conceptions of deterrence involve two serious, complicating semantic distortions. The first is that the word used to translate "deterrence" is also the word used to translate the American political concept of "containment": *sderzhivaniye,* meaning "constraint," "holding in check," "deterrence," "containment." The second problem is that, in the Soviet perception, the *American* concept of "deterrence" is not defensive but coercive, and the usual term used to identify it is not *sderzhivaniye,* but *ustrashen-*

iye: deterrence in the sense of intimidation, coercion, compellence. Occasionally, the term *"sderzhivaniye putem ustrashneniya,"* deterrence through intimidation, is used. Some Soviet analysts with a more benign understanding of the American conception in the mid-1970s and again in the late 1980s have used the term *sderzhivaniye* in referring to Western deterrence, but these are the exception. The most important (and encouraging) exception is the use of *sderzhivaniye* in the term "mutual deterrence," implicitly accepting the equivalence of Western and Soviet defensive deterrence.[26]

The Soviet concept of deterrence is thus sharply divided into two categories: *sderzhivaniye*, constraint against an enemy attack and war, attributed invariably to Soviet policy and occasionally to American policy; and *ustrasheniye*, coercive political-military pressure, attributed only to American (and NATO) policy. While this bifurcation into "defensive deterrence" and "offensive deterrence" is obviously self-serving and has propaganda implications and applications, it also does reflect and embody a different real Soviet perception. When *American* (and other Western) use of the term "deterrence" is rendered as *ustrasheniye*, it automatically characterizes Western policy as one of intimidation, coercion, and compellence. Soviet commentary consequently reacts negatively even to routine Western references to deterrence, entirely compatible with reduced tension and détente, as though it were incompatible and the reassertion of a confrontational element in Western policy, if not indeed a sign that Western policy remains basically confrontational with only détente window dressing. And Soviet leaders, receiving reports and full texts of Western pronouncements, of course read them in Russian translation.

A not unimportant illustration is the statement in the official communiqué of the Warsaw Pact meeting of July 8, 1989, that "the strategy of nuclear deterrence [*ustrasheniye*] confirmed afresh at the recent session of the NATO Council remains a dangerous anachronism at variance with the interests of common security." It was

---

26. In an article in a journal sponsored by the Soviet Ministry of Foreign Affairs, *Mezhdunarodnaya zhizn'* (*International Affairs*, in the English-language version), I have drawn attention to the discrepancy in Soviet usage and argued strongly for use of the term *sderzhivaniye* to render the Western, as well as the Soviet, concept of deterrence. Whether that will have any effect is problematical, but at least the point was made to the Soviet international relations community. See Raymond L. Garthoff, "Point of View: Reflections of an American," *Mezhdunarodnaya zhizn'*, no. 7 (July 1989), pp. 77–79, and *International Affairs*, no. 8 (August 1989), pp. 72–74.

described as one of "the concepts of confrontation and reliance on force established in the years of the cold war."[27] Similarly, at a seminar on military doctrine of the Conference on Security and Cooperation in Europe (CSCE) meeting in early 1990, a seminar attended by most chiefs of staff of Eastern and Western countries, General of the Army Mikhail Moiseyev attacked the concept of nuclear deterrence, and said that "so long as the ideas of 'nuclear deterrence' [*ustrasheniye*] are put into practice in the structure, strategy, and preparation of the armed forces of NATO, so long as the actual possibility of use of nuclear weapons is entertained, we will have to keep our armed forces in readiness to fulfill defensive missions under any possible development of the situation."[28]

Innumerable other examples over the years could be cited, describing not merely one or another Western action or application of deterrence as compellence, but envisaging the whole Western concept and strategy of deterrence as intimidation by force.[29]

American misperceptions of Soviet acceptance of deterrence stem, in part, from the very Soviet criticisms of American deterrence. Seeing our own policy as defensive deterrence, rather than offensive compellence, Americans believe it is our defensive deterrence that the Soviets criticize and reject. Why should the Soviets do so unless it is impeding some offensive design on their part? In addition, various Soviet actions, in particular the armed interventions in Hungary in 1956, Czechoslovakia in 1968, and Afghanistan in 1979, are seen as aggressive and as demonstrating that the Soviet Union is not pursuing deterrence.

The American self-perception of the United States and NATO, our intentions, and all our actions, as defensive also engenders a widespread public view that the Soviet Union does not even *need* a deterrent. The official and intellectual communities' concept of deterrence as a two-sided game does legitimate the idea of Soviet as well as American deterrence, but this point is absent from the

27. "Communiqué of the Meeting of the Political Consultative Committee of the Member States of the Warsaw Pact," *Pravda*, July 9, 1989, p. 1.

28. *Tezisy vystupleniya M. A. Moiseyeva o voyennoi doktrine Sovetskogo Soyuza* (Theses of the Statement by M. A. Moiseyev on the Military Doctrine of the Soviet Union), Vienna, January 16, 1990, official Soviet transcript, p. 10.

29. For a detailed review of Soviet perceptions of American deterrence policy and overall military strategy and doctrine, see Raymond L. Garthoff, "Soviet Perceptions of Western Strategic Thought and Doctrine," in Gregory Flynn, ed., *Soviet Military Doctrine and Western Policy* (London: Routledge, 1989), pp. 197–309.

general public and domestic political commentary in the United States.

Perhaps the main American misperception has been in its evaluation of the intensity of the Soviet drive for expansionism. Always greatly exaggerated, nonetheless this assumption of a communist (ideological) drive for Soviet (geopolitical) expansion persisted throughout the cold war and has only attenuated in recent years. Stalin's consolidation of control in Eastern Europe after World War II, and early apparent tentative attempts on the periphery (Iran, Greece, and above all Korea), seemed to confirm this diagnosis. Absence of further Soviet moves, including armed intervention in Western Europe, were attributed to the success of containment.

Americans thus saw deterrence as directed not only to preventing Soviet military attack and war, but also to preventing Soviet political and geopolitical expansion. The Soviet confusion of the concepts of deterrence and containment by defining both with the same Russian word was, by curious chance, not entirely an error. And the initial American nuclear monopoly encouraged such a broadened conception of what "deterrence" could do.

As American nuclear superiority waned and was overtaken by strategic parity and mutual deterrence, possible Soviet attack, even though now a real Soviet capability, clearly continued to be deterred. The focus of American concern thus shifted to possible Soviet aggrandizement below the protective shadow of our deterrent shield. Even, at the extreme, a Soviet conventional war in Europe might not be deterred. But more likely were Soviet compellent demands on the basis of local Soviet military, political, subversive, and other means. Hence, notwithstanding an unimpaired U.S. nuclear deterrent, deterrence of this wider range of "threats" seemed to require more. And the Soviet interest in deterrence was seen as limited to maintaining a U.S.-USSR strategic nuclear standoff, below which the Soviet Union could continue to pursue expansionist aims.

This concept, called by some "counterdeterrence" or "deterring our deterrent," gained influence in the late 1950s and early 1960s as the United States moved away from reliance on "massive retaliation," and sought "graduated deterrents" in a strategy of "flexible response."[30]

30. Many contributed to this shift in thinking, including General Maxwell Taylor, as well as civilian theorists such as Henry Kissinger. The term "counterdeterrence,"

In practice, the Soviet Union has always been very cautious in its involvements in the third world (excepting the Cuban missile venture). Nonetheless, several local conflicts in which Soviet or Soviet-aligned countries enjoyed some success have been seen by many Americans, even if incorrectly, as involving effects of a Soviet counter-terdeterrent: the Egyptian-Syrian war with Israel in October 1973, the victory of the Soviet-supported faction in the civil war in Angola in 1975–76, the Ethiopian repulse of Somali attack in 1977–78, the Sandinista victory in Nicaragua in 1979, the insurgency since 1980 in El Salvador, and the Soviet direct intervention in Afghanistan in 1979. In all these cases except Afghanistan, the Soviet Union would not have escalated by direct intervention—to say nothing of threatening nuclear response—to any U.S. action. (In Afghanistan the United States would never have considered a direct counterintervention even if it had held a nuclear monopoly.) But from the latter 1970s to the mid-1980s the Soviet buildup in its strategic nuclear forces, while in fact aimed at consolidating and preserving parity with the United States, was perceived here as a threatening increase aimed at gaining superiority, and as a strategic counterdeterrent backdrop to Soviet geopolitical expansionism. This was the conclusion even though the U.S. reaction in *all* cases was not based on evaluation of the strategic balance.

The stability of mutual deterrence and the absence in fact, as contrasted with initial political and public perceptions, of a counter-deterrent undermining extended deterrence gradually became evident. By the latter 1980s, parity was well established, and the absence since Afghanistan in 1979 (and even there, Soviet withdrawal by 1989) of new Soviet involvements and the return to a less tense U.S.-Soviet relationship led to a cooling of fears of Soviet attack or local advance in the shadow of Soviet strategic counterdeterrence.

Thus strategic parity and mutual deterrence gradually became accepted as a nonthreatening situation. But does it provide security for the long run? And are there alternatives that may better provide security? What is *Soviet* thinking on these matters? These questions are discussed in the chapters that follow.

---

defined as the neutralization of the adversary's deterrent to meet "lesser challenges not directly and mortally threatening" that adversary, was (I regret to say) my contribution. See Raymond L. Garthoff, *The Soviet Image of Future War* (Washington: Public Affairs Press, 1959), p. 3.

Chapter Two

Deterrence in
Soviet Political-Military Policy

MARXISM-LENINISM is based on historical determinism, a belief that socio-economic forces, through a struggle of classes, are the driving force of history. With the advent of the Soviet Union as a socialist state, the question of war between states as a possible form of class struggle arose—indeed, it was the central fact of international life to the Bolshevik leaders. Successive Soviet leaders have seen the greatest danger to the socialist cause (identified with the Soviet Union) as coming from the capitalist military threat; the one mortal danger faced during the first half-century of Soviet rule after victory in the Russian Civil War and the defeat of foreign interventions was the attack by Germany in World War II. Since that war the greatest threat in Soviet eyes has been the unparalleled destructive power of the American nuclear arsenal. Marxist-Leninist ideology sanctions the use of military power (and any other means) available to the socialist (Soviet) leaders whenever, *but only if*, it is expedient in advancing the socialist cause without jeopardizing achievements already gained, above all the security of the Soviet Union. Military power has been considered necessary to *deter* possible attack and to *defend* the socialist cause, and its use is sanctioned if that is deemed expedient to *advance* that cause. Military power has *not*, however, ever been seen as the decisive element in moving the historical process, which it is believed will advance when conditions are ripe through indigenous progressive revolutionary action.

Ideological and Historical Foundations

With the failure of "world revolution" after the successful conclusion of the Russian Civil War,[1] the new Soviet state turned to recov-

1. The years 1920–21 saw several separate though interrelated "wars" come to an end. Communist insurrections in 1919 in Germany and Hungary were put

ery and then to achievement of "socialism in one country." A brief
"breathing space" *(peredyshka)* was originally posited, but it soon was
supplanted by a more indeterminate long-term period of "peaceful
coexistence." Soviet leaders gave priority to internal economic development and to assurance of political control. They saw the principal
role of military power on behalf of world socialism as contributing
to the survival of the first socialist state, although they considered
the main factor in securing that survival to be political division
and rivalry among the imperialist great powers, not Soviet military
strength. Thus preventing an attack on the Soviet Union led to an
active diplomacy designed to ensure against a united imperialist
front against the Soviet Union: the Treaty of Rapallo in 1922 with
the other post-Versailles pariah state, Germany, was the most notable
first step. This approach also led to Soviet wavering between alignment with Britain and France, or with Germany, in 1938–39 and
finally Stalin's decision to sign a pact with Hitler in August 1939.

   Deterrence of renewed military intervention by the capitalist powers was the underlying strategic conception for military power, com-
plementing diplomatic efforts, although the term was not then yet
in vogue. Later, when the Soviet Union was attacked, the role of the
armed forces was of course defense and defeat of the attacker. This
task was not made easier by the fact that the operational-strategic
military doctrine of the Red Army had maintained an offensive
thrust, notwithstanding the defensive deterrent military-political
policy. Military power was also used offensively in a war with Finland
in 1939–40, and to facilitate the absorption of the Baltic states and
Bessarabia in 1940, even though these actions were from the Soviet
standpoint "defensive" preparations for possible war with Germany.

   A deterrent concept has also governed the period since World
War II, except that a socialist camp or commonwealth came into

---

down. The White Russian armies were decisively defeated by March 1921 with
General Petr Wrangel's withdrawal from the Crimea. The Western Allies (Great
Britain, France, and the United States) by 1920 withdrew their expeditionary forces
from northern Russia, the Caucasus, and Siberia (as did the Japanese soon after),
and the Red Army attacked retreating forces in Poland only to meet a rebuff and
forced Soviet withdrawal. The failure of the Polish campaign was especially important
in dispelling any notions that the Red Army could count on support of the popular
masses in other countries in an offensive war. Lenin and other Soviet leaders drew
this lesson very clearly. Peace treaties were signed accepting non-Soviet states and
noncommunist rule in Finland, Latvia, Estonia, and Lithuania as well as Poland.
Only in Outer Mongolia did local communist and Soviet forces succeed in establishing
a satellite communist state.

being, and of course it is recognized that military power in the nuclear age is enormously more dangerous, and therefore in its potential use more important, even if at the same time less usable. The principal role of Soviet military power has consistently been to dissuade imperialist powers from resort to *their* military power against the Soviet Union (and, after World War II, against the other Eastern European countries of the socialist camp) in an effort to thwart the progressive course of history driven by socio-economic revolutionary dynamics—not by military conquest. The Soviets also see other ideologically sanctioned uses of military force, but the basic Marxist-Leninist ideological framework predicates a fundamentally deterrent role for Soviet military power.[2]

The Soviets have, nonetheless, faced a doctrinal dilemma. While jettisoning Stalinist views on the inevitability of war and the necessary or desirable role of war as a catalyst of socialist advance in the world, as communists they were predisposed to assume that socialism would survive and triumph, even if a world nuclear catastrophe occurred. If they openly discarded that view, they long believed, it could place in question not only their whole worldview but also their basis for legitimacy. Hence from the late 1950s to the mid-1980s there were occasional reaffirmations of confidence in the ultimate triumph of socialism even if a world nuclear war should, despite Soviet efforts to prevent it, occur. Such confidence was most authoritatively expressed in the Party Program adopted in 1961. The Soviet leaders, nonetheless, from the mid-1950s on have acknowledged that general nuclear war would threaten the whole existence and future of world civilization and mankind. From the late 1960s on they have drawn further conclusions from that fact, deepening Soviet interest in strategic arms limitations and reductions and in seeking prevention of any nuclear war. Ultimately, in the latter 1980s, "new thinking" on this matter led to a new conception of requirements for security.

Before, however, turning to recent Soviet thinking, it is necessary to note that a crucial turn came in the early post-Stalin years. Indeed, there are intriguing signs that even before Stalin's death some of his key lieutenants, and soon successors, had begun to challenge the tenets of "Marxism-Leninism-Stalinism" on the inevitability of war

2. In addition to the summary discussion in these paragraphs, see Raymond L. Garthoff, *Soviet Military Policy: A Historical Analysis* (Praeger, 1966), chaps. 1, 4, 10, 12.

while imperialism remained. Stalin, in his final theoretical pronouncement in late 1952, reaffirmed that "in order to prevent the
inevitability of wars, imperialism must be destroyed." And he went
further and asserted that "some comrades" held the "incorrect" view
that "Lenin's thesis that imperialism inevitably gives rise to wars
must be considered obsolete."[3] Based on the later record, these
anonymous mistaken comrades appear to have included some, and
perhaps even a majority, of Stalin's successors.[4] In any case, the
new Soviet leadership proclaimed in 1956 at the Twentieth Party
Congress:

> As is well known, there is a Marxist-Leninist thesis that so long as
> imperialism exists wars are inevitable. . . . But at the present time this
> thesis has radically changed. The world camp of socialism has come
> into being and has become a mighty force . . . [possessing] material
> means to prevent aggression. . . . [W]e must maintain the greatest
> vigilance. . . . But there is no fatal inevitability of war. Now there are
> powerful social and political forces that possess serious means to
> prevent the imperialists from unleashing a war, and if they should
> attempt to start one, to give a crushing rebuff to the aggressors, foiling
> their adventuristic plans.[5]

Stalin had attributed to the unspecified comrades, who had dared
to challenge a thesis of Lenin, the idea that war was obsolete owing
to the "powerful popular forces" in the world opposing a war. (And,
indeed, Georgy M. Malenkov in the Central Committee Report to
the Party Congress in 1952, who also said only that imperialist
contradictions *may* lead to war, had adduced this as an important
restraint on the United States against attacking the Soviet Union.)[6]

3. I. V. Stalin, "Economic Problems of Socialism in the USSR," *Bol'shevik*, no.
18 (September 1952), pp. 18–19. Similarly, an authoritative unsigned editorial in
Pravda on September 9, 1952, flatly declared: "The fate of the globe will ultimately
be decided by the inevitable clash between the two worlds."
4. See Raymond L. Garthoff, "The Death of Stalin and the Birth of Mutual
Deterrence," *Survey*, vol. 25 (Spring 1980), pp. 10–16, for discussion.
5. First Secretary N. S. Khrushchev, "Report of the Central Committee of the
CPSU" (February 14, 1956), *XX s"yezd Kommunisticheskoi partii Sovetskogo Soyuza:
Stenograficheskii otchet* (The 20th Congress of the Communist Party of the Soviet
Union: Stenographic Account), vol. 1 (Moscow: Gospolitizdat, 1956), pp. 37–38. This
statement, which also appeared in *Pravda*, February 14, 1956, was endorsed in
speeches by others, including Malenkov and Mikoyan. See "Speech of Comrade G.
M. Malenkov," *Izvestiya*, February 19, 1956, p. 3; and "Speech of Comrade A. I.
Mikoyan," *Pravda*, February 18, 1956, pp. 5–6.
6. G. M. Malenkov, *Report to the Nineteenth Party Congress on the Work of the*

The Presidium and Central Committee in 1956, however, stressed that in addition to "powerful social and political forces" opposing war, the Soviet Union also now possessed "serious means," "material means"—a nuclear deterrent—to prevent war. In fact, of course, the Soviet nuclear deterrent in the mid-1950s was still marginal in capability, but it *was* coming into being.

Malenkov was the first Soviet leader to state publicly, in March 1954, that a world war in the nuclear age "would mean the end of world civilization."[7] Malenkov, to be sure, was soon pounced upon by factional opponents, Khrushchev in particular, for thus echoing a similar statement by President Dwight D. Eisenhower on December 8, 1953.[8] But this criticism was clearly an effort to embarrass him on a matter of premature public doctrinal departure, rather than an expression of real disagreement. Indeed his very critics, once in power, soon sounded the same theme themselves.

On the same day, a year after Stalin's death, that Malenkov first publicly acknowledged the complete nonexpediency of nuclear war, his Politburo colleague Anastas Mikoyan seconded him and added to that judgment an explicit reference to the deterrent role envisaged for Soviet nuclear weapons: "Atomic and hydrogen weapons in the hands of the Soviet Union are a means for deterring aggressors and for waging peace."[9]

The post-Stalin leaders have been well aware of the ideological, political, and military doctrinal implications of their changed view of the evolution of the world in the nuclear era. Above all, their central conclusion was the need to prevent nuclear war. Ideologically, by 1960 it was argued that "a contemporary nuclear war, no matter how one looks at it, can in no way be a factor that would accelerate the revolution and bring nearer the victory of socialism." Indeed, it would result only in "catastrophe."[10]

Central Committee of the C.P.S.U.(B) (Moscow: Foreign Languages Publishing House, 1952), pp. 33–37, quotation from p. 40.

7. "Speech of Comrade G. M. Malenkov," *Pravda*, March 13, 1954, p. 2.

8. "Address before the General Assembly of the United Nations on Peaceful Uses of Atomic Energy, New York City, December 8, 1953," *Public Papers of the Presidents: Dwight D. Eisenhower, 1953* (Washington, 1960), pp. 813–22.

9. "Speech of Comrade A. I. Mikoyan," *Kommunist* (Yerevan), March 12, 1954, pp. 2–3.

10. A. Belyakov and F. Burlatsky, "Lenin's Theory of the Socialist Revolution and the Present Day," *Kommunist*, no. 13 (September, 1960), pp. 15–16. This article was in particular directed against the views of the Chinese Communists.

Similarly, the "Declaration of the Conference of Representatives of the Communist and Workers Parties" in Moscow in November 1960, in addition to reaffirming that war was not inevitable, spoke of the death of hundreds of millions in a nuclear war, "the serious threat to all mankind," and of the "historic mission" of communists "to save mankind from the nightmare of a new world war."[11] These views were incorporated into the new Party Program adopted at the Twenty-second Party Congress in 1961, although as noted that document still expressed confidence that even in the case of a world nuclear war socialism would survive and capitalism would not.

Soviet political pronouncements in the 1950s and 1960s continued to reflect belief in the evolution of a "correlation of forces" in the world arena comprising basic political and economic, as well as military, factors.

Nuclear Deterrence

Nonetheless, Soviet leaders recognized that nuclear weapons had an essential, if not sufficient, role in preventing war. Thus the official Party *History* in various editions from the 1960s through the mid-1980s stressed that since the 1950s "not one state of the capitalist world could now threaten the Soviet land with thermonuclear weapons without risk of receiving a crushing retaliatory strike. That strengthened the defense capability of the USSR, created a reliable defense shield for the countries of the socialist commonwealth, and assumed important significance in defending the general peace."[12] Nuclear deterrence was thus established as a chief factor in dissuading attack on the Soviet Union and its allies, and generally in preventing war.

More specifically, the initial Soviet advances in developing intercontinental ballistic missiles gave a major boost to Soviet confidence in its nuclear deterrent. Within a few days of the first Soviet ICBM test in 1957 General Pokrovsky was stating in *Izvestiya* that "no

11. *Programmnyye dokumenty bor'by za mir, demokratiyu i sotsializm* (Programmatic Documents of the Struggle for Peace, Democracy and Socialism) (Moscow: Gospolitizdat, 1961), p. 63.

12. *Istoriya Kommunisticheskoi partii Sovetskogo Soyuza* (History of the Communist Party of the Soviet Union), 7th ed. (Moscow: Politizdat, 1985), p. 521, and see p. 568. See also 5th ed. (1977), p. 544, and 4th ed. (1973), p. 557, with only slight wording changes.

aggressor on earth can now evade retaliation from ballistic missiles armed with powerful nuclear warheads," and Khrushchev was soon bragging that now "the United States is just as vulnerable as all other countries."[13] Pronouncements of Soviet military leaders ever since the beginning of the 1960s have incorporated references to the role of Soviet military power in general, and strategic nuclear means in particular, as a powerful and crucial deterrent to American attack.

The major treatise *Military Strategy*, prepared by a collective of Soviet military theoreticians headed by Marshal Vasily Sokolovsky and issued in three editions in 1962, 1963, and 1968, stated that Soviet military power was the chief deterrent to the imperialists launching war. In its words, despite the inherent aggressive tendencies of world imperialism, the Communist Party had concluded that war was not fatally inevitable, that "political and economic potentialities for preventing a world war" were being created, and that "these potentialities are determined above all by the whole military might of the socialist camp, which is already now an insuperable barrier in the path to the unleashing of a new world war by imperialist madness."[14] While credit was here given to the military might of the socialist camp, it was clearly Soviet military power and especially strategic nuclear retaliatory capability that was most in mind.

Marshal Rodion Malinovsky, then minister of defense, in 1962 contrasted Soviet reliance on nuclear deterrence with the idea that "the best defense is an attack," saying, "We advance a different [concept]: the best means of defense is warning the adversary of our strength and readiness to destroy him at the first attempt to carry out an act of aggression."[15]

Marshal Sergei Biryuzov, chief of the General Staff, counterposed an alleged policy of imperialism favoring the unleashing of a war with a policy of socialism "not to permit a thermonuclear catastrophe," based on a Soviet nuclear deterrent. "Of primary, decisive significance in preserving the peace between states of the

13. Maj. Gen. Eng.-Tech. Service G. I. Pokrovsky, "On Intercontinental Ballistic Missiles," *Izvestiya*, August 31, 1957, p. 3; and "Conversation of N. S. Khrushchev with . . . Henry Shapiro," *Pravda*, November 19, 1957, pp. 1–2.

14. Marshal V. D. Sokolovsky, ed., *Voyennaya strategiya* (Military Strategy) (Moscow: Voyenizdat), 1st ed. (1962), p. 452; 2d ed. (1963), p. 499; 3d ed. (1968), p. 459.

15. Marshal R. Ya. Malinovsky, *Bditel'no stoyat' na strazhe mira* (Vigilantly Stand Guard over Peace) (Moscow: Voyenizdat, 1962), p. 25.

two social systems is the fact that the Soviet Union has at its disposal the most modern nuclear weapons possessing enormous destructive power. It can reach and completely destroy an aggressor in a short time. The policy of the Soviet state, directed at deterring an aggressor and preserving peace in the whole world, required counterposing to the nuclear weapons of the imperialists our powerful Soviet nuclear-missile weapons so as to provide a shield not only to defend our motherland, its state interests and our allies in the Warsaw Pact, but to stop the warmongers holding in their hand the atomic bomb threatening the whole world."[16]

These statements from the Khrushchev period have been echoed by all succeeding Soviet ministers of defense and other military leaders. Thus in a typical reference then Chief of the General Staff Marshal Nikolai Ogarkov referred in 1982 to the Soviet "strategic nuclear forces" as "the main factor deterring the aggressor."[17] Some statements more generally refer to Soviet military power as a deterrent; others, especially by the military chiefs of the missile forces, ascribe the chief role specifically to the Soviet intercontinental missile forces. And there is no difference on the deterrent role between public statements and those made in confidential publications such as the General Staff journal *Military Thought.* For example, Marshal Vladimir Tolubko, then chief of the Strategic Missile Forces, on their twentieth anniversary in 1979 writing in *Military Thought* described strategic nuclear missiles as "the main factor deterring the aggressive aspirations of imperialism," although he also then claimed—in a statement that would not be made today—that they were also "the main means of achieving final war aims."[18]

These two functions of strategic nuclear forces—deterrence of war, and retaliatory destruction of the enemy in case deterrence should fail—have in logic and in practice always been recognized both in the Soviet Union and in the United States. Both countries have avowed a deterrent purpose while building up war-fighting forces, defining military forces in terms of requirements for the war-waging role and rationalizing that as also maximizing deterrence.

16. Marshal S. S. Biryuzov, "Policy and Nuclear Weapons," in Marshal A. A. Grechko, ed., *Yadernyi vek i voina* (The Nuclear Age and War) (Moscow: Izvestiya, 1964), pp. 17–18.

17. Marshal N. V. Ogarkov, *Vsegda v gotovnosti k zashchite otechestva* (Always in Readiness to Defend the Fatherland) (Moscow: Voyenizdat, 1982), p. 49.

18. Marshal V. F. Tolubko, "Missile Shield of the Motherland," *Voyennaya mysl'* (Military Thought), no. 12 (December 1979), p. 6.

There have, however, been differences stemming from the different conceptions of the two sides on the relation between policy, doctrine, and strategy.

Military Policy, Doctrine, and Strategy

In American usage, "doctrines" have usually been popularized slogans for national policies on the world scene—from the Monroe Doctrine through those named for most of the presidents of the nuclear era—the Truman, Eisenhower, Nixon, Carter, and Reagan doctrines leap to mind. A small academic and professional military community has also used the term "military doctrine" to describe the codification of officially accepted precepts on the preparation for and conduct of military operations in war. "Military science" has been used to describe objective principles of the conduct of war, and "the military art" the subjective skill in that use of military forces. "Military strategy" in the strict sense is the application of military science and art in the concrete planning and direction of military operations on a large scale and affecting the course and outcome of a war. ("Tactics" is the subordinate parallel application at lower levels in managing the course and outcome of battle.)

Where does "deterrence" fit? Basically it has been seen in the United States as a political-military policy, a national policy expressing a political aim and undergirding military policy, programs, and strategy. With the fluidity characteristic of American theorizing on political and military affairs, deterrence has also been regarded as a military doctrine and even a military strategy. The effects have been described to some extent in the preceding chapter, but these brief comments are introduced only to provide a somewhat familiar base for comparison with Soviet thinking.

Military theory, and military doctrinal elaboration, have traditionally enjoyed greater attention in the Soviet Union (as in several other European great powers) than in the United States. Under Stalin, however, even before World War II and especially after it, military theoretical thinking was stifled in a straitjacket of what was termed "Stalinist military science."[19] In the early post-Stalin period, military theoreticians (a respectable career in the Soviet military, in contrast to its status in the United States) began to free military science

19. See Raymond L. Garthoff, *Soviet Strategy in the Nuclear Age*, 2d ed. (Praeger, 1962), pp. 61–71.

(and its main source, military history) from the rigidities of Stalinist dogma, and to develop "laws of war," and more limited military "laws of armed conflict." By the early 1960s, "military doctrine" was revived as the central concept, in a form that remained essentially unchanged until certain important modifications in the late 1980s.

And deterrence? In the first edition of *Military Strategy* the reference to deterrence cited earlier in this chapter was in the context of a paragraph on "Soviet military doctrine," but that reference was changed in the second edition and thereafter to "Soviet state policy."[20] Deterrence was thus identified as Soviet *policy*, rather than as part of Soviet military doctrine.[21]

By 1962–63 the new concept of military doctrine had been established authoritatively. From then (until expanded in 1987) it was held that military doctrine is a "set of views accepted by a state for a given (definite) period of time on the essence, aims, and character of a possible future war, on the preparation of the country and the armed forces for it, and on the means of its conduct." Also, "military doctrine has two closely interrelated and interdependent aspects— the socio-political and the military-technical."[22]

The political or socio-political aspect of doctrine would, in Western parlance, be termed the political-military aspect. It includes the political nature (or essence) of war, the political causes of war, the aims of war (and hence of strategy), evaluation of the political, economic, morale, and other factors affecting a nation's ability to prepare for and to wage war, and also the correlation of such factors in relation to probable enemies. Accordingly, as noted in an authori-

20. Sokolovsky, ed., *Voyennaya strategiya*, 1st ed., p. 452; 2d ed., p. 499; 3d ed., p. 459. American scholars have been indebted to Harriet Fast Scott for her translation with detailed annotations and comparisons of all three editions of this important Soviet book. The present instance, however, shows the hazards of overreliance on the research of others; she failed to note this change from the first to the later editions, citing only the later version of the paragraph. See Harriet Fast Scott, trans. and ed., *Soviet Military Strategy, by V. D. Sokolovskiy, Marshal of the Soviet Union* (New York: Crane, Russak, and Co., 1975), pp. 381, 383–84.

21. Marshal Malinovsky, in 1962, also made a reference not later reiterated placing in the political aspect of Soviet military doctrine (further discussed in the following paragraph) "the realistic task of prevention of war," not by a Soviet military deterrent but "as a consequence of the new alignment of forces in the world arena," with creation of a "socialist camp" and the rise of peace-loving social forces and even states in the capitalist world (a description taken from the 1961 Party Program). See Malinovsky, *Bditel'no stoyat'*, p. 5.

22. "Military Doctrine," *Voyennyi entsiklopedicheskii slovar'* (The Military Encyclopedic Dictionary; hereafter *VES*), 2d ed. (Moscow: Voyenizdat, 1986), p. 240.

tative senior Soviet military theorist's early exposition, "the bases of military doctrine are determined by the political leadership of a country, inasmuch as only it is able properly and competently to decide matters of military programming [*stroitel'stvo*], proceeding from an evaluation of the character of future war and an account of its own political tasks and military-economic potentialities and those of a potential enemy."[23]

The political aspect of Soviet military doctrine has always been described as defensive and nonaggressive, reflecting Soviet state policy.[24] After 1977, and again after 1981, renewed emphasis was placed on the "exclusively defensive orientation" of Soviet military doctrine.[25] As will be discussed in chapter 4, two major changes were introduced in 1987 when the very definition of military doctrine was changed to incorporate the objective of prevention of war, and when defensive dominance was for the first time applied to the military-technical level of doctrine.

The military, or in Soviet parlance "military-technical," level of military doctrine is not merely technical. It embraces (in Soviet terms) the entire scope of military science on the "laws of armed combat" and the military art—military strategy, the operational art, and tactics.[26] This is the area most often thought of in the West as

23. Col. Gen. N. A. Lomov, *Sovetskaya voyennaya doktrina* (Soviet Military Doctrine) (Moscow: Nauka, 1963), p. 5. See also the article "Military Doctrine," *Sovetskaya voyennaya entsiklopediya* (The Soviet Military Encyclopedia; hereafter *SVE*) (Moscow: Voyenizdat, 1977), vol. 3, pp. 225–29. Lomov, after earlier service on the General Staff, was at this time chair of the strategy faculty of the General Staff Academy.

24. For authoritative examples, see Marshal A. A. Grechko, *Vooruzhennyye sily Sovetskogo gosudarstva* (The Armed Forces of the Soviet State), 2d ed. (Moscow: Voyenizdat, 1975), p. 345; and "Military Doctrine," *SVE*, vol. 3, pp. 225, 229.

25. See "Military Doctrine," *VES*, 1st ed. (1983), p. 240. The 1986 edition used the expression "exclusively defensive character." See also, in the confidential General Staff journal, an entire article by a leading theorist, Col. Gen. I. G. Zav'yalov, "The Defensive Orientation [*napravlennost'*] of Soviet Military Doctrine," *Voyennaya mysl'*, no. 1 (January 1981), pp. 15–26.

26. See the above encyclopedia definitions of military doctrine; and Grechko, *Vooruzhennyye sily*, pp. 349–56. For the most extensive Western commentary, see Harriet Fast Scott and William F. Scott, *Soviet Military Doctrine: Continuity, Formulation, and Dissemination* (Boulder, Colo.: Westview, 1988), pp. 130–59. The Scotts' study demonstrates extensive and in many respects thorough research, but in my judgment the conclusions are in many cases incorrect, leaving an impression of much greater continuity in doctrine and ascribing a view of an unchanging, hostile Soviet policy and aims that I do not believe is justified by the historical record, or even the sources cited, to say nothing of other data and sources not used.

"military doctrine," and the difference between Western and Soviet definitions of doctrine has given rise to some innocent misunderstandings and sometimes deliberate misrepresentations. The most important example has concerned the question of the defensive character of Soviet military doctrine.

Soviet military doctrine at the political level has always been held to be defensive, but until recently (1987) at the "military-technical level" governing strategy, operations, and tactics it has been unabashedly offensive (as incidentally the comparable doctrine of most great powers has been). There is no necessary contradiction between a defensive *policy* (or, in Soviet terms, the political level of military doctrine) and an offensive *strategy* for waging war if war should come. But some Western commentators, through ignorance or willfully, have cited Soviet military statements describing the offensive as the principal form of warfare as though it implied or indicated an aggressive intention, and as though such statements "disproved" Soviet claims of defensive doctrine and intention.

An offensive strategic concept for waging war if it should come (as has characterized, for example, the U.S. Strategic Air Command from its inception, and the Soviet Army in Europe from the 1950s at least until 1987) may in fact be necessary, prudent, wise, and serve as a deterrent—or it may be unnecessary, imprudent, unwise, and a stimulus to perceptions of a threat. (It may even to some extent, although it cannot completely, be both.) But the issue is not addressed by misunderstanding or misrepresenting Soviet military doctrine.

From 1963 until 1987, while deterrence was accepted as a crucial element of Soviet state and military policy, it was not described as a constituent element of military doctrine, even at the political level of doctrine. Military doctrine governed the preparations of the armed forces and the country for the contingency of waging war should deterrence and prevention of war fail. Leaders regarded the preparation of military forces capable of waging war, especially general nuclear war, both as a contribution to deterrence and as preparation for the dire contingency of war.

Deterrence and Soviet Strategic Planning

Relatively little is known about Soviet war planning for the contingency of general nuclear war, apart from what may be surmised from the character of Soviet strategic nuclear forces. Available evidence, however, suggests that once deterrence had failed, the armed forces were given the traditional mission of seeking to prevail in conflict. Available evidence on Soviet military doctrinal development, from such sources as the curriculum of the General Staff Academy and writings in the restricted General Staff journal *Military Thought,* shows a concentration on preparations for waging continental land and sea theater campaigns, alternatively with and without use of nuclear weapons.[27] Such campaigns are, in Soviet terms, considered "strategic." Little is said about waging what in the United States is generally regarded as strategic, that is intercontinental, warfare. The most detailed discussions, mostly from the 1960s, do examine the requirements for command and control, and discuss targeting priorities on both counterforce targets (especially nuclear but also other major military targets), and war-sustaining targets (administrative-political control centers, war production and transportation facilities).[28] There is even one mathematical model for strategic nuclear forces (in *Military Thought* in 1967) similar to American models for gauging force requirements for strategic duels in which each side strives to emerge less completely destroyed than the adversary.[29] In both countries, while such analyses may serve as a basis for force programming and even war plans for force application, they do not represent scenario outcomes that any political leader in either country would regard as victory in a war.

The Soviet Union, acquiring intercontinental nuclear striking forces years later than the United States, from the outset had to give high priority to counterforce targets, above all U.S. strategic nuclear forces. Nonetheless, it also included (in what proportion Western analysts do not know) other targets that the Soviet Union regarded as strategically significant to U.S. capacity to wage nuclear war. The United States, in contrast, had virtually a "free ride" from counterforce, damage-limiting targeting from the mid-1940s to the mid-1950s, and enjoyed a massive force superiority into the late 1960s. Of course, even before the Soviet Union fielded its first marginal strate-

27. This statement is based on the author's review of the entire two-year course at the Voroshilov General Staff Academy in 1973–75, and a full file of *Military Thought* from 1959 to the present.

28. In particular, see Maj. Gen. Kh. Dzhelaukhov, "Dealing Deep Strikes," *Voyennaya mysl'*, no. 2 (February 1966), pp. 33–41. Dzhelaukhov was on the strategy faculty of the General Staff Academy.

29. Maj. Gen. Eng.-Tech. Service I. Anureyev, "On Determining the Correlation of Forces in Nuclear Arms," *Voyennaya mysl'*, no. 6 (June 1967), pp. 36–45.

gic bomber forces in the mid-1950s, the United States had begun to target even potential nuclear production and delivery facilities.

It should be noted that while the United States enjoyed the advantage of a period when it alone possessed nuclear weapons and long-range nuclear delivery systems, its forces—and war plans—were not prepared to meet some uniquely "deterrent" war application. At all times, the actual war plans (those from the late 1940s have been declassified) called for targeting political, economic, and military targets as part of a war-fighting strategy. The U.S. policy and purpose was deterrence (and containment), but in case of war was designed to contribute to winning the war. So, too, to judge from confidential Soviet discussions of strategy, were later Soviet war plans. In both cases, policymakers expected the preparation of war-waging strategic forces to have a deterrent effect by dissuading a potential attacker from believing he could gain from launching a war.

In 1955, in a rejuvenation and reevaluation of Soviet military doctrine undertaken after Stalin's death, the Soviet military concluded that a surprise initial nuclear attack could decisively cripple an enemy's retaliatory capability and prevent his victory. This significant upgrading of the potential role of surprise was first advanced by a senior Soviet officer and military theoretician, Marshal Pavel Rotmistrov, in an article in *Military Thought* in February 1955. This thesis was a sharp change from previous doctrine, which had held that surprise was only a transitory factor and that the course and outcome of a war were decided by a contest of the basic military, economic, and multi-political potentials of the adversaries. Indeed, the editors of the journal agreed to publish the article evidently only after intervention by the first deputy minister of defense, soon minister, Marshal Georgy Zhukov.[30] The change in doctrine did *not* conclude that a surprise attack would necessarily be decisive; but failure by the side attacked to take measures to prevent its success could make it so.

30. See Marshal of the Tank Troops P. A. Rotmistrov, "On the Role of Surprise in Contemporary War," *Voyennaya mysl'*, no. 2 (February 1955), pp. 14–24; and an unsigned lead editorial article "On Some Questions of Soviet Military Science," *Voyennaya mysl'*, no. 3 (March 1955), pp. 3–18. In the latter article the editors in self-criticism disclosed that they had, "without justification," held back Rotmistrov's article, "thus displaying a lack of the boldness required to raise a new and timely question of great significance for a correct understanding of the character of contemporary war" (p. 4). This article also disclosed Marshal Zhukov's role in criticizing the lag in military science and implied his role in leading to the reconsideration and publication of Rotmistrov's article.

The original article, and others in the subsequent discussion including authoritative unsigned editorial articles by *Military Thought*, spelled out the measures required to prevent surprise from becoming decisive. Most significant was the conclusion that in the event of an enemy surprise nuclear attack, the country attacked—the Soviet Union—must ensure that its own strategic nuclear retaliatory forces would be launched before they could be destroyed, and preferably preemptively, to weaken the attacking force by attrition. These discussions, unleashed by Marshal Zhukov and reflected in less explicit public statements by Zhukov, his successor Marshal Rodion Malinovsky, and other Soviet military leaders over the next seven to ten years, bore witness to a Soviet decision to consider launching its nuclear forces in a preemptive attack in the case of detection of an incipient or imminent enemy nuclear attack.

Unlike most developments in Soviet military doctrine, this one quickly drew the attention of the U.S. national security community. Ever since, official and unofficial American analyses of Soviet doctrine have given considerable attention to Soviet concepts of preemptive attack, often in terms distorting the actual record of evidence, either by interpreting the Soviet concept of preemption as a euphemism for a first-strike initiative, or by assuming the Soviet decision meant dedication to obtaining an effective preemptive capability, and later by assuming a decision in 1955 was still valid twenty or twenty-five years later without taking account of evidence of later changes.[31]

This matter requires some review here precisely because what it really represented, apart from a general belated recognition of what the destructiveness of nuclear weapons implied for military thinking, was a Soviet determination to preserve its strategic nuclear retaliatory forces both to ensure deterrence and, failing deterrence, for waging war.

Marshal Rotmistrov made very clear that the concept of preemptive action was *not* a euphemism for a surprise first strike or "preventive war," but a last-minute seizure of the initiative from an enemy already attempting a surprise attack on the Soviet Union: "The duty of the Soviet armed forces is to not permit surprise attack by the

---

31. ·The most comprehensive discussion of the Soviet military doctrinal revisions on surprise and preemption in the 1950s remains Raymond L. Garthoff, *The Soviet Image of Future War* (Washington: Public Affairs Press, 1959), pp. 64–73; and see Garthoff, *Soviet Strategy in the Nuclear Age*, pp. 84–87.

enemy on our country, and in case an attempt is made, not only
to repulse the attack successfully, but also to deal to the enemy
simultaneous or even preemptive surprise blows of terrible crushing
power." Past use of surprise by aggressors provided a "lesson of
history that we cannot ignore, and we must always be ready for
preemptive [or forestalling] actions against the cunning of aggressors." And finally, "Striving to seize and hold the strategic initiative
must not be understood as intention to start a preventive war against
the enemies of the USSR who are preparing to attack us. The Soviet
Union threatens no one and does not intend to attack first even when
some government conducts a provocative military policy, surround-
ing our country with a net of bases and feverishly coaching its satel-
lites for war against us."[32]

Preemption as set forth in this and other confidential Soviet military discussions in 1955 represented a contingent response to an
enemy decision and attempt to attack by surprise. It would not be
Soviet choice of war, or choice of the time for hostilities, nor would
it necessarily imply any relative military standing of the two sides or
satisfaction of requirements for a disarming strike against the other
side's forces. It would be a prompt "or even preemptive" response to
an enemy decision and an imminent and irrevocable enemy attack.

Regrettably, some American analyses of the Soviet upgrading of
the importance of surprise and articulation of a preemptive response
to possible enemy attack failed to make clear that the Soviet conclusion was *not* that it could win a war by use of a surprise attack and
should therefore plan and prepare to strike first preemptively, but
on the contrary represented a heightened defensive concern that
unless they recognized the importance of surprise and succeeded in
preventing its successful use against them, they could lose. In addition, analysts have often incorrectly assumed the Soviet concept of
preemption and its adoption established a new military "requirement": to be able by preemptive action to disarm the enemy before
he could strike. While that would no doubt be the most desirable
outcome, nothing in the doctrinal discussions nor in later Soviet
military programs and force buildups indicated that it was so intended. It was only a contingent response for launch under attack or
even preemptively *if* timely and reliable intelligence established that

32. Rotmistrov, *Voyennaya mysl'*, no. 2 (February 1955), pp. 20–21.

an enemy attack was imminent and irrevocable, criteria hard to establish until an attack was actually under way.

The Soviet military recognition of the need to avoid being successfully surprised, and to launch a response before that could occur, was made in 1955 at the height of the era of the bomber. There might then have been time for receiving reliable information on an incoming American air attack and deciding to launch Soviet bombers before the U.S. force struck, and even perhaps to destroy part of it at the advanced overseas bases required by most of the U.S. strategic air fleet of the day. Preemption became more necessary, but also more problematical, as intercontinental land-based and submarine-based missiles took over in the 1960s and 1970s.

It should also be noted that Soviet embrace of preemption in doctrine (Soviet capability to preempt remained very low) came five years after the U.S. government adopted preemption (in NSC-68), and seven years after adoption in fact by the U.S. Strategic Air Command. A rough five-year lag, while not always prevailing, has often marked Soviet attainment of capabilities (nuclear weapons, MIRVs, strategic cruise missiles) and doctrines (preemption in 1955, flexible response in 1965–66).

The preemptive concept was not publicly avowed, indeed was publicly denied. And it clearly was intended to enhance possibilities for successfully waging war if war should be forced upon the Soviet Union. Nonetheless, it was also intended to bolster deterrence by making the possibility of successful surprise appear less attainable to a potential aggressor, that is, the United States. Thus some military commentators even in public utterances discussed the strategic threat and the need "to nip in the bud any desire of the aggressors to carry out a surprise attack on our Soviet motherland."[33]

Preemption was thus not an aberration but a supporting element in deterrence. Moreover it remained the extreme recourse in a continuum of possible (and possibly necessary) forms of retaliation: if possible, preemption; if not, launch on warning of attack; if not, launch under attack; and finally retaliatory launch by survivors after an enemy attack. From 1955 until the late 1960s, when the Soviet strategic nuclear capability was weak and vulnerable, preemption seemed the most desirable option *if* its stringent conditions could be

33. Marshal I. Bagramyan, "The Historic Victory of the Soviet People," *Oktyabr'*, no. 5 (May 1955), p. 114.

met. But as the Soviet strategic missile forces became more numerous, less vulnerable, and more capable of rapid reaction, the balance of risk shifted from prompt and preemptive, but conceivably premature, response, to waiting for more reliable and certain indications that an attack was under way before launch. Then preemption gave way from the late 1960s to launch under attack, and by the late 1980s probably to retaliatory launch.

By the latter 1970s neither superpower could possess a "disarming" first-strike capability to prevent or greatly reduce a retaliatory strike. The other side of the coin was that both superpowers would continue to possess an indestructible capability to destroy the society of the enemy; any attacker would be devastated. Mutual deterrence had been established.

Mutual Deterrence

Even in the 1950s and early 1960s, both the United States and the Soviet Union anticipated the coming of mutual deterrence. The United States sought to bolster the invulnerability of its strategic forces and its (and its allies') nonnuclear forces to strengthen deterrence to withstand both direct challenge and indirect circumvention. And in at least some respects, the United States was "deterred"—not from attacking the Soviet Union, which it did not intend, but from pressing its advantage while it still had some.

As early as the mid- to late 1950s, the United States went through a period of "self-deterrence" by exaggerating Soviet capabilities and misreading Soviet intentions. Analytical studies prepared for the U.S. Air Force by the RAND Corporation, making use of all available intelligence but with truly "worst-case" assumptions, devised theoretically ingenious but practically and politically incredible Soviet air strikes capable of disarming the U.S. Strategic Air Command. While useful in pointing out certain vulnerabilities in U.S. Air Force warning, deployment, and operational practices, and perhaps in boosting SAC's budgets, the authors and many recipients also went beyond that to see a peril to deterrence. In the widely cited words of one of the principal authors of the original study, there was only "a delicate balance of terror."[34]

34. See Albert Wohlstetter, "The Delicate Balance of Terror," *Foreign Affairs*, vol. 37 (January 1959), pp. 211–34.

The SAC air base vulnerability issue was soon followed by a feared "bomber gap," then the notorious "missile gap" of 1959 to 1961. Again, by assuming the worst, abetted by some real uncertainties in information, Soviet deterrent and even compellent capabilities were imagined until enough intelligence was received from satellite photographic reconnaissance in 1961 to puncture the wildly inflated estimates.

The Soviet Union, meanwhile, fed such American fears and attempted to bluff its way into enjoying the fruits of deterrence before it possessed an adequate capability.

Nikita Khrushchev had two targets for his campaign of bluff and deception. One was the West, where he hoped both to cover Soviet strategic weakness as a defensive move, and to use the image of Soviet power to gain international political weight and some concrete geopolitical advantages, above all to force the Western powers out of Berlin. Khrushchev's second target was the Soviet people and political establishment. He wanted to substitute a nuclear deterrent, first notional and later real, for the large conventional armed forces traditionally maintained by the Soviet Union.

These attempts failed, utterly with respect to Berlin, and partially with respect to the Soviet army. He was able to effect part of the reductions in the armed forces that he sought, but only part. Khrushchev did succeed in getting the Soviet armed forces to focus on the one contingency of nuclear war—deterring nuclear war, but if deterrence failed then waging such a war. Khrushchev was interested only in deterrence, and in political uses of military power. The military leaders were quite prepared to support a policy of deterrence; there was no thirst for war. But they also believed that if war should come their task was to fight as successfully as possible, and for that they wanted resources and a war-waging (and at least in aspiration war-winning) military doctrine.

After Khrushchev was removed, the military were able to reassert a broader doctrine of preparation for waging both nuclear and, preferably, nonnuclear war. Deterrence remained Soviet policy, but Khrushchev had failed to substitute deterrence for a war-waging military doctrine.

Mutual deterrence, while equally applicable to the United States and the Soviet Union, meant something very different in one important sense. For the United States, it was the loss of a nuclear superiority, and while deterrence of direct Soviet attack was secure, the credibility of extended deterrence protecting American allies became a source of concern in the West. Ironically, there is no indication that this credibility was ever questioned by the Soviet leadership.

For the Soviet Union, mutual deterrence, and its stabilization and assurance under a growing parity in strategic capabilities, marked a historic advance over previous strategic inferiority. It even carried the promise of attaining political parity with the United States, until then the only global superpower.

Throughout the 1970s and 1980s, the Soviet Union sought to consolidate its attainment of strategic parity. While feeling much more secure than before, Soviet leaders have been very concerned about what they have seen as persistent U.S. attempts to deprive them of parity (and even of their deterrent) through new military technological breakthroughs: MIRV, which they caught up with in the latter 1970s; and in the latter half of the 1980s above all the Strategic Defense Initiative and space-based offensive weaponry, as well as a forward-deployed Pershing II and ground-launched cruise missile (GLCM) threat to their central command and control system, other cruise missiles and stealth technology, antisubmarine warfare superiority, and finally advanced high-precision arms and information and control technology for managing the theater battle.

The United States, on the other hand, far from seeing its technological advantages and advances as promising renewed superiority, saw an increasing threat from growing Soviet nuclear and conventional capabilities in the 1970s and 1980s.

Mutual deterrence has, nonetheless, been far more sturdy and robust than the expectations of those on either side who feared its disruption, and any on either side who may have harbored hopes of surmounting it.

Chapter Three

Prevention of Nuclear War in Soviet Policy

SOVIET LEADERS, as noted earlier, have acknowledged the catastrophic consequences of nuclear war, and hence its unacceptability as an instrument of policy, ever since the 1950s. During the 1960s and early 1970s, however, there was a debate over whether war in the nuclear era had ceased to be an instrument of policy.[1] Nominally, the debate was over a theoretical issue resolved by acknowledging that while nuclear war would be a continuation of policy (by both aggressor and defender), it could not rationally serve as an instrument of policy. This judgment was consistent with the Soviet policy of maintaining military forces for deterrence. The underlying significance of the debate, however, was over whether nuclear war, if deterrence should fail, could really be waged, thus requiring (and justifying) extensive preparations for waging such a war. A persistently recurring central defense policy issue therefore has been: to what extent should virtually limitless "requirements" for waging possible wars be met? Other important interrelated issues have involved Soviet arms control and foreign policy, and of course Soviet internal economic and other priorities.

As discussed in the preceding chapter, Soviet thinking has gener-

1. See the discussion in Raymond L. Garthoff, "Mutual Deterrence and Strategic Arms Limitation in Soviet Policy," *International Security*, vol. 3 (Summer 1978), pp. 117–21; reprinted in Sean M. Lynn-Jones, Steven E. Miller, and Stephen Van Evera, eds., *Soviet Military Policy* (MIT Press, 1989), pp. 171–206. This article has more complete reference to the debates in the 1960s than later versions of the analysis, which provide additional data and discussion relating to the 1970s and 1980s. For these later versions, see Garthoff, "Mutual Deterrence and Strategic Arms Limitation in Soviet Policy," in Bernard F. Halloran, ed., *Essays on Arms Control and National Security* (Washington: U.S. Arms Control and Disarmament Agency, 1986), pp. 137–86; and Garthoff, "Mutual Deterrence, Mutual Security, and the Future of Strategic Arms Limitation," in Derek Leebaert, ed., *The New Soviet Military Thinking* (Cambridge University Press, forthcoming 1990).

ally assumed deterrence to be provided by an assured military capability for retaliation, backed up by a capability for waging war if deterrence fails. Deterrence, however, while intended to dissuade a potential attacker, has not been regarded as equivalent to or exhaustive of measures to prevent war. Other aspects of foreign policy, arms control, and even military doctrine have come to be seen as having a significant contribution to make along with or beyond deterrence in preventing the ultimate catastrophe of nuclear war.

Even during the 1960s, military writings that continued to stress doctrine and requirements for waging a general nuclear war, such as the authoritative treatise *Military Strategy* edited by a team led by Marshal Vasily Sokolovsky (editions in 1962, 1963, and 1968), also accepted and even elaborated on the colossal death and destruction of nuclear war. By the third edition of that book in 1968 language had been added explicitly referring to "the unacceptability of nuclear war" to the Soviet Union, and "the necessity for its prevention."[2] Major General Vasily Zemskov, the editor of *Military Thought*, wrote in that confidential journal of the General Staff in 1969 that "realistically considering" that a nuclear war "cannot and should not serve as a means of resolving international disputes," the "Communist Party of the Soviet Union and the Soviet Government are pursuing a consistent line toward preventing a world war, including a nuclear war, and toward excluding it from the life of society."[3]

By the time of the Twenty-fourth Party Congress in April 1971, Soviet political and military leaders ceased to call for strategic superiority as an objective. In the mid-1970s Leonid Brezhnev (like Georgy Malenkov and then Nikita Khrushchev before him) frequently stressed the senselessness and danger of a catastrophic world nuclear war.[4]

As early as the mid-1970s, the distinguished Soviet military theoretician Major General Mikhail Cherednichenko mused that in the situation of polarized political conflict in the nuclear-missile age, strategy had become "not only a means of achieving objectives of war, but also a means of preventing [war]," which was "one of the

2. Marshal V. D. Sokolovsky, ed., *Voyennaya strategiya* (Military Strategy), 3d ed. (Moscow: Voyenizdat, 1968), p. 239.

3. Maj. Gen. V. I. Zemskov, "Wars of the Contemporary Era," *Voyennaya mysl'* (Military Thought), no. 5 (May 1969), p. 57.

4. For example, see "Speech of Comrade L. I. Brezhnev," *Pravda*, July 22, 1974, pp. 2–3; June 14, 1975, pp. 1–2; and November 25, 1976, p. 1.

main factors in world politics." Other Soviet military analysts also stressed that "the prevention of world nuclear war had become a reality of today and a real possibility for the future," and still others that the danger of world nuclear war had become "the main danger to humankind."[5]

In January 1977 Brezhnev explicitly disavowed the goal of military superiority aimed at a first strike and reaffirmed the goal of deterrence and "preventing both first and second strikes and nuclear war altogether."[6] Brezhnev and his successors in the 1980s continued to emphasize the necessity for preventing nuclear war, the catastrophic nature of such a war, and the inability to win such a war. There has been a progression of ever more far-reaching statements, from assertions of the need to prevent a world nuclear war to calls to prevent all nuclear war, and in the latter half of the 1980s to prevent all war, and in particular any war between the Soviet Union and its allies and the United States and its allies.

To be sure, some Western commentators have termed these statements of the Soviet political and military leaders the "Tula line" (Brezhnev's statement of January 1977 having been made in a speech at Tula), and disparaged its significance for Soviet military doctrine and strategy. Indeed, many in the West assumed and alleged that Soviet pronouncements on the political level were merely propaganda or deception, and not related to "real" Soviet military doctrine.

To evaluate these and similar Soviet declarations, this chapter reviews developments in Soviet military doctrine from the mid-1960s to the mid-1980s, on both the political and military levels, and actual Soviet practice both in its military programs and in arms limitation and reduction negotiations and other political actions.

5. Maj. Gen. M. Cherednichenko, "The Evolution of Views on the Content and Functions of Military Strategy," *Voyennaya mysl'*, no. 12 (December 1974), p. 21; Col. Ye. Rybkin and Col. S. Dmitriyev, "V. I. Lenin on the Essence, Character, and Types of Wars," *Voyennaya mysl'*, no. 1 (January 1975), p. 62; and Gen. Army I. Shavrov, "Nuclear World War—The Main Danger to Humankind," *Voyennaya mysl'*, no. 6 (June 1975), title and p. 22.

6. L. I. Brezhnev, "Outstanding Exploit of the Defenders of Tula: Speech of Comrade L. I. Brezhnev," *Pravda*, January 19, 1977, pp. 1–2. In an early reiteration, Brezhnev broadened his reference and clarified that the Soviet Union "does not and will not seek military superiority over the other side" for any reason, not just for purposes of preparing a first strike, and vowed instead to maintain parity, "the existing approximate balance of strength." L. I. Brezhnev, "The Great October Revolution and the Progress of Mankind: Report of Comrade L. I. Brezhnev," *Pravda*, November 3, 1977, pp. 2–3.

Changing Soviet Military Doctrine on Nuclear War

In the mid-1960s Soviet military doctrine abandoned an assumption that war between the Soviet Union and Warsaw Pact versus the United States and NATO would inevitably be general nuclear war. It was, instead, recognized that in an era of parity in intercontinental nuclear forces, at a level of potential reciprocal devastation threatening human civilization, both sides had an interest in averting catastrophe, and this fact could be acknowledged and acted on by both sides. While a strong desire to avert war remained, a range of possible offensive and defensive war scenarios below the level of general nuclear war and reciprocal annihilation also came to be recognized.[7] This change in Soviet military doctrine was profound and has significantly affected Soviet foreign policy and arms control policy as well as military policy. In the military sphere, it affected strategy, plans, organization, and force structure. As Marshal Nikolai Ogarkov has described it, there has been a general divide between the 1950s and 1960s, when nuclear weapons were regarded as another means of warfare, and the 1970s and 1980s, when a "radical reevaluation" of the role of nuclear weapons led to "a break from previous views on their role and place in war" and "*even on the possibility of waging war at all with the use of nuclear weapons.*"[8]

A new emphasis in Soviet national policy statements on justifying a policy of averting nuclear war began in 1967 and intensified in the 1970s and 1980s. Moreover, such national policy statements by General Secretary Brezhnev and his successors and other Soviet leaders are cited as authoritative in the military doctrinal discussions. For example, an article in *Military Thought* in 1970 stressed that the Soviet strategic nuclear capability had made general nuclear war no longer inevitable because of its deterrent effect on the

---

7. See Michael MccGwire, *Military Objectives in Soviet Foreign Policy* (Brookings, 1987), for a pioneering analysis of this important turning point. MccGwire suggests, on the basis of a careful analysis, that a key decision was made in December 1966. Change began, however, in the mid-1960s, gaining momentum after Khrushchev's ouster in 1964, and for reasons discussed later in this chapter I believe early 1965 was the watershed change. At the same time, as MccGwire also notes, it took several years for some aspects of the change to become apparent and to take effect, particularly with respect to changes in force structure.

8. Marshal N. V. Ogarkov, *Istoriya uchit bditel'nosti* (History Teaches Vigilance) (Moscow: Voyenizdat, 1985), p. 51; emphasis added.

United States. Without suggesting that general war might ever have been considered in the Soviet interest, the author went out of his way to stress that *nuclear* war certainly would *not* be in the Soviet interest. "A world nuclear war, despite all of the just nature of our struggle, we cannot consider as a feasible, rational means of resolution of international problems. A deep responsibility for the fate of peoples and the achievements of civilization, and the nature of Marxist ideology, underlie the striving of the peoples and the governments of the socialist countries and communists of the whole world not to permit a nuclear war."[9] The author then cited in support of this position a statement by General Secretary Brezhnev in late 1967, in line with the change in Soviet military doctrine directed toward averting nuclear war, that "under contemporary circumstances world war with the employment of nuclear missile weapons would lead to the death of hundreds of millions of people, to the annihilation of entire countries, to the contamination of the atmosphere and surface of the earth. Communists cannot fail to draw from that the most serious political conclusions. The struggle for the prevention of the threat of a new world war has now become one of the most important conditions for the successful construction of socialism and communism and the development of the whole world revolutionary process."[10]

Ideological justification is thus provided for a deeply pragmatic consideration. Citation of Brezhnev's statement in a discussion of Soviet military doctrine in the confidential General Staff journal suggests its relevance not only to Soviet declaratory doctrine and internal and external propaganda, but also to military policy.

The change in military doctrine beginning in the latter half of the 1960s was made possible by recognition that the Soviet attainment of strategic nuclear parity would give the United States also a powerful incentive to avert general nuclear war. Colonel General Mikhail Povaly, soon after serving as deputy chief of the General Staff and head of its Main Operations Directorate—the chief Soviet war planner—wrote in a key article on "Policy and Military Strategy" in

9. Col. Ye. Rybkin, "The Marxist-Leninist Conception of the Essence of War and Its Sources," *Voyennaya mysl'*, no. 8 (August 1970), p. 14.

10. L. Brezhnev, *Izbrannye proizvedeniya* (Selected Works) (Moscow: Politizdat, 1981), vol. 1, p. 196. The original speech was "Fifty Years of the Great Victories of Socialism," delivered on November 3, 1967.

Military Thought in 1970 that "the growth of the military potential and possession of strategic nuclear forces by the USSR has an enormous deterrent effect on the policy of the imperialist states and on the nature and content of American military strategy."[11] He noted the continuing possibility of a general nuclear war, and that "the strategic nuclear forces of the sides would be the main, decisive element in *such* a war." He stressed, however, that "now American political leaders and strategists have begun to understand that, in connection with the creation of a powerful nuclear potential in the Soviet Union, general nuclear war becomes hopeless and extremely dangerous for the United States as a means for achievement of its aggressive policy. . . . Therefore more and more Western political leaders and military strategists are returning to the idea of the possibility of waging nonnuclear war, even in Europe."[12]

Soviet military analyses, especially in *Military Thought,* had begun in the mid-1960s to give serious attention to the growing Western interest in "flexible response" and limited nuclear and nonnuclear wars. They stressed that American interest in limited war arose "not because of good intentions," but because growing Soviet military power and other political factors in the world made resort to general nuclear war more dangerous for the United States.[13] It was noted that wars could be limited by "political and military aims," by territorial limits, and by the employment of various weapons, notably use or nonuse of nuclear weapons.[14] American views of escalation were similarly examined in detail, as it was held that "even the theory of 'limited war' has not encompassed the problem as a whole. There have continued searches for a military strategy that would provide for the waging of wars of any kind: general nuclear war, or limited war with or without the use of nuclear weapons." Western concepts of flexible response *and* theories of escalation and escalation domi-

11. Col. Gen. M. Povaly, "Policy and Military Strategy," *Voyennaya mysl'*, no. 7 (July 1970), p. 18. This article was one of a series on military strategy presented from 1970 through 1973 in the confidential General Staff journal.

12. Ibid., pp. 18–19, 19–20; emphasis added. This final sentence quoted above repeated almost verbatim a statement by General Cherednichenko in the same journal five months earlier (cited later in this chapter), suggesting that both may have been hewing closely to a classified assessment.

13. See Col. V. Mochalov, "Types of Wars According to the Pentagon," *Voyennaya mysl'*, no. 9 (September 1964), pp. 70–78, esp. pp. 72–73.

14. Ibid., pp. 73, 74.

nance were thus seen as having arisen from this impulse to find a war-waging strategy.[15]

Although the Soviet discussions followed and were keyed to Western theories, in fact there were parallels in Soviet and American thinking about limited war and flexible response reflecting the fact that both sides faced essentially the same problems. This fact was obscured because neither took sufficiently seriously the expressed views of the other—both tended instead to impute more ominous and aggressive designs to the adversary.

These Soviet discussions of the mid- to late 1960s and early 1970s encompassed possible nonnuclear or limited nuclear war in Europe, as well as nonnuclear local wars in various regions of the globe. The dangers of escalation in Europe were particularly stressed.[16] Discussions of U.S. strategy repeatedly assured that "such doctrines have no chance of success" in meeting imputed aggressive American aims,[17] but they were much more equivocal on the question of limiting war. In the first place, they treated such wars as the Korean War and the war in Vietnam as limited wars waged by the United States—not successfully, but nonetheless limited wars.[18] Controlled escalation, particularly in a limited nuclear war in Europe, was perhaps another matter: "Any attempt to put such a theory into practice would prove fatal to its initiators," according to one discussion in 1965.[19]

Yet even in the mid-1960s some discussions in the General Staff journal cautiously addressed the *Soviet* view of limited war and concluded that "the limitation of war is currently possible," providing examples of restraint and limitation in Soviet military experience.[20] Moreover, there were direct signs of a debate among Soviet military men, beginning even before Khrushchev's ouster but developing in the several years following. In May 1963 a Soviet officer declared: "One must not lose sight of the fact that the imperialists, fearing an

15. See in particular Capt. lst Rank A. Kvitnitsky and Capt. (Res.) Yu. Nepodayev, "The Theory of the Escalation of War," *Voyennaya mysl'*, no. 9 (September 1965), pp. 51–59, esp. p. 52. See also Nepodayev, "On the 'Nuclear Threshold' in NATO Strategy," *Voyennaya mysl'*, no. 6 (June 1966), pp. 58–64.

16. See V. Perfilov, "Limited War in U.S. Foreign Policy," *Voyennaya mysl'*, no. 4 (April 1971), pp. 82, 88.

17. Ibid., p. 90.

18. Ibid., pp. 82–89.

19. Kvitnitsky and Nepodayev, *Voyennaya mysl'*, no. 9 (September 1965), p. 59.

20. Mochalov, *Voyennaya mysl'*, no. 9 (September 1964), p. 77.

inevitable nuclear missile retaliatory strike, might unleash against us one or another form of war *without* using nuclear weapons." The author then went on to say that "from this proceeds a practical conclusion—*our* armed forces must be prepared to deal an appropriate rebuff *with conventional weapons*," while of course "keeping nuclear missile weapons in the highest state of readiness."[21] Early in 1964 several articles by much more prominent military figures discussed the need for Soviet military science to study requirements for waging conventional war, as well as nuclear war. Most notably, the deputy editor of *Military Thought* in that confidential journal asserted that military science permitted, indeed required, that Soviet military doctrine not only prepare to deal with "the most probable future war" the imperialists might unleash, "a world nuclear-missile war," but also address "other means of waging war that can arise either in the framework of nuclear war [that is, limited nuclear war] or in a war without the use of nuclear weapons."[22] After Khrushchev's fall in October 1964 such discussion expanded.

The new political leadership did not intrude into the military-technical level of military doctrine as Khrushchev had done. And in rare comments in this area, Leonid Brezhnev and his colleagues, in sharp contrast to Khrushchev, endorsed the view of the military leadership. Thus in an address to military academy graduates in July 1965 Brezhnev reassured his audience that "in paying special attention to nuclear-missile weapons, we have not forgotten the great role that remains, as before, with conventional weapons."[23] Even

21. Major D. Kazakov, "The Theoretical and Methodological Foundation of Soviet Military Science," *Kommunist vooruzhennykh sil* (Communist of the Armed Forces), no. 10 (May 1963), pp. 71–72; emphasis added. (Hereafter *KVS*.)

22. See Maj. Gen. S. Kozlov, "The Development of Soviet Military Science after World War II," *Voyennaya mysl'*, no. 2 (February 1964), p. 67; and see also Maj. Gen. V. Reznichenko, "Questions of Contemporary Combined Arms Battle," *Voyennaya mysl'*, no. 3 (March 1964), p. 32. General Kozlov, then deputy chief editor of *Military Thought*, in June 1965 became chief editor. General Reznichenko headed the tactics faculty at the Frunze (Command and Staff) Academy. References also appeared, without elaboration, in the open military press. For example, see Marshal of the Tank Troops P. Rotmistrov, "Historic Victory," *Moscow News*, no. 19, May 11, 1963, p. 3; Col. Gen. S. M. Shtemenko, "The Ground Forces in Contemporary War and Their Combat Preparation," *Krasnaya zvezda* (Red Star), January 3, 1963, p. 2; and Col. Gen. I. Glebov, "Development of the Operational Art," *Krasnaya zvezda*, April 2, 1964, p. 3.

23. "All Efforts and Knowledge—For the Motherland, for the Cause of the Party: Speech of Comrade L. I. Brezhnev," *Krasnaya zvezda*, July 4, 1965, p. 3. His remarks

more important, military outlays were increased to accommodate a buildup in conventional capabilities.

A later book on the Soviet armed forces, intended for use in military academies as well as wider readership, made clear the connection with the ouster of Khrushchev, the central change from an overemphasis on nuclear war, and the role of the professional military in this change. "After the October 1964 Central Committee Plenum," it stated, referring to the meeting that removed Khrushchev, "certain erroneous views associated with an overevaluation of the potential of the atomic weapon and its influence on the character of war and on the further development of the armed forces were overcome in military science circles."[24]

On November 6, 1965, Minister of Defense Marshal Rodion Malinovsky issued classified Order 303, "On the Journal *Military Thought*," defining "the most important trends of theoretical research that respond to actual problems of developing military affairs." Among them was study of the military art "chiefly under conditions of the employment of nuclear weapons, but also under conditions of the conduct of military operations with conventional weapons."[25] The directive also called for generalization of the experience of local wars.

A later history of the General Staff Academy disclosed that the academy had begun to include instruction in preparation for nonnuclear wars in 1965, just after Khrushchev's ouster. The history highlighted the roles of the Politburo and the Central Committee in "defining the requirements for the organization of the defense of the country," and the provision by the Central Committee and the

---

also strongly implied a Soviet readiness to meet limited military challenges with limited responses.

24. [Col.] S. A. Tyushkevich and others, *Sovetskiye vooruzhennyye sily: Istoriya stroitel'stva* (The Soviet Armed Forces: History of Development) (Moscow: Voyenizdat, 1978), p. 476.

25. The order, never made public, is quoted at length in an editorial article, "Under the Banner of the Great Lenin," *Voyennaya mysl'*, no. 2 (February 1966), pp. 13–14. A conference of military historians in early 1965 was told that "quite recently we witnessed how one-sidedness and subjectivism" in the military sphere involved "an underevaluation of the role of aviation and tanks in modern warfare." Col. A. Grylev, "Certain Questions Concerning Methods of Research in Military History," *Voyenno-istoricheskii zhurnal* (Journal of Military History), no. 7 (July 1965), p. 9 (reporting on a conference held March 1, 1965). The whole subject of military history was given renewed attention in accordance with the recognition that future wars might not be totally different from past wars.

Council of Ministers not only of the newest strategic missile arms but also "great attention to the development and improvement of conventional arms." It went on to stress the academy's task in "the new stage of construction of the Soviet armed forces" beginning in 1965 as "perfecting the theory and practice of the conduct by all services of the armed forces of contemporary operations of various scale and nature, both with the employment of nuclear weapons and with the employment only of conventional armaments."[26] In late 1964 or 1965 orders were also given for a secret text on *General Tactics*, prepared and issued by the Frunze (Command and Staff) Academy in 1966. This secret text was devoted entirely to warfare with conventional weapons only (although of course noting in a prefatory comment the possibility of escalation to nuclear war, and the "decisive influence" of such weapons on the battle if employed).[27] Almost at the same time another volume, called *Tactics*, with the same editor (Major General Vasily Reznichenko of the Frunze Academy), was openly published for the official Officer's Library series, but it dealt predominantly with tactics of nuclear warfare.[28] Clearly, the Soviet leaders wished to retain their public opposition to ideas of limited war, including conventional war, while preparing to be able to wage such war effectively if the West were prepared to keep a war limited to nonnuclear weapons.

Openly published military discussions also surfaced the general requirement: "The Soviet armed forces must be prepared to assure the destruction of the enemy not only when nuclear weapons are employed, but also when only conventional weapons are employed."[29] Revealing discussions and open signs of direct debate, however, continued to be restricted to the confidential discussions.

In one of the most interesting discussions of this period, in *Military*

26. Gen. Army V. G. Kulikov, ed., *Akademiya general'nogo shtaba* (Academy of the General Staff) (Moscow: Voyenizdat, 1976), pp. 179, 178, 181.

27. Maj. Gen. V. G. Reznichenko, ed., *Obshchaya taktika: uchebnik* (General Tactics: A Textbook) (Moscow: Voyenizdat, 1966), Secret. (A translation by the Office of the Assistant Chief of Staff for Intelligence, U.S. Army, has recently been declassified.)

28. Maj. Gen. V. G. Reznichenko, ed., *Taktika* (Tactics), Officer's Library series (Moscow: Voyenizdat, 1966). Except for the important distinction between nuclear and nonnuclear warfare, it closely paralleled the secret version in organization and coverage.

29. Col. I. Prusanov, "The Party's Work in Strengthening the Armed Forces under Conditions of the Revolution in Military Affairs," *KVS*, no. 3 (February 1966), p. 10.

Thought, two writers described the "special reliance" being placed by the imperialists on "local and limited wars as a means of achieving the same aggressive aims" under conditions when the military power of the Soviet Union would serve as a "global paralyzation" of American strategic nuclear power. They went on to discuss limited and local wars, noting that "local wars are the result of limited aims (limited from the standpoint of global, not necessarily local, scale)." But local wars with limited aims may not, they noted, be "limited in their impact on the general world situation"; "they may disturb important political, economic, and military-strategic interests of the main groupings of powers opposing one another and provoke a conflict with them. A conflict into which the nuclear powers are directly drawn will threaten to turn into a general world war." The authors concluded that "the unique combination of the threat of nuclear war hanging over the world and local wars being constantly waged is a most important feature of the contemporary epoch."[30]

Nonetheless, despite the dangers of escalation of a local or other limited war, some contributors to the Soviet internal military debate stressed the possibility of avoiding such involvements and escalation by Soviet restraint. One of the authors of the above-cited warning, for example, took issue with a writer who had stressed the danger of escalation. Major General Nikolai Pukhovsky, a veteran Soviet military theoretician on the faculty of the General Staff Academy, had written a book published in 1965 in which he warned that a local war unleashed by the United States could rapidly escalate into a world thermonuclear war. He said, "Such an outcome of a local war is most likely because any local war by the [Western] aggressors will have as its mission undermining the might of the world system of socialism and, as soon as that system moves to defend its interests and strikes the aggressor, it is entirely likely that he will then seek to change the correlation of forces to his advantage by means of nuclear weapons, and that would immediately make the war a world thermonuclear war."[31] He thus implied Soviet nuclear response to any Western local use of nuclear weapons, and even perhaps Soviet escalation to wider use of nuclear weapons.

The commentator in *Military Thought*, Colonel Yevgeny Rybkin,

30. Maj. Gen. K. Stepanov and Lt. Col. Ye. Rybkin, "On the Character and Types of Wars in the Contemporary Epoch," *Voyennaya mysl'*, no. 2 (February 1968), p. 67.

31. Maj. Gen. N. V. Pukhovsky, *O mire i voine* (On Peace and War) (Moscow: Mysl', 1965), pp. 182–83.

tore this statement to shreds. First, he pointed out that "*not* every local war has the aim of the direct undermining of the world socialist system," that such wars are usually imperialist wars against the national-liberation movement, even though indirectly they deal a loss to "the socialist camp." Second, he noted that of numerous local wars in this century, "only two" had been transformed into world wars (the attack by Austria-Hungary on Serbia in 1914 and by Germany on Poland in 1939). While accepting the general formula that it was "entirely possible" that the imperialists might resort to nuclear weapons in a local war, "again it is doubtful that that would 'immediately' lead to world war. *Everything would depend on the concrete circumstances. And in any case it is in the interests of the Soviet Union* and of all progressive mankind *to end a local war or to limit it* and defeat an aggressor with limited forces." While not specifically saying a local defeat would be preferable to escalation, he did not say escalation should be undertaken by the Soviet Union even to ward off defeat in a local war, and he implied it should not. He then concluded by saying, "The working out of this problem is one of the important tasks of the development of Soviet military theory at the contemporary stage."[32]

There were other discussions during the last half of the 1960s envisaging the possibilities of limited nuclear war, even in Europe. Colonel General Nikolai Lomov, a distinguished professor and General Staff officer who had long contributed to the study of military doctrine, referred to the possibility of a local (limited) war in Europe, probably without use of nuclear weapons but "not excluding the possibility that tactical nuclear weapons would be employed." He stressed, however, that in the case of limited nuclear warfare "the probability of escalation into a nuclear world war would always be great and might under certain circumstances become inevitable."[33]

32. Lt. Col. Ye. Rybkin, "The Book 'On Peace and War,'" *Voyennaya mysl'*, no. 7 (July 1966), p. 78; emphasis added. Another Soviet military analyst, writing in *Military Thought* in 1980, added to the dangers of a world war arising from a local imperialist-generated war the case of "the aggressive policy of the present leaders of China," clearly having in mind the Chinese attack on Vietnam in early 1979. "In the contemporary world, where there are no isolated events, local wars, as history bears witness, are fraught with danger of a great war." Maj. Gen. Avn. V. V. Serebryannikov, "Leninist Principles of the Analysis of War and the Present Day," *Voyennaya mysl'*, no. 3 (March 1980), pp. 11–12.

33. Col. Gen. N. A. Lomov, "The Influence of Soviet Military Doctrine on the Development of the Military Art," *KVS*, no. 21 (November 1965), pp. 16, 18.

An important volume on *Methodological Problems of Military Theory and Practice* that was published in 1966 suggested that in addition to general nuclear war and wars limited to conventional arms, wars might "encompass only some regions, with [nuclear] weapons of limited yields" and that "if the employment of nuclear weapons is limited (in terms of numbers and yield of nuclear strikes, and also by definite regions of the world), then the operation of the laws of armed conflict will acquire a somewhat different direction. Conventional arms and armaments and corresponding means and forms of armed conflict will then play a greater role."[34] Two years later, Marshal Vasily Sokolovsky and General Cherednichenko also referred to both "the possibility of wars occurring with the use of conventional weapons" alone and "the limited use of nuclear means in one or several theaters of military operations."[35] These possibilities were not further elaborated.

In 1970, however, a series of articles in *Military Thought* disclosed the extent to which the Soviet military establishment was working on various scenarios for limited war in the belief that there were real possibilities for avoiding a general nuclear war. General Cherednichenko, a close collaborator of the late Marshal Sokolovsky and member of the faculty of the General Staff Academy, contributed a particularly important article in February 1970. He stressed that the United States had turned to consideration of limited war, limited nuclear or conventional only, in response to Soviet strategic military advances.[36]

General Cherednichenko's discussion of limited nuclear war took as its point of departure the views of Western military theoreticians, but he went beyond them to indicate his own views. Thus he cited the Western view that "limited nuclear war *can* occur as the result of escalation from conventional war when the necessity may arise for the use of nuclear weapons against military targets on the battlefield."

34. Col. M. V. Popov, "Laws of Armed Conflict and Principles of the Military Art," in Maj. Gen. N. Ya. Sushko and Lt. Col. T. R. Kondratkov, eds., *Metodologicheskiye problemy voyennoi teorii i praktiki* (Methodological Problems of Military Theory and Practice) (Moscow: Voyenizdat, 1966), p. 108, and see Col. S. I. Krupnov, "Dialectics of the Evolution of the Means and Forms of Armed Conflict," p. 127, in the same volume.

35. Marshal V. Sokolovsky and Maj. Gen. M. Cherednichenko, "Military Strategy and Its Problems," *Voyennaya mysl'*, no. 10 (October 1968), p. 36.

36. Maj. Gen. M. Cherednichenko, "Some Characteristics of the Contemporary Military Art," *Voyennaya mysl'*, no. 2 (February 1970), p. 40.

He stressed, however, the difficulties in limiting damage and civilian casualties and in separating operational-tactical from strategic nuclear weapons, and expressed doubt whether escalation to strategic nuclear weapons could be prevented. "There is no guarantee that an aggressor, suffering setbacks, would not turn to more powerful means, to strategic nuclear weapons." His conclusion was that "limited nuclear war, thus, *can* quickly be transformed into general nuclear war."[37] His skepticism was strong, but he did not conclude that limited nuclear war would *inevitably* and inescapably escalate—nor that the Soviet Union would not seek to prevent such escalation.

General Cherednichenko gave much more attention to, and was more optimistic about, the possibility of limiting war to conventional weapons. He noted that "more and more, Western military strategists are returning to the idea of the possibility of waging nonnuclear war, even in Europe."[38] He doubted that conventional war could become a general war on the scale of World War II but noted that it is "difficult to determine the scale, intensity and length of a conventional war under contemporary conditions"—a statement he could not have made if the option of large-scale conventional war was one Soviet strategy had rejected. Moreover, he said these "characteristics of the military art" not only are being analyzed by foreign sources, but also "to one or another extent they are *objectively determined* by the contemporary level of development of arms and military technology and the prospects for their further development."[39]

The debate over giving priority attention to preparing for wars limited to conventional weapons was essentially decided by the late 1960s. Soon after, discussions of conventional warfare began to appear, especially in the confidential *Military Thought.*[40] Several

37. Ibid., p. 41; emphasis added. General Cherednichenko suggested, drawing from Western discussion, that limited nuclear war would also be held to a restricted region, would use "mainly" tactical nuclear weapons, delivered by missiles, aircraft, and naval vessels, of small and medium (up to 600 KT) destructive power, employed to an operational depth of 300–500 kilometers, against military targets. But he expressed great doubt over the ability to limit use to military targets and to contain the impact within any region, and he concluded there would unavoidably be enormous devastation and high population losses. Ibid., pp. 46–47.

38. Ibid., p. 47. Note the similar later statement by General Povaly cited above in this chapter.

39. Ibid., p. 49; emphasis added.

40. For example, Col. D. Samorukov, "On Combat Operations with the Employment of Conventional Means of Attack," *Voyennaya mysl'*, no. 8 (August 1967), pp. 30–41.

books that had been published in the early or mid-1960s (including Marshal Sokolovsky's *Military Strategy* and the volume on *Methodological Problems of Military Theory and Practice*) appeared in revised editions in 1968 and 1969 with references that precluded conventional war deleted and with new references to the fact that "wars are possible without the employment of nuclear weapons."[41]

Books written in the late 1960s that still emphasized nuclear war were subjected to critical reviews in mass military media. For example, readers of the Armed Forces newspaper *Red Star* were warned that a book on *Nuclear Weapons and the Development of Tactics* written by instructors at the Frunze Academy and published in 1967 was guilty of "overestimating nuclear weapons, absolutizing their role in close combat, and underestimating the potential of conventional arms."[42] A book on *The Offensive*, also by an instructor at the Frunze Academy and published in 1970, was criticized in the Army ground forces' journal *Military Herald* because it "dwelt to an excess" on nuclear weapons, and as a consequence "loses some of its value." The review charged that the book "belittled the importance of conventional weapons in armed conflict," and most pointedly and

41. Col. Gen. A. S. Zheltov and others, eds., *Metodologicheskiye problemy voyennoy teorii i praktiki* (Methodological Problems of Military Theory and Practice) (Moscow: Voyenizdat, 1969), p. 359. The 1966 edition had already introduced the idea of preparing for all kinds of wars, "world and local," and "with or without the use of nuclear weapons," but the 1969 edition went further in emphasizing the possibility of conventional war. It also deleted the reference to limited nuclear wars earlier cited, evidently either because of the new concentration on conventional war or because the subject was under review.

The Sokolovsky volume, which had appeared in 1962 and was first revised in 1963, was changed in many respects in the 1968 edition, reflecting the new flexibility and preference for conventional war. For example, a section discussing general nuclear war, while essentially retained, instead of representing *the* view of future war was now introduced by the statement: "Nuclear missile war, *if it nonetheless arises*, will be waged by different methods in comparison with past wars." Sokolovsky, ed., *Voyennaya strategiya*, 3d ed., p. 332; emphasis added. A discussion of possible limited nuclear use in local wars, on the other hand, *added* in the second edition, was *deleted* in the third, paralleling the deletion of a similar reference from *Methodological Problems*. See Sokolovsky, ed., *Voyennaya strategiya*, 2d ed., pp. 374–75. For a very useful translation of the third and last edition, with notations of changes in each edition, see Harriet Fast Scott, ed. and trans., *Soviet Military Strategy, by V. D. Sokolovsky, Marshal of the Soviet Union* (New York: Crane, Russak, and Co., 1968).

42. Maj. Gen. Yu. Novikov, review of [Colonels] P. M. Petrus', P. V. Shemansky, and N. I. Chul'sky, *Yadernoye oruzhiye i razvitiye taktiki* (Nuclear Weapons and the Development of Tactics) (Moscow: Voyenizdat, 1967), in *Krasnaya zvezda*, June 28, 1968, p.4.

significantly disagreed that employment of nuclear weapons "constitutes the main trend in combat operations."[43]

Thus by the early 1970s, in particular after the Party Congress in
1971, the Soviet leaders seem to have decided that while limited
nuclear *responses* should not be precluded, any concept advocating
limited nuclear war was fraught with such danger that it should be
abjured. As the United States turned increasingly in the direction of
limited nuclear options, beginning with the so-called Schlesinger
Doctrine in 1974 and continued in Presidential Directive 59 (PD-59)
in the Carter administration, the Soviets sought, through a vigorous
political and propaganda campaign, to argue against the feasibility
of any concepts of limited war and to concentrate more on keeping
any war nonnuclear.

Soviet understanding of Western interest in limited nuclear war
"options," and Western understanding of Soviet views on limited
nuclear war, have both been seriously distorted by differing perspec-
tives. Western interest in limited nuclear options has only been in
terms of building more credible extended deterrence, and in the
worst case, in limited nuclear use if needed to respond to and terminate a massive Soviet conventional attack. The Soviet side, however,
has regarded the Western consideration of and threat to use limited
nuclear options not as intended to restrain or respond to a Soviet
attack, which the Soviets have never intended to launch, but rather
as a Western strategic doctrine intended to avoid the consequences
of general nuclear war while making military gains from a Western
position of strength.[44]

A unique new source of information on Soviet military doctrine
in the mid-1970s has recently become available. Detailed lecture
notes, transcribed by a student at the Voroshilov General Staff Academy in the period 1973–75, outlined four scenarios for a major war:

43. Col. V. Baschenko, "The Book 'The Offensive,'" *Voyennyi vestnik* (Military
Herald), no. 6 (June 1971), pp. 125–27. Review of Col. A. A. Sidorenko, *Nastupleniye*
(The Offensive) (Moscow: Voyenizdat, 1970). Sidorenko's book, incidentally, is widely
cited by American analysts because it was selected for translation by the U.S. Air
Force; the critical review is rarely, if ever before, cited.

44. This distorted Soviet view was a mirror image of the similar distorted view of
those American commentators who inferred aggressive intent and desire to exploit
nuclear capability from Soviet doctrinal writings about waging nuclear war and
pursuit of "victory." Sometimes these arguments, on both sides, may have been
cynical propaganda by those who knew better, but in most cases they represent real
but misplaced views.

(1) surprise attack with unlimited use of nuclear weapons; (2) an attack with limited use of nuclear weapons later escalating to unlimited use of nuclear weapons; (3) attacks by forces in a theater of military operations using only nonnuclear weapons, including the variant of a nonnuclear attack later escalating to use of operational-tactical nuclear weapons in the primary theater of military operations; and (4) gradual escalation from a local war.[45] All variants posited enemy (Western) decision on initiation of the war and of the use of nuclear weapons.

Soviet use of nuclear weapons in all cases was posited only after the enemy had first decided to resort to them. The Soviets would strive to keep any war nonnuclear but recognized that the enemy might escalate to nuclear weapons, probably to a limited use in the main theater of military operations, Europe. These limited nuclear strikes would most likely be caused by escalation "when the dangers of complete destruction of the grouping of enemy armed forces and the loss of important and vital strategic enemy territories may become apparent."[46] The Soviets were not sanguine either that a conventional war would fail to escalate to limited use of nuclear weapons, or that a limited nuclear war, particularly in the Western (European) theater of military operations, could be long maintained without further escalation.[47] Initial limited use of nuclear weapons by the enemy, met by limited use in Soviet counteraction, or enemy escalation from a conventional war to limited use of "operational-tactical" nuclear weapons in a primary theater of military operations, in particular Europe, were posited. The most likely scenario would be a conventional war escalating to limited use of nuclear weapons, and then further escalating to use of strategic nuclear weapons.[48] The Soviet Union, according to this source and others, would meet limited theater uses but *not* escalate. The lecture materials did state, how-

45. These materials have recently been declassified by the U.S. government; see *The Voroshilov Lectures: Materials from the Soviet General Staff Academy*, vol. 1: *Issues of Soviet Military Strategy*, comp. by Ghulam Dastagir Wardak (Washington: National Defense University Press, 1989), pp. 244–48.

46. Ibid., pp. 247–48, and see pp. 72–75.

47. Ibid., pp. 74–75, 247–48.

48. Ibid., pp. 244–48. Essentially the same probable development of hostilities is presented in a published work by professors of the Frunze Academy in 1982. See Lt. Gen. M. M. Kir'yan and others, *Voyenno-tekhnicheskii progress i vooruzhennyye sily SSSR* (Military-Technical Progress and the Armed Forces of the USSR) (Moscow: Voyenizdat, 1982), pp. 312–15.

ever, that Western use of nuclear weapons in the theater should be preempted, if feasible, by Soviet "operational and tactical nuclear delivery means," although not unless the enemy had used or had clearly decided to use nuclear weapons.[49] (This would, by Soviet definition, have excluded the use of SS-20s in the Soviet Union, even in "second use" in a limited nuclear war, but not the employment of shorter-range systems deployed in Eastern Europe.) The Soviets seemed confident they could wage a limited nuclear war, but for that very reason were concerned that the West would therefore at some point further escalate.[50] They did not regard escalation to general nuclear war involving strikes on the Soviet Union and the United States as inevitable, but they did show concern over the danger and even likelihood of such escalation. Thus despite the new strong attention to seeking to keep any war nonnuclear, limited nuclear response options remained. And doctrine and training have also continued to prepare for the worst possibility—a general nuclear war launched by the West directly or in escalation.

The strong Soviet preference for keeping any war nonnuclear if possible has been reinforced. Perhaps the strongest confirmation of the continuing validity of the doctrine of contingent nuclear or nonnuclear war was the appearance in 1984 of a new edition of the authoritative Officer's Library volume *Tactics*, again edited by a team led by General Reznichenko. This volume amalgamated the 1966 secret and open publications, and discussed general troop tactics *both* with and without the employment of nuclear weapons.[51] A new edition published in 1987 went even further in stressing nonnuclear warfare, in particular high-precision strike systems.[52]

Thus Soviet military doctrine on the strategic and operational level was developed to conduct war without use of nuclear weapons. The very nature of military strategy was affected. As one of the leading Soviet military theoreticians noted in 1974, because of both political changes in the world and the appearance of nuclear-missile weapons, there had been "an intensive development of military strategy, a search for new strategic conceptions and a further increase in

49. *Voroshilov Lectures*, vol. 1, p. 248.

50. Ibid., pp. 247–50, 312–13.

51. See Lt. Gen. V. G. Reznichenko and others, *Taktika* (Tactics) (Moscow: Voyenizdat, 1984), pp. 13, 14, 42, and throughout.

52. Lt. Gen. V. G. Reznichenko and others, *Taktika* (Moscow: Voyenizdat, 1987), pp. 16, 23–25, and throughout. This same edition was again issued without further change in 1988.

its role not only as a means of achieving the objectives of war, but also as a means of its prevention," and this had indeed become "one of the main factors in world politics."[53]

A closely related subject given little direct attention in Soviet writings (and almost no attention in Western analysis) has been the development of Soviet military thinking on conflict termination—preventing the continuation and escalation of armed conflict if it should occur (see chapter 5).

The Soviet-American agreements on détente and arms control of the early 1970s, the Antiballistic Missile (ABM) Treaty and Strategic Arms Limitation Talks (SALT) I Interim Agreement on strategic offensive arms signed in 1972, the political accord on Basic Principles for Mutual Relations of that same year, and the Prevention of Nuclear War agreement in 1973, posed a question for Soviet military theory and practice. On the one hand, they seemed to mark major achievements in meeting Soviet aims of preventing a nuclear war. But, at the same time, American strategic capabilities were little affected, and intentions could change. Some Soviet military men feared the agreements would be used to justify reduced Soviet defense efforts. Without reviewing here an interesting debate and decisions on this question, it will suffice to note that these agreements were held to reduce the danger of war, but not to prevent it.[54] They were strongly endorsed, but not held to have yet dispelled the threat. Most important, they failed to dispose of the need for countervailing Soviet strategic nuclear power to ensure that nuclear war would not occur. Nonetheless, these developments were depicted as a significant trend. In the words of General Mal'tsev, then commandant of the Lenin Military-Political Academy, in 1974: "Of fundamental significance is the determination of the United States and the USSR, established in [these] documents, to make every effort together to eliminate the danger of war, and in particular war involving the use of nuclear and other weapons of mass destruction, to curb and ultimately to end the arms race, especially in strategic arms, and to strengthen détente."[55]

53. Cherednichenko, *Voyennaya mysl'*, no. 12 (December 1974), p. 21.
54. This military debate is discussed in Raymond L. Garthoff, *Détente and Confrontation: American-Soviet Relations from Nixon to Reagan* (Brookings, 1985), pp. 352–54.
55. Gen. Army Ye. Mal'tsev, "Political-Military Aspects of International Détente," *Voyennaya mysl'*, no. 8 (August 1974), p. 4.

Soviet military theorists stressed the ideological, political, and military necessity for preventing nuclear war. Nuclear war would be "qualitatively different from other wars." Not only was preventing nuclear war thus a priority objective of the Soviet Union, but a course toward the prevention of war "constitutes one of the essential conditions for successfully accomplishing the tasks of building socialism and communism." The agreements signed in the early 1970s "are lessening the danger of a world war." And, most important, "The prevention of nuclear world war has therefore become a reality of the present day, and a realistic possibility for the future."[56]

Even after the steady deterioration of relations between the United States and the Soviet Union and the rise of tension from 1980 to 1985, Soviet political and military spokesmen reaffirmed the possibility, and even greater need, for prevention of nuclear war. Thus, for example, at the nadir of relations Marshal Nikolai Ogarkov, in an article in the fall of 1983 bristling with charges that the United States was not only increasingly aggressive but was "strenuously pursuing material preparation for a new war," also reaffirmed the Soviet policy of working to prevent a new war.[57]

In November 1984, in his first public utterance after being relieved of his position as chief of the General Staff, Marshal Ogarkov again coupled a renewed attack on the aggressiveness of the Reagan administration with a strong statement on the necessity of preventing war. "War can and must be prevented," he said. "The lessons of history require it. And at the present time both the social-political and military-technical preconditions to do this exist." He stated that the "countries of the socialist commonwealth headed by the Soviet Union" are "the decisive factor in preventing war." More specifically, "the constant combat readiness of the armed forces is the main deterrent and an insurmountable barrier to an aggressor and his strivings to ignite a new world war," and he further defined the military deterrent as a defense capability at the level of "assured destruction of any aggressor."[58] Marshal Sergei Akhromeyev emphasized the same themes: a continuing, even growing, Western threat, but an "objective possibility and real necessity for collaboration of states with dif-

56. Rybkin and Dmitriyev, *Voyennaya mysl'*, no. 1 (January 1975), pp. 61–62.
57. Marshal N. Ogarkov, "A Reliable Defense for Peace," *Izvestiya*, September 23, 1983, pp. 4–5, and *Krasnaya zvezda*, September 23, 1983, p. 2.
58. Marshal N. Ogarkov, "The Unfading Glory of Soviet Arms," *KVS*, no. 21 (November 1984), pp. 23–24.

ferent social systems in the cause of prevention of nuclear war," also giving particular emphasis to the defense capability of the Soviet Union and the inability of the imperialists despite the SDI and other efforts to acquire military superiority and a disarming capability.[59]

Prevention of nuclear war has thus been seen as affecting both the political and military levels or dimensions of Soviet military doctrine, and is so presented in the confidential General Staff organ as well as in public utterances of military and political figures. There is no need to recite numerous illustrations of continuing Soviet statements on this point. Before turning to other applications of this objective in concrete military (including arms limitation) policy, it may, however, be useful to note that even when the prospects for U.S.-Soviet arms control or other agreements seemed most dark, indeed when arms talks had just been broken off, the objective and its necessity continued to be affirmed. Thus, for example, Colonel General Nikolai Chervov, then head of the General Staff directorate responsible for arms control, wrote in *Military Thought* at the end of 1983: "Humankind is now experiencing an exceptionally dangerous period in its history. There hangs over it the shadow of a world nuclear war with its catastrophic consequences. . . . The prevention of nuclear war, restraining the arms race, is today the most impera-tive, the most burning task facing humankind."[60]

As the discussion in the following chapter will show, this objective has been given renewed stress in Soviet military as well as political pronouncements on security policy in the "new thinking" of the Gorbachev period, applied both to the political and military dimen-sions of military doctrine, and to the prevention of nuclear and all war. At this point, it may suffice to note one early example of the new thinking by some Soviet military theoreticians even before Gor-bachev's pronouncements. General Dmitry Volkogonov, in an article in *Pravda* in August 1985, stressed that "the issue is no longer victory or defeat, but existence or annihilation," and that "true security now consists not in seeking ways to achieve victory in war, but in abilities to prevent a nuclear cataclysm."[61]

59. Marshal S. Akhromeyev, "The Superiority of Soviet Military Science and Soviet Military Art—One of the Most Important Factors of Victory in the Great Fatherland War," *Kommunist*, no. 3 (February 1985), pp. 60–61.

60. Col. Gen. N. F. Chervov, "Disarmament: Who Is Opposed?" *Voyennaya mysl'*, no. 12 (December 1983), pp. 3, 4.

61. Lt. Gen. D. Volkogonov, "War and Peace in the 'Nuclear Age,'" *Pravda*, August 30, 1985, pp. 3, 4.

Military Programs

I have reviewed the increasing Soviet attention in military doctrinal discussions from the latter 1960s on to show the new stress on
limiting hostilities to nonnuclear weapons. That emphasis has also
permeated the Soviet military structure and weapons development
and procurement, most of which of course took some time to effect.
It is useful to note a few important examples.

First was the reversal of the reductions in conventional ground
forces and weaponry that had been made in the Khrushchev period.
From the mid-1950s to the early 1960s, the basic Soviet Army
structure had been reduced from 175 divisions (at varying manning
levels) to 140 line divisions. Then from the mid-1960s to the mid-
1980s that structure was gradually increased to about 200 divisions.
Many were at low peacetime levels, but the number at higher manning also rose, as well as the weapons and equipment investment
and planning for wartime mobilization. In the late 1960s and early
1970s, for example, the number of conventional artillery pieces, and
also field antiaircraft systems, were greatly increased—after having
been reduced in the early years of the decade when the emphasis
had been on nuclear warfare. In 1967 the post of "commander-in-
chief, ground forces" was also reestablished in the Soviet armed
forces, reversing the abolition of the position under Khrushchev in
1964. This move reflected the greater role of the army ground forces
in preparing for nonnuclear war.

A second example is the qualitative change in tactical airpower,
providing the longer-range and larger delivery capacities needed for
prolonged conflict and delivery of more bulky conventional ordnance. A third example is the qualitative change in the Soviet navy,
moving from smaller, short-lived ships heavily armed for short engagements to heavier, more balanced, long-endurance ships expected to survive and fight with conventional weapons.

A fourth example, affecting ground, air, and naval forces, is the
shift in training to give greater attention to warfare without use of
nuclear weapons (although all training must make allowance for the
possibility of rapid transition to nuclear warfare if the enemy were
to escalate to nuclear weapons). Training for possible nuclear warfare also occurs, and was even given some renewed attention in the
early 1980s, but it remains more limited. In contrast, in 1960–64 *all*
training had been based on an assumption of nuclear warfare.

During the "transitional" phase in the mid- to late 1960s, two major Warsaw Pact exercises for the first time began with conventional-only *phases*: "October Storm" in the fall of 1965, and "Vltava" in the fall of 1966. Then in September 1967 came the first large-scale entirely nonnuclear field maneuver, "Dnepr" (a Soviet Army exercise, incidentally, rather than a Warsaw Pact one).

The Soviet Union also acquired large numbers of nuclear delivery systems, including many tactical delivery systems (artillery and rocket), during this period. One reason was to prepare for the contingency of nuclear warfare, limited or unlimited. But another reason was to prevent the United States and NATO from having an advantage in nuclear delivery capability, at any level, that might lead it to escalate. In other words, Soviet nuclear delivery systems were intended to serve in the first instance to deter the other side from resorting to comparable nuclear systems by depriving it of any advantage in doing so, thus working to keep any hostilities nonnuclear. Finally, the Soviets began making these systems dual-capable to the extent possible, to increase conventional capability while retaining the deterrent to use of nuclear systems. New tactical ballistic missile systems with much greater accuracy and conventional ordnance delivery capability have been replacing earlier types suitable only for nuclear weapons delivery.

Thus in military operational doctrine, in training, in force composition, and in weaponry the Soviet actions have given convincing signs of seriousness in their efforts both to prepare for conventional warfare and to induce the other side as well to refrain from resort to nuclear weapons.

Theater Nuclear Forces

During the early and mid-1970s, with the SALT negotiations limited to strategic intercontinental and submarine-based ballistic missiles, the Soviet military moved to modernize and enhance theater intermediate-range missile and bomber forces. The SS-20 represented, from the Soviet standpoint, a much overdue replacement for their aging, vulnerable, and excessively large SS-4 medium-range and SS-5 intermediate-range missiles, which had faced Europe since the late 1950s. Substitution of the variable-range SS-11 (and follow-on SS-19) missiles, begun in the late 1960s and early

1970s, was no longer sensible. Since those missiles had intercontinental range, they had to be counted against the Soviet ICBM ceiling
in SALT. While the 360 SS-11s already deployed to cover Eurasian
targets could be absorbed under the SALT I freeze ceiling, when
the Soviet leadership agreed, in December 1974, to accept lower
equal strategic forces ceilings in SALT II, it was decided that they
could not afford under equal ceilings to make even that allotment,
much less hundreds more, designated for Eurasian rather than intercontinental targets. Moreover the SS-20 (using two stages of the
now-abandoned SS-16 mobile ICBM) was available and suitable.
Accordingly, the Soviet leaders approved plans of the Defense Ministry for a force of nearly 500 SS-20 launchers facing both Europe
and the Far East (and covering the Southern Asian rim as well).[62]

The Soviet decision to modernize its theater intermediate-range
missile capability, and similar decisions to modernize shorter-range
tactical-operational missile systems, had two purposes: (1) to contribute to the prevention of any nuclear war in Europe by counterbalancing and "standing off" Western theater nuclear systems, thus
making less likely Western initiation of or escalation to nuclear
warfare; and (2) to provide effective theater nuclear forces if, despite
their efforts to prevent it, a limited nuclear war in Europe should
occur.

The Soviet decision to deploy the SS-20 proved very unwise. It
excited Western concerns and prompted a NATO decision to deploy
counterbalancing intermediate-range missile forces. Although some
Western defense planners (and defense intellectuals) favored deploying such U.S. systems to strengthen deterrence "coupling" independent of new Soviet deployments, the political decision in NATO
would not have been made but for the SS-20.

The NATO decision in 1979 to deploy new, longer-range American nuclear missile systems in Europe—systems capable of striking
targets in the Soviet Union—was a severe blow to Soviet efforts to
reduce the likelihood of escalation to nuclear weapons if hostilities
should occur in Europe. This fact explains the strong, though unsuccessful, Soviet campaign from 1979 through 1983 to prevent that
deployment. Aside from the political contest over deployment, it is
worth noting several aspects of the Soviet position that throw light
on their military priorities.

62. See Raymond L. Garthoff, "The Soviet SS-20 Decision," *Survival*, vol. 25
(May–June 1983), pp. 110–19; and MccGwire, *Military Objectives*, p. 506.

Despite the widespread Western view that the Soviets deployed SS-20s to obtain political-military leverage on Western Europe unless a countering American deployment were made, in fact the Soviet position from the outset undercut any such purpose for their deployment. Rather than threatening Western Europe, explicitly or even implicitly, with its regional nuclear capability, to the contrary the Soviets stressed that *they* regarded any limited use of nuclear weapons as inevitably unleashing general nuclear war. They were far more concerned about possible American resort to the threat or use of limited nuclear warfare than they were tempted by it themselves. While this appeared to some in the West as an attempt to "decouple" the U.S. nuclear deterrent to permit Soviet pressure or even conventional attack, it represented a Soviet effort to deter NATO pressure or limited nuclear attack.

The deployment of the U.S. Pershing II and GLCMs (ground-launched cruise missiles) in Europe contributed also to a hardening of Soviet military doctrine against limited nuclear war. The prospect that Americans might launch nuclear missile attacks deep into the territory of the Soviet Union as part of a war in the European theater, but not face parallel attacks on the United States, drastically changed the terms from those the Soviets had considered in their military doctrinal development and strategic planning from the mid-1960s to the late 1970s.

In the negotiations on intermediate-range nuclear forces (INF), the Soviets made strenuous, albeit unsuccessful, efforts to exchange major reductions in their own INF for no American deployment. They were more interested in preventing American deployment than in preserving their own. This position became very clear in 1987 when a new and more flexible Soviet leadership, faced with the fact of the Pershing II deployment, was prepared to eliminate altogether their own intermediate-range missiles (which had faced Europe since 1959) in exchange for removal of the new American missiles, even without limits on French and British nuclear forces. The Soviets have been far more interested in balancing, reducing, or eliminating theater nuclear forces than in possessing such a capability even when they enjoyed superiority in numbers and strike capability.

A steady stream of statements by Soviet political leaders and by leading Soviet military men in the first half of the 1980s emphatically rejected the feasibility of limited nuclear war. Marshals Ogarkov, Akhromeyev, Dmitry Ustinov, and Viktor Kulikov among others all flatly argued that, in Ustinov's words, "there can be no kind of 'limited' nuclear war at all."[63] Or as Marshal Ogarkov repeatedly stated, "It is impossible in practice to confine a nuclear war within any kind of limited framework."[64] These statements pervaded materials intended for Soviet military readers as well as other publications. The strong Soviet interest in seeking to persuade Western leaders that they do not have limited nuclear "options" provides a good reason for the public Soviet stand. But Soviet views on the possibility of any extended or viable limited nuclear war, always considered a low probability, hardened in their military doctrinal literature as well. At the same time, it is likely that military plans continue to provide flexibility, allowing for Soviet limited nuclear responses if the circumstances warrant.

Those in the West who argued on the basis of Soviet military doctrine and weapon programs that the Soviet Union was pursuing a nuclear war-fighting strategy were simply wrong. So were those in the Soviet Union who misread NATO strategy in the same way. On the other hand, those in the West who feared a Soviet effort to deny to NATO a usable nuclear response, while correct in seeing the Soviet moves as a counter to possible U.S. nuclear use, erred in believing the Soviet purpose was compellence. The Soviet purpose, like that of the West, was deterrence.

Strategic Nuclear Forces

Mutual deterrence remained the bedrock of efforts to prevent nuclear war, based on consolidation and maintenance of parity in strategic nuclear forces and capabilities. From rough equality in numbers of strategic delivery means (missiles and aircraft) at the

63. Marshal D. F. Ustinov, *Sluzhim rodine, delu kommunizma* (We Serve the Motherland and the Cause of Communism) (Moscow: Voyenizdat, 1982), p. 49.

64. Marshal N. V. Ogarkov, *Istoriya uchit bditel'nosti* (History Teaches Vigilance) (Moscow: Voyenizdat, 1985), p. 89; he used virtually the same words in *Vsegda v gotovnosti k zashchite otechestva* (Always in Readiness to Defend the Fatherland) (Moscow: Voyenizdat, 1982), p. 16, and on several other occasions. Marshal S. F. Akhromeyev on several occasions also said that limited nuclear war was "impossible"; for example, see "The Great Victory and Its Lessons," *Izvestiya*, May 7, 1985, p. 2.

For a fuller review of Soviet statements in the 1981–85 period rejecting limited nuclear war, see Mary C. FitzGerald, *Changing Soviet Doctrine on Nuclear War* (Halfax, Nova Scotia: Center for Foreign Policy Studies, Dalhousie University, 1989), pp. 62–82.

beginning of the 1970s, the Soviet Union also reached rough equality in numbers of warheads by the end of the decade. Soviet—like parallel American—efforts in the 1970s and first half of the 1980s were devoted basically to ensuring parity in capability for retaliatory destruction, mixed with continuing if futile efforts to limit damage by counterforce capabilities for destroying part of the adversary's strike capability before it could be launched. Both objectives were justified, in both countries, as enhancing deterrence. But there remained recognition and (if, by some, reluctant) acceptance that there was no realistic prospect of limiting counterforce damage.

In the first place, no adversary could distinguish counterforce damage limitation capability from the disarming capability for a first strike or from offensive compellence grounded in that first-strike capability. While perhaps useful for defensive deterrence, such a capability would be incompatible with mutual deterrence. Even its active pursuit would raise suspicions and fears in the adversary—as the programs of both the Soviet Union and the United States did in the late 1970s and first half of the 1980s. In both countries, the significance of modernization and enhancement of strategic missile forces and possible new strategic defense programs (avowed in the United States in Reagan's SDI; not avowed in the Soviet Union, but feared by suspicious Americans) was exaggerated and gave rise to unwarranted alarm as to the intentions of the adversary. But most important, effective disarming counterforce capability was unattainable, as became increasingly evident. Mutual deterrence had become the dominant factor not so much because it became acceptable to both sides, as that it was insurmountable. Although many military leaders and some political analysts in both countries remained reluctant or even recalcitrant about the virtues of mutual deterrence, it not only existed and exists but was much more readily welcomed by political leaders.

The renunciation of strategic superiority and acceptance of parity by the Soviet political leadership in the 1970s led to increasingly open acceptance of mutual deterrence by the early 1980s. For example, the Soviet armed forces mass journal *Red Star* in 1981 endorsed "strategic parity as a factor of mutual deterrence," which, it went on to note, "makes possible the process of strategic arms limitation."[65]

65. S. Tarov, "Constructive Initiatives," *Krasnaya zvezda*, February 13, 1981, p. 3.

Soviet international security commentators have endorsed not only mutual deterrence, but "the principle of the mutual vulnerability of the sides" based on "mutual assured destruction"—which, although less desirable than disarmament, short of that is "the best way to stabilize the strategic balance."[66] Moreover, mutual deterrence was—correctly—seen as a Soviet achievement canceling the previously one-sided American deterrent-compellent advantage: "The creation by the Soviet Union of a strategic arsenal comparable not only in numbers of forces [*sistemy*] but in qualitative terms with the strategic arsenal of the United States radically changed the situation.... [T]he tendency toward mutual deterrence of the sides— not merely in words, but in fact—is becoming the dominating [factor]."[67]

Mutual deterrence has remained a bedrock of Soviet efforts to prevent nuclear war. The Soviet efforts to minimize the possibility of nuclear war have extended beyond maintaining mutual deterrence to other measures relating to strategic nuclear forces. In the first place, there has been the major effort to reach, and later to preserve and expand, agreements to limit strategic arms.

In the first significant step toward reliance on arms control to serve a key security objective and reduce the possibility of nuclear war, the Soviets decided in 1968–69 to give a higher priority to assured deterrence than to war-waging damage limitation. They decided to accept, and indeed to press for, minimal ABM systems in the strategic arms limitation negotiations (SALT). The ABM Treaty of 1972 reflected a Soviet preference to reduce strategic nuclear war-waging prospects by accepting mutual vulnerability. Soviet agreement to negotiate such a treaty, in 1968, had come soon after a corresponding change in military doctrine ended an important debate on ballistic missile defense that had been under way within the Soviet military and political establishment.[68]

66. G. A. Trofimenko, in "Formulation of the Military-Political Strategy of the Reagan Administration," *SShA: ekonomika, politika, ideologiya* (USA: Economics, Politics, Ideology), no. 5 (May 1982), pp. 123–25. This statement was made in a roundtable discussion directed to analyzing U.S. policy, but in a passage reflecting Soviet acceptance of these postures and American departure from them. In the same discussions another analyst, Radomir Bogdanov, also referred to "the concept of 'mutual assured destruction'" as a "positive, constructive element underlying certain conceptions of deterrence." *SShA*, no. 6 (June 1982), pp. 118–19.

67. G. A. Trofimenko, "Strategic Seesaw in Washington," *SShA*, no. 12 (December 1980), p. 54.

68. For a detailed account, see Raymond L. Garthoff, "BMD and East-West

The ABM Treaty, negotiated in 1969–72, following the unilateral Soviet curtailment of its own ABM deployment at Moscow in 1968–69, represented far more than recognition of limited capabilities of current systems. The decision to work for a binding bilateral commitment of indefinite duration banning nationwide ballistic missile defense reflected a change in Soviet military doctrine to give priority to preventing nuclear war through ensuring a strategic nuclear retaliatory deterrent at the expense of options for war-waging damage limitation in a nuclear war that must not be fought.

The strategic arms limitations negotiated in the SALT I Interim Agreement in 1972 and the SALT II Treaty in 1979 were modest. But they did involve scaling back planned Soviet ICBM deployments in 1969–72 and planned MIRV (multiple independently targeted reentry vehicle) deployments in 1975–76. In addition, if ratified SALT II would have required a 10 percent reduction in Soviet force levels (and none in those of the United States).[69] Moreover, the Soviets had been prepared to reduce strategic forces further if the persistent problem of U.S. and allied forward-based forces capable of strategic strikes on the Soviet Union could have been resolved rather than repeatedly deferred. Nonetheless, the Soviet leadership in the 1970s, not unlike that of the United States, was content to stabilize the existing level of parity and to continue its programs of modernization without serious constraint.

The Soviet leaders also gave increasing attention from the late 1960s on to crisis prevention and crisis management. This Soviet interest contributed to the Accident Measures Agreement of 1971, the hot line upgradings in 1971 and 1984, the U.S.-USSR agreement in 1972 on measures to prevent naval incidents at sea, and other measures.[70] In this connection, they gave particular attention to reaching an agreement on political measures for "Prevention of Nuclear War," to which I shall turn presently.

As discussed in the preceding chapter, the Soviet military in the mid-1950s had developed a concept of preemptive action as a

Relations," in Ashton B. Carter and David N. Schwartz, eds., *Ballistic Missile Defense* (Brookings, 1984), pp. 286–314.

69. For a careful and insightful analysis of Soviet military programs that makes a convincing case that far larger reductions were made in planned Soviet strategic weapons programs, see MccGwire, *Military Objectives*, pp. 235–41, 480–500.

70. See John Borawski, ed., *Avoiding War in the Nuclear Age: Confidence-Building Measures for Crisis Stability* (Boulder, Colo.: Westview Press, 1986), for chapters by appropriate specialists devoted to each of these agreements.

response to an imminent and irrevocable enemy decision to attack.
This concept, developed in the pre-missile age, was largely if not
entirely superseded in the latter 1960s by the concept of launch on
warning or under attack.[71] Launch under attack, while a step toward
stability from preemption, remains a potentially destabilizing and
dangerous possibility. Inherently, the possibility of launch on warning (or launch on first impact, or on multiple impacts) does contribute
to the uncertainties any potential attacker must consider and thereby
to deterrence, but it would be dangerous if in fact carried out in
response to any action except a proven major assault. Moreover, the
very prospect might intensify a crisis and thus weaken efforts to
prevent nuclear war.

The Soviet concept of launch on warning (or under attack) has
never meant a commitment to launch without deliberate decision,
but represented a contingent response if a major enemy attack were
detected. In addition to the means of detection, reconnaissance,
communications, and control highlighted in Soviet military discussions, it also was necessary to have, and by the early 1970s the
Soviets were acquiring, rapid-response missile systems to replace
the slow-reaction, liquid-fueled Soviet missiles of the early and mid-
1960s.

One of the most authoritative early discussions of the concept of
launch on warning replacing preemption, again in the same confidential General Staff organ in which preemption had first been
discussed twelve years earlier, was presented by the commander in
chief of the Strategic Missile Forces, Marshal Nikolai Krylov. "With
the presence in the armament [of the Soviet armed forces] of launchers and missiles completely ready for action, as well as systems for
detecting enemy missile launches and other types of reconnaissance,
an aggressor is no longer able suddenly to destroy the missiles on
the territory of the country subjected to aggression prior to their
launching. They will have time during the flight of the missiles of
the aggressor to leave their launchers and inflict a retaliatory strike
against the enemy."[72] In an important article on Soviet military

71. Many statements appeared in Soviet military literature in the latter 1960s
and 1970s, especially in the confidential *Military Thought*. The point was also made,
inadvertently, in the SALT talks in 1970. See Garthoff, "Mutual Deterrence and
Strategic Arms Limitation in Soviet Policy," in Hallaron, ed., *Essays on Arms Control
and National Security*, pp. 153–56.
72. Marshal N. I. Krylov, "The Nuclear Missile Shield of the Soviet State,"
Voyennaya mysl', no. 11 (November 1967), p. 20. See also Maj. Gen. N. Vasendin

strategy in the same journal in 1979, the head of the chair of strategy at the General Staff Academy reflected the accepted doctrine on launch on warning when he wrote: "Decisions on dealing a retaliatory strike on an aggressor must be taken in calculated minutes after detection of his launch of ballistic missiles."[73]

By the late 1970s and early 1980s, political figures were also occasionally referring in public statements to retaliatory launch under attack as a presumptive consideration for any would-be attacker. For example, an official of the Central Committee staff, in arguing against the idea of limited nuclear attack options, stated that scenarios for limited strategic counterforce strikes were totally unrealistic "deceptions," since "in reality nothing could hold back war if it began in some such 'limited' framework. . . . No one should forget that an aggressor's missiles could not reach their targets before an all-destructive retaliatory salvo would follow."[74]

Although the Soviet concept of preemption was always contingent, defensive, and the forward extreme of a continuum from retaliation, the change in the late 1960s to launch under attack was significant. In the first place, advances in swift technical intelligence collation, communications, and rapid reaction by improved missile systems made launch under attack or even on warning more feasible. But it was made possible not only by such technical advances and the arrival of parity, but also by the Soviet decision to avert nuclear war even at the cost of losing whatever residual advantages preemption might carry if the other side then attacked. When all-out nuclear war had been assumed to be the only or even the most likely form of war, as it had been in the early 1960s, preempting when the enemy was about to launch an attack made sense: going first in the last resort. But if general nuclear war could be averted, and would be comparably devastating for both sides no matter who struck first, it became more prudent to rely on launch under attack. This change helped shift the basis for later decisions on force structure and possible strategic arms limitations.

It remains uncertain to what extent the Soviets have actually

---

and Col. N. Kuznetsov, "Contemporary War and Surprise," *Voyennaya mysl'*, no. 6 (June 1968), p. 42; and Gen. Army S. P. Ivanov, "Soviet Military Doctrine and Strategy," *Voyennaya mysl'*, no. 5 (May 1969), p. 47.

73. Col. Gen. V. N. Karpov, "On the Theory of Soviet Military Strategy," *Voyennaya mysl'*, no. 10 (October 1979), p. 25.

74. V. Kortunov, "Disastrous Relapses into a Policy of Strength," *Kommunist*, no. 10 (July 1980), pp. 103–04.

prepared their forces and command communications for carrying out a launch on warning, although "operationalizing" the concept has probably gone further than it earlier did with respect to preemptive response, for which they were even less prepared. The concept is important as a guideline in military planning for contingent response in lieu of preemption, even though this does not mean that in all conditions it could be fully implemented.

Thus by 1987 Soviet writers, commenting on the Soviet pledge not to use nuclear weapons first, add that "in *contemporary* Soviet military doctrine the conception of preemptive strikes is also absent."[75] Thinking about launch under attack is best discussed in the context of the related concept of non-first use of nuclear weapons.

No First Use of Nuclear Weapons

For many years Soviet leaders pursued a campaign for "no first use" of nuclear weapons through both private and public diplomacy, and finally in 1982 unilaterally committed their nation not to be the first to use nuclear weapons. This pledge has been widely ignored or discounted as propaganda in the West.

How can one judge whether a Soviet pledge not to use nuclear weapons first is serious? While first use itself would certainly be instantly verifiable (unless both sides resorted to use almost simultaneously), how can the proclamation of intent be evaluated? And what does it really mean?

75. A. G. Arbatov, A. A. Vasil'yev, and A. A. Kokoshin, "Nuclear Weapons and Strategic Stability," *SShA*, no. 9 (September 1987), p. 12; emphasis added. See chapter 5 for further discussion of recent Soviet thinking.

Throughout this volume, preemption is discussed in terms of strategic action in initiation of hostilities and war. During the course of a war, either side might of course seek to preempt some military action planned by the other side, but that is an entirely different matter. Some Western analysts have confused the two categories and argued that the Soviet Union still held a preemptive doctrine, because of doctrine on tactical or operational levels during the course of a war (in particular, a surprise preemptive air, tactical rocket, or artillery strike against enemy forces planning an offensive operation, called "counterpreparation" [*kontrpodgotovka*]. This argument was even advanced by American participants at the official CSCE seminar on military doctrines in Vienna in January 1990 who should have known better. (Information from participants in the seminar.) For the wartime field doctrine, see "Counterpreparation," *Slovar' voyennykh terminov* (Dictionary of Military Terms) (Moscow: Voyenizdat, 1988), p. 137. The dictionary does not carry an entry for preemption.

One can review the recent history of Soviet interest in the subject, and the nature of their stated position.[76] One can also judge whether it fits the broader framework of their thinking and policy. Is it a logical and understandable step in terms of Soviet objectives, insofar as we can determine them? Finally, has it affected their military doctrine and military forces?

This analysis concludes that the effort to promote a no-first-use position by other nuclear powers, and the unilateral pledge by the Soviet Union, in fact reflects serious deliberations within the Soviet military and political establishment since the late 1960s and is actual Soviet policy as part of its endeavor to prevent nuclear war.

Efforts to obtain American acceptance of what the Soviet leaders saw as a basic interest of *both* sides in preventing nuclear war had only limited success. Nonetheless, they stemmed from a serious Soviet interest. The idea of pledges by the nuclear powers not to be the first to use nuclear weapons had a long, undistinguished history. In the 1950s it was one element debated in terms of a step at some advanced stage of "general and complete disarmament." In the late 1960s it was discussed in connection with negotiations and measures to curb nuclear proliferation. Starting from that base, in early 1969 the Soviets sounded out the new Nixon administration privately, and then raised in Geneva, in the multilateral disarmament forum, the idea of some limited, conditional steps on nonuse of nuclear weapons. The United States was not interested in pursuing the matter.[77]

Again in the SALT negotiations, in December 1970, the Soviets privately raised with the head of the American delegation the idea of supplementing strategic arms limitations with commitments not to be the first to use nuclear weapons. When advised that the U.S. position remained that first use must remain available in individual

76. The Soviet Union opened its first political campaign against first use in November 1953, after Stalin's death and shortly after their first thermonuclear test, charging that first use of nuclear weapons would be a "war crime." Diplomatic proposals and propaganda on no first use were pressed from 1955 on, as were proposals for nuclear-free zones and an end to nuclear testing. A new phase of renewed effort began in the late 1960s, as described below.

77. For a good summary history, see Lawrence D. Weiler, "No First Use: A History," *Bulletin of the Atomic Scientists*, vol. 39 (February 1983), pp. 28–34. For a Soviet review, see V. Petrovsky, "An Important Problem in International Politics (On the Non-First Use of Nuclear Weapons)," *Mirovaya ekonomika i mezhdunarodnyye otnosheniya* (World Economy and International Relations; hereafter *MEiMO*), no. 5 (May 1983), pp. 50–52, 57–58. Vladimir Petrovsky is a senior diplomat and now a deputy foreign minister.

or collective self-defense (that is, possible first use of nuclear weapons if necessary to meet a major nonnuclear attack), the Soviets did not pursue the matter further in SALT.[78] They turned, however, to a new approach in talks leading to the 1972 summit meeting.

Beginning in April 1972, in discussions with Henry Kissinger preparing for his forthcoming Moscow summit meeting with President Richard Nixon, Brezhnev proposed a remarkable bilateral U.S.-USSR "understanding" that the two powers would not use nuclear weapons against one another. He clarified this (through Ambassador Anatoly Dobrynin) to mean that the United States and the Soviet Union should be sanctuaries from nuclear attack even in a NATO–Warsaw Pact nuclear war (as well as in any other hostilities). Kissinger considered this idea political poison for the Western alliance, and rejected the proposition out of hand.[79]

The Soviets continued to seek agreement on nonuse, or no first use, of nuclear weapons. Eventually, the United States did agree to a Prevention of Nuclear War Agreement in 1973. This agreement, to which the Soviet leaders attached great importance at the time and since, was given very little weight by the United States.[80] The point of particular interest here is the strong Soviet interest in getting the maximum American commitment to nonuse of nuclear weapons against the Soviet Union through diplomatic means, and through concrete arms control limitations reinforcing the mutual deterrent standoff, as well as through unilateral military programs to support such a standoff by balancing Western nuclear forces with their own at all levels and by building up conventional capabilities.

In the early 1970s, as the Soviets sought to pursue no first use

78. Based on the author's participation in the negotiations. See also Garthoff, *Détente and Confrontation*, p. 182.

79. See Henry Kissinger, *White House Years* (Little, Brown, 1979), p. 1152, and *Years of Upheaval* (Little, Brown, 1982), pp. 274–76.

80. For the fullest account of the development of the Prevention of Nuclear War Agreement, see Garthoff, *Détente and Confrontation*, pp. 334–54. Petrovsky stated in 1983 that the Prevention of Nuclear War Agreement, in conjunction with other similar agreements with Britain and France, is "an important positive factor in weakening the danger of the use of nuclear weapons or threatening their use." See Petrovsky, *MEiMO*, no. 5 (May 1983), p. 52.

While supportive of the objective of prevention of nuclear war, some Soviet military commentaries in 1973–74 were concerned about the use of the PNW agreement as an argument justifying reduced military expenditures and stressed the continuing Western military threat notwithstanding the agreement. See Garthoff, *Détente and Confrontation*, pp. 352–54.

quietly through diplomatic channels with the United States, steps were also considered in the Soviet establishment for possible variations of bilateral or even unilateral pledges of no first use. While the Soviet military establishment since the late 1960s has supported efforts to reduce the possibility of nuclear warfare, there were those who wanted to retain the option of Soviet first use if necessary under some contingencies, in particular in a conventional war with China. Thus they opposed any international commitment. For example, an argument was made by Colonel Yevgeny Rybkin in a Soviet military journal in 1973—evidently against unnamed advocates of a no-first-use declaration—that "it would be premature to declare the exclusion of the possibility of use of nuclear weapons in case of the unleashing of a [conventional] war by aggressors."[81]

Sometime in 1973–74 a secret directive was issued in the name of the Central Committee of the Party instructing that the Soviet Union would make its military plans and preparations on the basis that it would *not* be the first to use nuclear weapons. This decision, and directive to the military, was referred to in the confidential *Military Thought* by the same Colonel Rybkin in January 1975. His 1973 objection to no first use had been overridden, and he noted that the Soviet military was now "guided by the instructions of the Central Committee of the CPSU that the Soviet Union shall not be the first to employ nuclear weapons." It was also noted that "at the same time, the Soviet armed forces should be ready and prepared for any nuclear 'escalation.'" But the main lesson was that a nuclear world war, should it occur, would have "catastrophic consequences," and that the risk in any use of nuclear weapons was too great to assume so long as the choice was in Soviet hands.[82]

In 1976, at or following the Twenty-fifth Party Congress, a decision was evidently made to intensify international diplomatic efforts to agitate the no-first-use issue. In November the Communist Party chiefs of the countries of the Warsaw Pact, meeting as the Political Consultative Committee of the Pact, formally proposed a draft treaty banning first use of nuclear weapons.[83] In his Tula speech in January 1977 Brezhnev noted the West had rejected this proposal, but he nonetheless reaffirmed Soviet support for a mutual renunciation of

81. See Col. Ye. Rybkin, "The Leninist Conception of War and the Present," *KVS*, no. 20 (October 1973), p. 35.

82. See Rybkin and Dmitriyev, *Voyennaya mysl'*, no. 1 (January 1975), p. 66.

83. The text is in *Pravda*, November 28, 1976, p. 1.

first use of nuclear weapons.[84] In November 1977 the Warsaw Pact members advanced this no-first-use proposal at the Belgrade Conference on Security and Cooperation in Europe (CSCE) as a confidence-building measure. In 1978 the Soviet Union made conditional unilateral pledges not to use nuclear weapons except in "extraordinary circumstances, aggression by another nuclear power against our country or our allies," and not to use nuclear weapons against nonnuclear states that had renounced nuclear arms.[85] In September 1981 the Soviet Union proposed a draft resolution in the UN General Assembly on "Prevention of Nuclear Catastrophe," condemning any nuclear first use or "doctrines allowing the first use of nuclear weapons."[86]

By this time something else of note had occurred (although it was not noted in the West). Soviet military publications quietly began to state that no first nuclear use was already Soviet military doctrine. The key statement was one for guidance of the Soviet military establishment by the chief of the General Staff, Marshal Nikolai Ogarkov, in 1979. Soviet military strategy, he said, accepts that even a world war can begin and be conducted without the use of nuclear weapons, although "expansion of hostilities *can* lead to its development into general nuclear war." However, he noted, "at the foundation of Soviet military strategy lies the postulate that the Soviet Union, proceeding from the principles of its policy, will not use that [nuclear] weapon first."[87] Later discussions in 1980–82 prior to the public pledge of no first use similarly stated that "at the foundation of Soviet military strategy is the principle that the Soviet Union will not be the first to use nuclear weapons."[88] In a booklet in early 1982 Marshal Ustinov, stressing "the aim of preventing a new war," stated

84. *Pravda*, January 19, 1977, pp. 1–2.

85. "Speech of Comrade L. I. Brezhnev," *Pravda*, April 26, 1978, pp. 1–2; and "Statement of A. A. Gromyko," *Pravda*, May 27, 1978, p. 4.

86. Text in *Pravda*, September 24, 1981, p. 4. The UN General Assembly on December 9, 1981, adopted a corresponding "Declaration on the Prevention of Nuclear Catastrophe" by a vote of 82 to 19, with 41 abstentions. Most U.S. allies abstained; the United States voted no.

87. See Marshal N. V. Ogarkov, "Military Strategy," *Sovetskaya voyennaya entsiklopediya* (Moscow: Voyenizdat, 1979) [signed to press September 2, 1979], vol. 7, p. 564; emphasis added.

88. This identical statement appeared in *Otkuda iskhodit ugroza miru?* (Whence the Threat to Peace?) (Moscow: Voyenizdat, 1982) [to press December 11, 1981], p. 12; and in "Who Threatens Peace?" *KVS*, no. 5 (March 1982) [to press February 18, 1982], p. 91.

that "only extraordinary circumstances—direct nuclear aggression against the Soviet Union or its allies—could compel us to resort to a retaliating nuclear strike as the extreme means of self-defense."[89]

Soviet officials have privately stated that a decision to take the final step to unilateral adoption of no first use flowed from decisions taken (though not announced) in connection with the Twenty-sixth Party Congress in early 1981.[90] Then, on June 15, 1982, Brezhnev made a public unilateral pledge: "The Soviet Union is assuming the obligation not to be the first to use nuclear weapons."[91] Although Brezhnev made this pledge to the United Nations Special Session on Disarmament and it was given heavy propaganda play, its motivations and implications were much more far-reaching.

Marshal Ustinov, the minister of defense, found it necessary in an article in *Pravda* some three weeks later to admit that questions had been raised as to the timeliness (and by implication soundness) of this Soviet unilateral renunciation. He said that this "exceptional, extraordinary" decision had not been easy: "It was no simple matter for the Soviet Union to make a unilateral commitment." In a remarkable admission, he acknowledged that "quite naturally, Soviet people . . . are asking whether the right moment has been chosen for such a step and whether by this unilateral commitment we are not incurring excessive danger for our people, our Motherland, the cause of socialism and progress in the whole world?"[92] It is highly unusual for Soviet leaders to pose even hypothetical questions as to the wisdom of their decisions, and least of all on a matter of national life and death. There is reason to believe these questions arose particularly among some Soviet military men.[93] Ustinov not only justified the action by stressing the danger to world civilization from nuclear war, but stressed the Soviet view on the "impossibil-

89. Ustinov, *Sluzhim rodine, delu kommunizma,* p. 72.

90. In particular, this was mentioned in conversation before the public pledge by the late Academician Nikolai Inozemtsev, a full member of the Central Committee, and on another occasion after Brezhnev's public pledge by a senior Party official. Inozemtsev also said that the prevention of nuclear war had become the top priority of Soviet foreign policy.

91. L. I. Brezhnev, "The Second Special Session of the UN General Assembly," *Pravda,* June 16, 1982, p. 1.

92. Marshal D. F. Ustinov, "To Avert the Threat of Nuclear War," *Pravda,* July 12, 1982, p. 4. Ustinov's identification with the article not only gave his marshal's rank and minister of defense title, as usual, but also specifically and unusually identified him as a member of the Politburo.

93. I was advised of this concern within the Soviet military by a senior Soviet

ity" of victory in a nuclear war. Moreover, he nailed this down: "There is no place for any other opinions and appraisals" on this question.

Marshal Ustinov also discussed the "military implications" of the commitment, including its impact on "the strategy and tactics of the Soviet armed forces," and on combat readiness, armaments, and improvement of command, control, and communications. The change on the political level of military doctrine was thus tied to a number of concrete applications on the military-technical level. Finally, Ustinov dealt at length with the important point that an aggressor would know that "the advantages of a preemptive use of nuclear weapons would not lead it to victory," and that with contemporary weaponry and means of detection "the United States would not be able to deal a disarming strike to the socialist countries. The aggressor would not be able to escape an all-crushing retaliatory strike."[94] Therefore it would be deterred.

The Soviet decision on no first use of nuclear weapons had its origins in the revision of military doctrine begun in the late 1960s, in which the desirability and feasibility of avoiding nuclear war led to a shift from preemptive response to launch under attack, and to giving priority to prevention of escalation to nuclear war even if that risked ceding a preemptive strike option to the other side. And Marshal Ustinov drew as one of the military implications of the renunciation of first use of nuclear weapons a requirement for the Soviet armed forces "to devote still more attention to the problem of *preventing the escalation of a military conflict to the nuclear level.*"[95] This was repeated in later military writings, some of which stressed that the no-first-use pledge was *not* merely rhetorical but a "requirement for our military programming."[96]

This analysis of the no-first-use issue has proceeded from data in the public record (including, to be sure, disclosures by American participants of confidential diplomatic exchanges between Soviet and American leaders). It includes a number of references from

officer, and by a well-placed civilian, both in 1983; in both cases it was stated that the contingency of a war with China was a major reason for such reservations.

94. Ustinov, *Pravda*, July 12, 1982, p. 4.

95. Ibid.; emphasis added.

96. See, for example, Lt. Gen. N. Tetekin, "The Main Indicator of the Qualitative State of the Troops," *Krasnaya zvezda*, November 10, 1982, pp. 2–3. Quotation from Rear Adm. G. Kostev, "Our Military Doctrine in the Light of the New Political Thinking," *KVS*, no. 17 (September 1987), p. 13.

Soviet military writings not previously cited in Western analytical accounts, but these are for the most part open sources. These sources provide, in my judgment, a reasonable basis for concluding that the matter involved Soviet military doctrine and policy, not merely public propaganda. But this judgment might fail to convince a determined skeptic.

The disclosure in the confidential General Staff journal *Military Thought* in 1975 of a Central Committee "instruction" to the Soviet military against first use is, however, a significant datum confirming that judgment. An important additional source contributes direct evidence in support of that conclusion. The Voroshilov General Staff Academy lecture materials of the mid-1970s, cited earlier, for the whole range of possible scenarios for a major war stressed the Soviet effort to prevent escalation to nuclear war and posited *no* Soviet first use of nuclear weapons.[97] These secret lecture materials do not necessarily divulge all contingencies in Soviet war planning, but there is no reason to doubt their accurate reflection of authoritative Soviet military thinking as of 1975, and they are consistent with and amplify other confidential Soviet military writings, especially those in *Military Thought.*

The Soviets considered their adoption of a policy of no first use of nuclear weapons consistent with launch under attack—or, indeed, with preemption. In Soviet thinking, launch on warning or under attack is timely retaliation, and even preemptive launch as an enemy is unleashing or about to unleash his attack—explicitly stated to be the only circumstance justifying preemption—is regarded as anticipatory retaliation. This would not be a euphemism for evasion of no first use; it would be in response to the enemy's irrevocable prior *decision* to use nuclear weapons. Uncertainties about an irrevocable enemy decision and imminent attack are, of course, reduced by shifting from preemption to a launch under attack, and this change was in accordance with the new emphasis on avoiding first use of nuclear weapons (if preemption were undertaken on an incorrect reading of the enemy's intentions and actions, it would constitute inadvertent first use). The overriding aim has been to avoid the

97. As discussed below, this would not preclude Soviet preemption by tactical nuclear weapons in a situation where NATO was known (believed) to have already decided upon use of such weapons, that is, a case of prior NATO decision on first use and a Soviet choice only to wait and absorb the first NATO strike or, if able to do so, to preempt it.

nuclear devastation of the Soviet Union—by enemy attack, or by enemy retaliation after a Soviet preemptive or other attack.

The General Staff Academy materials on Soviet military strategy in the mid-1970s are very revealing on this subject, being of course far more frank and explicit on it than published military writings could be. They state that "the most important task is the timely detection of enemy direct preparations for launching a nuclear attack" in order to enable the *political* leadership to "make a timely decision on committing friendly nuclear forces into action," that is, presumably, to preempt an impending attack or to be ready for launch upon warning of an attack. The warning system must be capable of detecting enemy missile launchings and transmitting that information to the Supreme Command "within three to four minutes" so that it could make a decision to launch Soviet retaliatory nuclear strikes "by the commencement of an enemy nuclear attack," in other words, a launch on warning.[98] Thus Soviet doctrine has not regarded launch on warning, and even preemption, as Soviet initiation of use of nuclear weapons, but as a timely response to an enemy decision to initiate nuclear war, and thus as compatible with a policy of no first use and with the basic goal of preventing nuclear war if at all possible.[99]

In his 1979 *Military Encyclopedia* pronouncement on Soviet military strategy, Marshal Ogarkov in an unusual, explicit distinction stressed that by then Soviet military doctrine not only excluded "deliberate attack," but also did "not provide for any kind of preemptive strikes."[100]

In the context of public acknowledgement of a policy of no first use (about a decade after the effective adoption of no first use in Soviet strategy toward the West), Soviet leaders considered it necessary to assure the public of effective deterrence through Soviet ability to retaliate. Defense Minister Ustinov's assurances were cited earlier. A remarkable article soon after was more explicit and insistent. The author quotes a letter to the editor of the *Literary Gazette* (the organ of the Union of Writers; despite its title, an influential journal on topical political issues) from an ordinary Soviet citizen asking whether it had been desirable for the Soviet Union to make a solemn

98. *Voroshilov Lectures*, vol. 1, p. 246.
99. The equivalent and operative term in American military planning is "prompt retaliation," launching a retaliatory strike force before it is hit.
100. Ogarkov, *Sovetskaya voyennaya entsiklopediya*, vol. 7, 1979, p. 563.

pledge renouncing first use of nuclear weapons. The author argued that the Soviet renunciation was "a concrete act reducing the danger hanging over mankind and thereby strengthening international security." How? By denying a potential aggressor the possibility of escaping a devastating retaliatory strike, while assuring him that if he refrains from attack with nuclear weapons, he will not be attacked with nuclear weapons. The writer went on to explain to readers how a would-be aggressor would know that he could not succeed in making a disarming strike: "Because our military doctrine, while remaining defensive, will not be passive in nature. The guarantee of this is the combat readiness of Soviet strategic nuclear systems and modern early-warning systems." He then cast the concept of launch under attack in clear lay terms: "No matter how sophisticated and ultramodern new weapons may be, an ICBM nonetheless has a considerable distance to cross. It will not be a matter of seconds. *And nobody is going to stand around waiting for American warheads to start dropping on our heads.*" The author thus sought to reassure that parity in retaliatory power will prevent the enemy from believing he can gain from an attack, that is, that mutual deterrence is stable. But he did admit that political confrontation increases tension and that "the danger today . . . lies in the fact that casual statements [in the West] about first and preemptive strikes, about demonstrative detonations, and about the acceptability of either limited or protracted nuclear war depending on the circumstances, create a nervous atmosphere and increase the danger of the accidental outbreak of war. When people are nervous, things can go wrong. . . . If events get out of control no 'hot line' is going to be of any help." The antidote is to reduce tensions, and "by pledging not to be the first to use nuclear weapons, the Soviet Union made a substantial contribution to . . . reducing tensions."[101]

Political Action

Without discussing the matter at length, I should note the cardinal importance in the eyes of the Soviet leaders of the parallel line of policy in seeking to prevent nuclear war through a range of political

101. Yury Yartsev, "They Had Better Think Three Times," *Literaturnaya gazeta* (Literary Gazette), October 27, 1982, pp. 14–15; emphasis added.

action in the world. This finds expression in political campaigns designed to influence public opinion in the world and in particular countries on themes that the *Soviets* see as contributing to prevention of nuclear war. Weakening support in Western countries for American and NATO planned nuclear deployments in the early 1980s, for example, entered that pattern. So does encouragement of agreements on balanced arms reductions and disarmament.

In the disarmament field, apart from some political campaigns and from the actual negotiations on ABM, strategic nuclear forces, intermediate-range nuclear forces, and nuclear testing, there has been the broader Soviet campaign directed at all nuclear weapons. It comprises a major propaganda effort as well as some serious negotiating efforts. Although the Soviet aim of preventing nuclear war has the many important facets discussed earlier, it also includes a major long-term effort to stigmatize nuclear weapons, to constrain the possibilities of their use in every possible way, and to seek their reduction and optimally their eventual elimination. This has been a Soviet propaganda aim since the 1950s, but the new, serious efforts begun in 1971 and reinvigorated since 1986 have been part and parcel of the priority Soviet endeavor to prevent nuclear war.

Official NATO concerns over maintaining public support for nuclear deterrence have led to interpreting Soviet efforts to stigmatize nuclear weapons and to denuclearize Europe as attempts to undercut the Western deterrent. In fact, the Soviets have sought to reduce the possibility of nuclear war, not to prepare conditions under which they could launch a conventional (or nuclear) attack. Perhaps after Soviet military power retracts from central and eastern Europe this fact will become more clear.

In contrast to the Soviet efforts to stabilize and then reduce the strategic nuclear arms competition by the ABM and SALT I and II strategic forces agreements, in the field of conventional arms control the Soviet position in the Mutual and Balanced Force Reduction (MBFR) talks in the 1970s and early 1980s was a holding operation, seeking to inhibit any Western (in particular West German) buildup, while proceeding with a major qualitative (and in weapons, not units, quantitative) buildup of their own conventional forces. This buildup was in pursuance of their military doctrinal emphasis on keeping any war nonnuclear. No agreements were reached in the whole MBFR negotiation from 1973 to 1989, basically because neither side really wanted reductions or even an agreement. This situation has radically changed with the new Soviet unilateral measures and concessions to prime early agreement in the new conventional arms reduction negotiations under way since early 1989, as will be discussed later.

In addition to the SALT and START strategic arms negotiations, all of Brezhnev's successors have renewed efforts to engage the United States in political agreements to reduce the possibility of nuclear war. General Secretary Yury Andropov in one of his first public statements as leader, in March 1983, appealed to the United States to join in working toward "preventing a nuclear catastrophe."[102] A year later his successor, General Secretary Konstantin Chernenko, proposed five "norms" to regulate the conduct of the five nuclear powers. The first of these was for each "to consider the prevention of nuclear war the main aim of its foreign policy" and, working together, to prevent conflict situations from arising or to keep them from leading to nuclear war.[103] There was no Western reaction, despite Soviet diplomatic efforts (including a pitch by Gorbachev when he visited London in December 1984).

One diplomatic initiative to which the Soviets attribute significance was gaining President Reagan's agreement to include in the joint communiqué at the Geneva summit meeting in November 1985 the statement that "a nuclear war cannot be won and must never be fought" and stressing "*the importance of preventing any war between them, whether nuclear or conventional.*"[104] This agreed statement on preventing war was later cited frequently by Soviet writers as a positive development.[105]

Intensified Soviet efforts in the 1980s to press for a comprehensive nuclear test ban, to note another important example, are intended to serve a range of objectives in furtherance of putting the nuclear genie back in the bottle. Optimally, the Soviets hope to create pressures on the United States administration to negotiate and agree to end tests. Short of that, they aim to place the Soviet Union in a favorable light and the United States in an unfavorable one in world

102. "Answers by Yu. V. Andropov to Questions from a Correspondent of 'Pravda,'" *Pravda*, March 27, 1983, p. 1.

103. "Speech of Comrade K. U. Chernenko," *Pravda*, March 3, 1984, pp. 1–2.

104. "Joint Statement by the United States and the Soviet Union, Geneva, November 21, 1985," in *American Foreign Policy: Current Documents, 1985* (Washington: Department of State, 1986), p. 427; emphasis added.

105. For example, see Maj. Gen. S. A. Tyushkevich, *Voina i sovremennost'* (War and the Present Day) (Moscow: Nauka, 1986), p. 118.

opinion. And in any case, no less important is the aim of keeping the danger and threat of nuclear weapons in the public eye, and of intensifying opposition to any thought of their use. This renewed effort to achieve a ban on all nuclear testing has fostered Soviet acceptance of intensive on-site monitoring and inspection, and in 1985–86 led to an eighteen-month unilateral moratorium on nuclear testing notwithstanding continued American testing.

The January 15, 1986, Soviet proposal for the elimination of nuclear weapons by the end of the century has been the most comprehensive approach to date.[106] But there are many other elements in the Soviet disarmament campaign against nuclear weapons, including public agitation of the no-first-use issue.[107]

That the Soviet effort to prevent nuclear war includes disarmament propaganda should not obscure the fact that it also includes serious pursuit of arms limitation and reduction agreements that could importantly affect the capabilities of the United States and the Soviet Union. Nor should it distract attention from the fact that this effort also covers developments in military doctrine, military operational concepts, and military force structure and weapon programs.

Thus the prevention of nuclear war, and in general of war between East and West, has been pursued by a variety of policy means in addition to deterrence, and has been reflected in Soviet military doctrine. Soviet military doctrine on the "military-technical level"— strategy, operations, and tactics—nonetheless remains predicated on preparation in all respects for the possibility that deterrence and the whole panoply of other means designed to prevent war may not succeed in doing so. Military doctrine provides a strategic concept for waging war. The Soviet strategic concept calls for waging war without the use of nuclear weapons except in response to Western

106. "Statement by the General Secretary of the Central Committee of the CPSU, M. S. Gorbachev," *Pravda*, January 16, 1986, p. 1. For an analysis of the proposal, see Raymond L. Garthoff, "The Gorbachev Proposal and Prospects for Arms Control," *Arms Control Today*, vol. 16 (January–February 1986), pp. 3–6. The proposal is further discussed in chapter 4.

107. For example, Petrovsky has argued that "recognition of the impermissibility of first use of nuclear weapons is an important starting point for strengthening international stability, for a whole program of measures the ultimate purpose of which is to exclude the very possibility of a nuclear catastrophe. . . . A renunciation of the first use of nuclear weapons would create new possibilities for banning nuclear weapons, and finally for advancing to resolve the task of nuclear disarmament." See Petrovsky, *MEiMO*, no. 5 (May 1983), p. 58.

use. But since the Western powers (in particular the United States, with or without alliance consultation) might initiate use of nuclear weapons, the Soviet armed forces must be prepared for waging nuclear war in the European theater of war—but not against the territories of the nuclear powers (probably Britain and France as well as the United States, given their nuclear capability) in order to avert use against the territory of the Soviet Union if at all possible. Soviet military doctrine, while directed at averting any war with the West, and at preventing or containing nuclear war, nonetheless until the late 1980s held that if war between NATO and the Warsaw Pact were to break out, the Soviet strategic concept must be to strive for a rapid offensive thrust to the English Channel, defeating NATO forces in Germany and the Lowlands. Since the Soviet Union would not itself begin any war into western Europe, war would occur only at NATO's initiation and above all based on an American decision. The war could be terminated by Western defeat or surrender short of military defeat, but in any case by a successful Soviet–Warsaw Pact military campaign. In the words of a secret General Staff Academy lecture of 1975, probably unchanged a decade later, "final victory can be achieved only through the destruction of the enemy armed forces and the seizure of his territory."[108]

As I shall discuss, this strategic concept and the underlying military doctrine were radically changed in the late 1980s.

The Soviet efforts at prevention of nuclear war, implicit ever since the close of World War II, have had a consistent policy thrust since the mid-1960s and continuing into the late 1980s. While this element of continuity is important, significant new elements have entered under the Gorbachev leadership. They are marked not only by an intensification of policy efforts, but also by a new—indeed revolutionary—impact on Soviet military doctrine, and on the future role of deterrence.

108. This quotation is from *The Voroshilov Lectures: Materials from the Soviet General Staff Academy*, vol. 2 (forthcoming).

Chapter Four

Gorbachev's New Thinking

AT THE TWENTY-SEVENTH Congress of the Communist Party of the Soviet Union in February 1986, when General Secretary Mikhail Gorbachev addressed that august body with the authoritative Political Report of the Central Committee, he spoke of the "complete unacceptability of nuclear war" and of the insufficiency for security of defense or deterrence in the nuclear age. "The character of contemporary weapons," he said, "does not permit *any* state hope of defending itself by military-technical means alone, even by creating the most powerful defense." He accepted the reality of mutual deterrence, "when the whole world has become a nuclear hostage," but he argued that "security cannot indefinitely be built on fear of retaliation, that is on doctrines of 'deterrence' *[sderzhivaniye]* or 'intimidation' *[ustrasheniye]*." Rather, "Ensuring security more and more becomes a political task and can only be solved by political means." "It is high time," he said, "to begin a practical withdrawal from balancing on the brink of war, from a balance of terror, to normal civilized forms of mutual relations between states of the two systems." Finally, in reviewing the main tasks of the Party's external policy, he stressed, "In the future the most important direction of the Party's activity in the world arena remains the struggle against the nuclear danger."[1]

The ideological underpinning for this priority of the prevention of war was underscored in the revised Party Program adopted at the

1. M. S. Gorbachev, *Politicheskii doklad tsentral'nogo komiteta KPSS XXVII s"yezdu Kommunisticheskoi partii Sovetskogo Soyuza* (Political Report of the Central Committee of the CPSU to the Twenty-seventh Congress of the Communist Party of the Soviet Union, February 25, 1986) (Moscow: Politizdat, 1986), pp. 15, 81–82; emphasis added. Note that Gorbachev appears to be sensitive to the distinction between the two terms used in Russian to represent "deterrence," and intentionally covers both.

Congress, where the prevention of war, not victory in class struggle, was described as "the historic calling of socialism."[2]

Gorbachev reaffirmed the Soviet pledge not to be first to use nuclear weapons (which was greeted by applause) and went on to say: "But it is no secret that scenarios for nuclear attack on us do exist. We have no right not to take them into account. The Soviet Union is a convinced opponent of nuclear war in any variant." And what was his response to meet this threat? "Our country is for eliminating weapons of mass destruction, and limiting military potential to reasonable sufficiency."[3]

This line of argument and its terms are revealing and interesting. In the first place, Gorbachev throughout used the term "security" rather than "military security." He made no reference to a military balance and argued that deterrence is not enough: it is necessary to move beyond mutual deterrence to increased mutual confidence, and from national security to shared international security. Even in discussing the present situation, where mutual deterrence prevails, he advanced as his criterion for military forces "reasonable sufficiency."[4] While criteria for *perestroika* (restructuring) in the armed forces are very important, one must bear in mind the framework and broader policy aims reaffirmed and stressed by Gorbachev: eliminating nuclear weapons and preventing nuclear—and indeed any—war.

As I have discussed, the aim of preventing war (in particular, nuclear war) has been avowed by Soviet leaders since Nikita Khrushchev. The new element introduced by Gorbachev concerns not the aim so much as the means to realize it. While Leonid Brezhnev relied chiefly on a military buildup to achieve and then ensure parity and deterrence, Gorbachev has moved to define and carry out a broad political as well as military program calling for replacement of military means to ensure security by political means. This involves not only greater efforts to obtain negotiated bilateral arms reductions, but also new Soviet assessments of the threat and of Soviet political-military measures to provide security.

2. *Programma Kommunisticheskoi partii Sovetskogo Soyuza* (The Program of the Communist Party of the Soviet Union), new ed. (Moscow: Politizdat, 1986), pp. 21–22.

3. Gorbachev, *Politicheskii doklad*, p. 85.

4. During the period after the congress, the concept of "reasonable sufficiency" began to be developed, with a debate among adherents of differing views, as discussed later in this chapter.

Gorbachev's far-reaching new ideas on security and military doctrine caught the Soviet military and national security establishment largely unprepared, even though the reconsideration of military policy had begun after the April 1985 Central Committee plenum. It was well into 1986 and 1987 before any extensive discussion began on most of the new concepts such as "reasonable sufficiency." The objective of preventing war, and especially nuclear war, of course, was not new, but important implications and applications were affected by the emergent "new thinking." One of the earliest new steps was redefining both Soviet military doctrine and strategy to incorporate the objective.

The 1986 revised edition of the *Military Encyclopedic Dictionary*, originally issued only three years earlier, added this sentence to the definition of "military strategy": "A most important task for Soviet military strategy in contemporary conditions is the solution of the problem of preventing war." The definition of "military doctrine" was also revised to include specific reference to the goal of Soviet doctrine as not only defense but "the prevention of world war." And in its definition of "war," the concluding sentence dealing with global policy was amended to add explicit reference to "the struggle for the elimination of the threat of world war," and "the achievement of general security" in the world.[5]

A key editorial article in *Military Thought* in June 1986 spelled out for Soviet military leaders the basis for the new emphasis on prevention of war: "Humankind has entered a most dangerous period. In the first half of the 1980s the nuclear confrontation of the United States and the Soviet Union, of NATO and the Warsaw Pact, intensified. A threat of the end of world civilization has arisen. Questions of war and peace, questions of survival have been placed at the center of world politics by the objective course of the world process itself. In these circumstances, the conclusion of our Party that in the contemporary nuclear-space age one must not think in old categories, that a new approach to the problem of security was necessary, is an important matter of principle." While the Soviet Union was seen as being in the vanguard of an effort "to save humankind from nuclear catastrophe," the article stressed that despite ideological and national political differences and conflict, "the nuclear

5. *Voyennyi entsiklopedicheskii slovar'* (Military Encyclopedic Dictionary), 2d ed. (Moscow: Voyenizdat, 1986), pp. 712, 240, 151. (Hereafter *VES*.)

epoch has radically changed the content of world politics." The cycle of war and peace must be broken. "Now it is peaceful coexistence, or nonexistence. There is no third possibility inasmuch as the nuclear weapon is capable of removing the human species from the face of the earth. Hence the prevention of war is a task for all peoples irrespective of the state or social system in which they live."[6]

By the end of 1986, General of the Army Mikhail Kozlov, in an article in *Military Thought* stressing the need to maintain strategic parity with the United States, nonetheless declared that parity was not an end in itself and that it was necessary to pursue the objective of "reducing, and ultimately completely eliminating, the threat of nuclear war."[7]

The summit meeting between President Ronald Reagan and General Secretary Gorbachev in Reykjavik in October 1986 startled the world. While agreement was not reached, the fact that the two leaders had discussed and endorsed the elimination of nuclear weapons gave that aim a degree of serious standing it had not previously enjoyed. Many in the West were jolted that President Reagan had entertained the idea of an accord to eliminate all strategic nuclear weapons, particularly without consultation and agreement in the Western alliance or even in the government in Washington. Gorbachev, on the other hand, had been able to take such a stand by virtue of the earlier endorsement of the Politburo and Party Congress (and Warsaw Pact) for the January 1986 Soviet proposals for eliminating nuclear weapons (although some Soviet leaders may have been surprised by the Reykjavik "near-miss" as well).

Nor was the achievement of Reykjavik only rhetorical. Several concrete understandings advanced there undergirded both the intermediate-range nuclear forces (INF) agreement concluded in December 1987, and the basic terms for a strategic arms reduction treaty. Both stemmed from Soviet concessions justified only by the priority given in Moscow to maximum reduction of nuclear weapons. Gorbachev agreed to the elimination of all Soviet and American intermedi-

6. "A Concrete Program for Assuring Peace and Security," *Voyennaya mysl'*, no. 6 (June 1986), pp. 3–4. This was the second editorial article in the General Staff journal based on the Twenty-seventh Party Congress and went much further than the first (in no. 3, March 1986) in reflecting the "new thinking."

7. Gen. Army M. M. Kozlov, "The Preservation of Military-Strategic Parity—A Serious Factor in Assuring Peace and International Security," *Voyennaya mysl'*, no. 12 (December 1986), p. 12.

ate-range missiles in Europe, despite the larger number of Soviet weapons and exclusion from consideration of comparable weapons of the American allies, and to reduce Soviet missiles in Asia from more than 500 down to 100 warheads, with no American reductions. (Later the Soviets agreed to eliminate all their medium-range and also certain shorter-range missiles in Europe and Asia with no American reduction entailed.) In addition, at Reykjavik (although not then publicly disclosed) Marshal Sergei Akhromeyev first offered to reduce the Soviet SS-18 heavy ICBM force by half.

General Kozlov, in his important article in *Military Thought* two months later, stressed that "one of the main lessons of Reykjavik is that the new political thinking, which corresponds to the realities of the nuclear age, is an indispensable condition for getting out of the critical situation in which humankind has found itself toward the close of the twentieth century."[8] Kozlov also stressed to his military colleagues, in a paraphrase of Gorbachev's report to the congress, that "realistically evaluating the possibilities of contemporary means of armed conflict, the 27th Congress of the CPSU drew the new and fundamentally important conclusion that these [means], especially nuclear, do not allow any state hope of defending itself by military-technical means alone, even through creation of the most powerful defense."[9]

Mutual deterrence based on parity in strategic capabilities has continued to be affirmed under the new thinking. Strategic parity has even been described as an "epic of the twentieth century," ranking along with the Bolshevik Revolution and the Soviet victory in World War II, because it deters and prevents war. Soviet commentators speak of "the achievement of military-strategic parity with the strongest and most mighty capitalist power, the United States, permitting mankind to keep peace on earth and to save civilization from a nuclear missile catastrophe."[10] Strategic parity is of course seen not merely as serving Soviet security or even world peace through deterrence. It also has provided the foundation for mutual efforts to improve stability and security.

Life has so developed that both of our countries must proceed from the fact that strategic parity is a natural condition. Without a military-

8. *Ibid.*, p. 11.
9. *Ibid.*, p. 12.
10. S. Tikhvinsky, "Soviet Historical Science at the Threshhold of the Twenty-

strategic balance the maintenance of international stability is un-thinkable. Without it, it would hardly have been possible to conclude a number of treaties and agreements on the limitation of the arms race. An approximate equivalence of forces must be accepted as a foundation for international security, as a self-evident imperative.

But for this, new thinking is necessary to understand that for reliable defense today a considerably reduced number of arms is sufficient. Indeed, and this is obvious to everyone, the present level of the balance of nuclear potentials of the opposing sides is much too high. For the present this ensures both sides equal danger. But only for the time being. A continuation of the nuclear arms race will inevitably increase this equal danger and it could lead to such extremes that even parity would cease to be a military-political deterrent.[11]

Similarly, the new Party Program adopted at the Twenty-seventh Party Congress in 1986 not only described the "establishment of military-strategic parity between the USSR and the United States, and the Warsaw Pact and NATO" as "a historic achievement of socialism," but also argued that the preservation of parity is "an important factor for safeguarding peace and international security."[12]

Yet parity itself, as traditionally conceived, has come under challenge by the new thinking. In delivering the report of the Central Committee to the Party Congress, as earlier noted, Gorbachev introduced the concept of "reasonable sufficiency" as a criterion in determining military requirements.[13] He did not spell out how reasonable sufficiency itself would be determined but encouraged an open discussion of the issue. The military soon began to stress that the foundation for reasonable sufficiency was maintaining strategic parity.[14] Marshal (then General of the Army) Dmitry Yazov, minister of defense, emphatically expressed the continuing view that "military strategic parity remains the decisive factor in preventing war at the present time," that is, serves as the key to deterrence of war.[15]

seventh Congress of the CPSU," *Kommunist* (The Communist), no. 1 (January 1986), p. 99. Tikhvinsky is a prominent historian and has been head of the Historical Diplomatic Directorate of the Ministry of Foreign Affairs.

11. L. Tolkunov, "The Dilemma of the Age," *Kommunist*, no. 7 (May 1986), pp. 85–86. The late Lev Tolkunov was chairman of one of the houses of the Supreme Soviet and an influential member of the Party Central Committee.

12. "Program of the Communist Party of the Soviet Union, New Edition, Adopted by the Twenty-seventh Congress of the CPSU," *Pravda*, March 7, 1986, p. 3.

13. Gorbachev, *Politicheskii doklad*, p. 85.

14. See the discussion in Raymond L. Garthoff, "New Thinking in Soviet Military Doctrine," *Washington Quarterly*, vol. 11 (Summer 1988), pp. 136–45. One of the first was General Kozlov, earlier cited.

15. Gen. Army D. T. Yazov, "The Military Doctrine of the Warsaw Pact—A

The "old view" of parity held by most military leaders and analysts until the late 1980s, while keyed to deterrence, nonetheless was predicated on a war-waging capability rather than merely deterrence by punishment. In one of his last statements before being retired, Marshal Viktor Kulikov expressed this very clearly in early 1988 in the confidential General Staff journal: "From a military point of view parity is an approximate equivalence in military power of the sides, above all in nuclear and other strategic means of armed combat, *having a decisive significance for waging war,* and is the basic indicator of the correlation of military forces of the sides which we must take into account in making decisions on *political* and military questions."[16]

Debate, indirectly expressed, continued in 1987–88 on whether "parity" meant quantitative equality in strategic forces, or qualitative equality in the ability to deliver a retaliatory strike—that is, a parity in deterrent capability. While a minority of civilian commentators who have espoused a doctrine of unilateral minimum deterrence with inferior forces has not prevailed in the debate, the idea of qualitative rather than quantitative parity has. Thus even a relatively conservative military writer by 1989 accepts the idea that the traditional quantitative approach must be replaced by a qualitative one based on "reasonable sufficiency for defense," although "the measure of reasonable sufficiency is defined not only by us but also by the other side's actions." Most important, however, is the recognition that parity is defined in mutual deterrent capabilities. The new approach "requires that parity be regarded as a correlation of the two sides' strategic potential that provides capability to inflict unacceptable damage on the aggressor in a retaliatory strike."[17]

This acceptance of a retaliatory deterrent capability as the essence of parity has been reflected in military writings. For example, in 1988 this approach was made crystal clear in a discussion in *Military Thought:* "Military-strategic parity between the USSR and the USA, and between the WTO and NATO, has decisive significance

---

Doctrine of the Defense of Peace and Socialism," *Pravda,* July 27, 1987, p. 5. See also Yazov, *Oboronnoye stroitel'stvo: novyye podkhody* (Defense Programs: New Approaches) (Moscow: Voyenizdat, 1989).

16. Marshal V. G. Kulikov, "On Military-Strategic Parity and Sufficiency for Defense," *Voyennaya mysl',* no. 5 (May 1988), p. 4; emphasis added.

17. Col. V. Strebkov, "From the Standpoint of the New Thinking: Military Parity Yesterday and Today," *Krasnaya zvezda* (Red Star), January 3, 1989, p. 3.

for deterrence of aggression and prevention of war. Maintaining military-strategic parity doesn't mean an absolute equality of forces, but requires capabilities for assured dealing of an inevitable retaliatory strike."[18]

The acceptance by the military of mutual assured destruction capability as the foundation for parity and reasonable sufficiency of strategic forces underlies military support for Gorbachev's efforts to reduce strategic nuclear weapons (and indeed all nuclear weapons) on both sides to the fullest extent negotiable, while maintaining parity and mutual deterrence at lower levels of forces. While conceptually this was not a new departure in military and political thinking, the "new thinking" did give considerable impetus to practical policy measures.

Military Doctrine and the Prevention of War

In 1987 Soviet (and Warsaw Pact) military doctrine was publicly redefined, along the lines foreshadowed by the revision of the *Military Encyclopedic Dictionary*. In one of the first general public statements, Marshal Akhromeyev declared that "Soviet military doctrine *is* a system of fundamental views on the essence *and prevention* of war."[19] General (now Marshal) Yazov, the new defense minister, in his first major pronouncement on military policy and doctrine a few months later, repeated this statement, and in addition introduced a new, somewhat different formulation as well. He said that a "main feature" of Soviet and Pact military doctrine was "that it is *subordinated* to the accomplishment of the cardinal task facing humankind, the task of preventing war."[20]

This formulation was drawn from one first used in an important

18. Col. Gen. V. V. Korobushin, "On Increasing the Effectiveness of Military-Scientific Research," *Voyennaya mysl'*, no. 5 (May 1988), p. 40.

19. Marshal S. F. Akhromeyev, "The Fame and Pride of the Soviet People," *Sovetskaya Rossiya* (Soviet Russia), February 21, 1987, p. 1; emphasis added.

20. Yazov, *Pravda*, July 27, 1987, p. 5; emphasis added. His predecessor as defense minister, Marshal Sergei Sokolov, had not yet used this formulation on subordination, although he had stated earlier in the year that "the main tenet" of Soviet military doctrine was "not to permit a war, [but] to prevent it." Marshal S. L. Sokolov, "On Guard over Peace and the Security of the Motherland," *Pravda*, February 23, 1987, p. 2.

declaration on military doctrine of the Warsaw Pact signed in May 1987 by the leaders of all the Pact member states. The statement declared: "The military doctrine of the Warsaw Pact, just as of each of its members, is subordinated to the task of preventing war, nuclear and conventional."[21] This declaration included a proposal to NATO for consultation on the military doctrines of both alliances, and also served not only to coordinate Pact doctrine and policy, but also to advance Soviet military doctrinal development.

Soviet military writings since mid-1987 have frequently reiterated these statements and added others. For example, Rear Admiral Kostev in a discussion of military doctrine not only repeated the Warsaw Pact formula, but also declared that "the chief and primary task is to exclude nuclear war." Similarly, General of the Army Petr Lushev, then first deputy defense minister, stated, "Today there is no more important task than the struggle against the threat of nuclear war." And Lieutenant General Vladimir Serebryannikov noted, "For the first time in history military doctrine was given the thrust of not permitting war as its main principle."[22]

Authoritative Soviet military statements indeed soon made clear that not only was military doctrine "subordinated to the task of preventing war," but that military doctrine had itself been redefined to *incorporate* the prevention of war as its main task, as well as continuing to include the traditional tasks of setting out guidelines for waging war if it could not be prevented. A key editorial article in the General Staff journal *Military Thought* in January 1988 declared: "Contemporary Soviet military doctrine represents a system of officially accepted fundamental views on the prevention of war, military programs *[stroitel'stva]*, the preparation of the country and the armed forces for repelling aggression, and the means for waging armed combat in defense of socialism. From that definition it follows

21. "On the Military Doctrine of the Member States of the Warsaw Pact," *Pravda*, May 30, 1987, p. 1.
22. Rear Adm. G. Kostev, "Our Military Doctrine in the Light of New Political Thinking," *Kommunist vooruzhennykh sil* (Communist of the Armed Forces; hereafter *KVS*), no. 17 (September 1987), p. 12, and see p. 11 for the reiteration; Gen. Army P. Lushev, "In Defense of the Achievements of the Revolution," *Mezhdunarodnaya zhizn'* (International Affairs), no. 8 (August 1987), p. 68; and Lt. Gen. Avn. V. Serebryannikov, "The Correlation of Political and Military Means in the Defense of Socialism," *KVS*, no. 18 (September 1987), p. 14. See also Marshal S. Akhromeyev, "A Doctrine of Prevention of War, Defense of Peace and Socialism," *Problemy mira i sotsializma* (Problems of Peace and Socialism), no. 12 (December 1987), p. 25.

that Soviet military doctrine is directed not at preparation for war, but against it, for strengthening the foundations of international security. It proceeds from [recognition of] the inadmissibility of war, defines a complex of effective political and defensive measures aimed at averting war, not permitting an aggressor to unleash it with a calculation of any kind of advantage and in the illusory hope of winning victory." The article continued: "It is necessary to underline the fact that such a direct and sharp posing of the thesis on the prevention of war is incorporated in the definition of our military doctrine for the first time. Of course, the military activities of the Soviet Union and the other socialist countries previously also envisaged the struggle against war. But now that task is not only in policy, but also in military doctrine. It has moved into the foreground and become the main, determining element."[23]

Marshal Akhromeyev soon publicly stressed most of these same points, noting that preventing war had "become part of the content of military doctrine for the first time," and that while this task had earlier been undertaken by policy measures, "today in military strategy as well the struggle to prevent war has moved into the foreground and become decisive."[24]

While many statements continue to refer specifically to the need to prevent nuclear war, the statements incorporating the objective into military doctrine virtually all refer to the broader objective of preventing all war. General Yazov, in a key statement in 1988, made this explicit and discussed the point at some length. Proceeding from "the utter inadmissibility of war as a means of policy," he noted "this applies to nuclear war," implicitly but clearly including limited nuclear war because any nuclear war "would inevitably take on a global scale and lead to irreparable, catastrophic consequences for both sides and for all of humanity." But then he went on: "This is also true of conventional war," which "would have catastrophic consequences comparable to a nuclear cataclysm."[25]

23. "The Defensive Character of Soviet Military Doctrine and Preparation of the Troops (Forces)," *Voyennaya mysl'*, no. 1 (January 1988), p. 3.

24. Marshal S. F. Akhromeyev, "On Guard over Peace and Security," *Trud* (Labor), February 21, 1988, p. 2.

25. "Seventy Years on Guard over Socialism and Peace: Report of the Minister of Defense, General of the Army D. T. Yazov," *Krasnaya zvezda*, February 23, 1988, p. 2. In this article Yazov did not also note dangers of probable if not inevitable escalation of major conventional war into nuclear war, but he had done so in a similar discussion in his book a few months earlier. See Gen. Army D. T. Yazov, *Na strazhe*

Soviet military doctrine thus gained a new explicit incorporation in its political-military dimension of the need for averting nuclear, and indeed *all*, war involving the nuclear powers. This was stressed in the Warsaw Pact statement, and also in many internal Soviet statements. For example, a major article on the subject in *Military Thought* in 1989 concluded that under contemporary conditions "the conception of 'prevention of war' must, undoubtedly, relate both to nuclear and conventional war of any scale and social[-political] type between states possessing nuclear weapons and 'untraditional' forms of conventional arms approximating nuclear weapons in their effectiveness."[26]

The increasingly frequent references since 1985 to the expanded aim of preventing war, rather than specifically nuclear war, were an easy change in the political level of military doctrine. One of the first authoritative statements was in the joint declaration of Gorbachev and Reagan at Geneva in November 1985, in which the two leaders not only included the celebrated acknowledgement that "nuclear war cannot be won and must never be fought," but also "recognizing that any conflict between the USSR and the U.S. could have catastrophic consequences, they emphasized the importance of preventing any war between them, whether nuclear or conventional."[27] The initiative for this statement, according to Soviet officials, came from the Soviet side. While this reference was made in terms of avoiding any war between the two powers, it clearly also applied to any war that could involve them.

The expanded aim of preventing nonnuclear as well as nuclear war involves much more complex and serious potential applications to the military-technical level of military doctrine. Indeed, it threatens the foundation for military "requirements" to prepare for nonnuclear war, as well as to support a war-waging nuclear deterrent capability. Thus it can undercut the traditional basis for justifying resource allocations and affect unilateral force levels, as well as arms limitation and reduction positions and agreed constraints.

---

sotsializma i mira (On Guard over Socialism and Peace) (Moscow: Voyenizdat, 1987), p. 31.

26. Col. (Ret.) B. M. Kanevsky, "The Problem of Prevention of War: Concept, Potentialities, Mechanism," *Voyennaya mysl'*, no. 4 (April 1989), p. 49.

27. See *American Foreign Policy: Current Documents*, 1985 (Washington: Department of State, 1986), p. 427; and *Sovetsko-Amerikanskaya vstrecha na vysshem urovne, Zheneva 19-21 noyabrya 1985 goda* (The Soviet-American Summit Meeting, Geneva, November 19–21, 1985) (Moscow: Politizdat, 1985), p. 14.

In contrast, perhaps in reaction, some military men have tried to mobilize the objective of preventing nuclear war to *support* more traditional requirements (since the late 1960s) for forces capable of waging conventional war. Thus Admiral Kostev identified an important change in Soviet military doctrine (although without noting when it had changed). He cited the thesis that "if war is unleashed by the imperialists, it will inevitably assume the character of a nuclear-missile war, that is, a war in which the main means of destruction will be nuclear weapons and the main means of their delivery missiles. Today," Kostev declared, "that thesis does not correspond to the real situation. The extraordinary danger of nuclear war to a notable degree is understood in the United States and NATO. Hence, while not desisting from a policy of acting 'from positions of strength,' in their military strategy of 'flexible response' they provide for active preparation not only for nuclear [war], but for a long conventional war. In this connection, they are creating new means of combat that are by their characteristics almost indistinguishable from small-yield nuclear weapons. From this," he continued, "derives a necessity for all-round preparations by our country for armed defense not only with the employment of nuclear, but also highly effective nonnuclear, means of attack. The task is to not be weaker than a probable adversary."[28] This train of thought is obviously closer to the "new" military thinking introduced in the late 1960s than to the new political thinking of the late 1980s. Similarly, some discussions more generally now define the role of Soviet military power as not only for deterrence of imperialist attack, but for prevention of nuclear war. For example: "The military power of socialism is a means for deterrence of imperialist aggression, prevention of nuclear war, and preservation of peace."[29]

While noting that some conservative military writers may seek to co-opt the objective of preventing nuclear war to support traditional requirements, it remains within a framework in which that objective is real. Moreover, while local wars still occur, even the putative U.S.-Soviet nonnuclear world war that has been envisioned as a possibility (and still concerns those such as Admiral Kostev) is essentially discarded by most military leaders in their pronouncements. Thus, for example, then Defense Minister Marshal Sergei Sokolov in his 1987

28. Kostev, *KVS*, no. 17 (September 1987), p. 13.
29. Col. P. Skorodenko, "Military Parity and the Principle of Reasonable Sufficiency," *KVS*, no. 10 (May 1987), p. 21.

address on the anniversary of the end of World War II in Europe commented that "a world war in the nuclear-space age is obsolete, and has ceased to be a means of achieving political goals."[30]

The new criterion of reasonable sufficiency had by 1989 been refined to incorporate both deterrence and defense. Major General Stepan Tyushkevich, while noting a broader application to political relations, stated that "in military-technical and strategic terms reasonable sufficiency means a level of defense potential and character of activity of the armed forces that ensures prevention of war and sufficiency for defense."[31] And another discussion notes that "in Soviet military doctrine the solution of two interrelated tasks is considered necessary: to be in readiness to repulse any aggression that the military forces of imperialism may unleash, and to possess all that is necessary to deny those forces any hopes of dealing the USSR a first disarming strike without retaliation. In other words, our defensive policy and the defensive military doctrine that stems from it is a policy of preventing nuclear catastrophe."[32]

These developments reflect a radical revision in the military-technical level of Soviet military doctrine. The strategic concept for waging war in the continental theaters of military operations, above all in Europe, calling for a strategic nonnuclear offensive westward to destroy the NATO armies, has been replaced. The new doctrine calls for primary reliance on defense, and the new strategy calls for defensive repulse of attack for the initial period of the war. These represent major changes.

Until 1987 the long-standing Soviet view (shared by most modern armies) was that the offensive was the dominant form of warfare. To cite but one authoritative reference, an important article on Soviet military strategy in *Military Thought* in 1979 had stressed: "Only active, decisive operations with the use of all forces and means can lead to full victory over an aggressor," so that while Soviet aims were defensive, in case of an enemy attack they would assume the offensive.[33]

30. Marshal S. L. Sokolov, "Victory for the Sake of Peace," *Pravda*, May 9, 1987, p. 2.
31. Maj. Gen. (Ret.) S. A. Tyushkevich, "Reasonable Sufficiency for Defense: Parameters and Criteria," *Voyennaya mysl'*, no. 5 (May 1989), p. 56.
32. [Col.] B. M. Kanevsky and [Lt. Col.] P. M. Shabardin, *Problemy sovremennoi voyennoi politiki* (Problems of Contemporary Military Policy), Mezhdunarodnaya series 5 (Moscow: Znaniye, 1989), p. 21.
33. Col. Gen. V. N. Karpov, "On the Theory of Soviet Military Strategy," *Voyen-*

But by mid-1987 that view had drastically changed.[34] General Yazov and other military leaders soon began to assert that "Soviet military doctrine considers the defense as the main form of military operations in repelling aggression."[35] This was a striking change, but alone could have been essentially rhetorical. Other changes in doctrine, and more important in policy and military posture, in 1988–89 showed that the shift was not just declaratory. The impact on Soviet strategy is discussed in chapter 5, but it is also useful to note here briefly that beginning with the Warsaw Pact statement of military doctrine in May 1987, the stated doctrine not only gave primacy to the defensive but proposed that the two alliances in Europe reduce their forces to defensive sufficiency defined (to cite General Yazov) as "a level such that neither side, while assuring its defense, has the forces or means enabling it to mount offensive operations."[36]

These statements of the task of Soviet military doctrine do not resolve the practical policy issues of how much to spend to satisfy the requirement of "sufficiency for defense." They do, however, provide a basis for closely examining and challenging submissions of the Ministry of Defense and General Staff based on prior, more open-ended "requirements" for waging a war, nuclear or nonnuclear, to victory over the enemy.

More generally, the application of sufficiency, a defensive strategy, and prevention of war to military doctrine and strategy has not yet been fully worked out. As a military theorist who has devoted particular attention to this subject, Lieutenant General Serebryanni-

naya mysl', no. 10 (October 1979), p. 19. General Karpov was then head of the strategy faculty at the General Staff Academy.

34. Thus, for example, the *Soviet Military Encyclopedia* in 1978, all discussions on *Military Thought* to 1987, and the *Military Encyclopedic Dictionary* in its revised edition in 1986, all continued to state flatly that the offensive was "the main form of combat operations." See "Offensive" and "Strategic Offensive," *VES*, 2d ed. ([April 21] 1986), pp. 476, 711. So, too, did the basic military text on *Tactics*, signed to press as late as January 29, 1987. See Lt. Gen. V. G. Reznichenko and others, eds., *Taktika*, 2d ed. (Moscow: Voyenizdat, 1987), p. 56, and unchanged even in a 1988 reprinting.

The first statement explicitly ascribing a "profoundly defensive thrust" to the military-technical level of Soviet military doctrine was a statement by General Makhmut Gareyev, a deputy chief of the General Staff and former head of its Military Science directorate. See Statement by Deputy Chief of the General Staff of the USSR Armed Forces, Col. Gen. M. A. Gareyev, in "A Doctrine for Preventing War," *Krasnaya zvezda*, June 23, 1987, p. 3.

35. Yazov, *Na strazhe sotsializma i mira*, p. 32.

36. Yazov, *Pravda*, July 27, 1987, p. 5.

kov, has written: "It appears that scientific development of the theory of preventing war must be accomplished within the framework of studies of war and peace, military science, military doctrine, and the military art. In terms of substance, the theory and practical means of actions by the army to prevent war have not yet been worked out, inasmuch as in the past all attention was concentrated on working out means of conducting combat operations."[37] General Mikhail Moiseyev, chief of the General Staff, has no less frankly acknowledged that "one of the most complex tasks of military science is working out strategy for the prevention of war. Such a problem has never before been posed in our armed forces. Deep scientific study is required, working out concrete recommendations by the organs of command, the troops and the fleet."[38]

These fundamental changes in Soviet military doctrine stemmed directly from political initiatives of the new Gorbachev leadership in 1985. Marshal Akhromeyev, on several occasions in recent years, has emphasized that as "the new leadership" worked out new foreign policies, "an objective requirement arose for working out a new military doctrine . . . therefore in the period from 1985 to 1987 in the USSR, and in the other states of the Warsaw Pact, a new military doctrine was worked out. It was published in May 1987 and since that time has been the operative guidance for the armed forces of the USSR."[39]

Glasnost' *and New Thinking*

The "new thinking" on the need to prevent war has had some unanticipated results. *Glasnost'* has even led to a remarkable debate in the Soviet media over whether nuclear "second use," nuclear retaliation, would be justified! A Belorussian writer, Ales Adamovich,

37. Lt. Gen. Avn. V. Serebryannikov, "The Prevention of War: The Army's Contribution," *KVS*, no. 17 (September 1989), p. 25.
38. Cited in ibid., p. 25.
39. "A New Policy against the Arsenals of War," *KVS*, no. 1 (January 1990), p. 17. Akhromeyev had made a similar statement while visiting in the United States in July 1988. Colonel General Nikolai Chervov, who accompanied Akhromeyev on that occasion, confirmed to me at the time that the two-year period marked the time from the April 1985 Central Committee plenum to the May 1987 Warsaw Pact declaration. He noted that it required consultation and discussion with the other Warsaw Pact defense ministers, and although he did not say so, I had the impression that the requirements for multilateral consultation were used to spur the Soviet change in doctrine.

has contended that *no* use of nuclear weapons would be justified, that even nuclear retaliation for an enemy nuclear first strike would only "finish off" humankind.[40] Colonel General Dmitry Volkogonov rebutted that contention, not by challenging the argument on the consequences of nuclear war, but on the grounds that *readiness* for nuclear retaliation was essential in order to *deter* the potential enemy first strike.[41] (This argument of course underlies American, as well as Soviet, official doctrine.) Adamovich and others nonetheless repeated his challenge, while still others joined in rebuttal.[42] A debate continued in several journals over a period of months. Surprisingly, the journal *Sovetskaya kultura*, after carrying articles by both sides, concluded at least one stage of the debate in December 1987 not by reaffirming the official position on deterrence, but by noting that "the most authoritative specialists" had proved that victory in a nuclear war was unattainable by any side including a defender in retaliation, and stressing that a nuclear arms race and nuclear war simply must be prevented. Moreover, while imperialism was charged with nuclear war doctrines, the editors stated that "*all* so-called scenarios for a future war compiled in military headquarters are in their very foundations absurd."[43]

Aleksandr Bovin, an independent thinker and influential commentator, has gone so far as to write in *Izvestiya* that the argument that a nuclear retaliatory strike would be justified is "an empty, meaningless abstraction." He then drove the point home in a provocative way by arguing that "nuclear pacifism, applied to nuclear war . . . is the only reasonable, only morally and politically justified position."[44]

40. Ales Adamovich, "At the Forum and After," *Moskovskiye novosti* (Moscow News), March 8, 1987, p. 3.

41. Col. Gen. D. A. Volkogonov, comments at a literary conference, reported in "The Present Day and Literature," *Literaturnaya gazeta* (Literary Gazette), May 6, 1987, p.3. Adamovich was also present and stood his ground.

42. General Volkogonov repeated his position in "Imperatives of the Nuclear Age," *Krasnaya zvezda*, May 22, 1987, pp. 2–3. Meanwhile, a parallel debate had independently arisen in articles by Vladimir Begun and Vitaly Bovsh in the Belorussian Party journal *Politicheskii sobesednik* (Political Interlocutor), Minsk, issues 1 and 2, 1987, and rebuttals by Vasil' Bykov and others in "Who Stole the 'Lantern of Glasnost,' " *Sovetskaya kultura* (Soviet Culture), October 3, 1987, p. 6, and a round-robin including Adamovich, Begun, Bovsh, Bykov, and the editors in the same journal on December 10, 1987.

43. "From the Editorial Office," *Sovetskaya kultura*, December 10, 1987, p. 6; emphasis added.

44. A. Bovin, "Nuclear War and Policy," *Izvestiya*, February 5, 1988, p. 5.

This remains a politically delicate and extreme conclusion by some in applying the "new thinking." Yet it clearly is extending well beyond a Belorussian writer and a provocative journalist. In the first issue of the chief Party journal *Kommunist* in 1988, a vice president of the Academy of Sciences, Yevgeny Velikhov, in favorably reviewing a new book (of which Adamovich, along with Anatoly Gromyko, son of the late Soviet leader, is a coauthor) himself writes of nuclear war: "Not only is victory impossible in such a war, but so too is successful defense, which means that security cannot be achieved by military-technical means." The "necessity of recognizing that there cannot be victors in a nuclear war" is called foremost among the "key principles on which the new thinking is based." Finally, "it is senseless to seek one's own security in isolation from the security of the nuclear 'opponent'—security can only exist as a mutual threat reduction and in the scale of the world community as common security."[45]

Public opinion is increasingly a factor in this new age of *glasnost'* and *demokratizatsiya*. The Soviet public strongly supports a policy of nuclear disarmament and of seeking to prevent nuclear war, although there are some reservations as to the feasibility of such far-reaching goals as eliminating all nuclear weapons. In an opinion poll of Moscow citizens in early 1987, overwhelming majorities saw a world nuclear war as an unmitigated disaster—89 percent believed there would be no victor and that "the United States and the Soviet Union would be completely annihilated," and 83 percent believed human civilization would perish.[46]

45. Ye. Velikhov, "A Summons to Changes," *Kommunist*, no. 1 (January 1988), p. 53. The book he was reviewing is titled *Proryv: Stanovleniye novogo myshleniya* (Breakthrough: The Formation of the New Thinking) (Moscow: Progress, 1988); published concurrently in the United States as Anatoly Gromyko and Martin Hellman, eds., *Breakthrough/Proryv: Emerging New Thinking* (New York: Walker and Co., 1988). The book is something of an experimental venture, with both Soviet and American authors. The review in *Kommunist*, as well as the publication in Russian, makes clear it is not seen merely as an external propaganda venture.

Velikhov, and Adamovich, have both been active as deputies in the Supreme Soviet elected in 1989.

46. Some 88 percent believed limited nuclear war was impossible, and 93 percent that *no* purpose would justify the use of nuclear weapons. (A similar 93 percent were certain the Soviet Union would never use nuclear weapons first; only 8 percent were confident that the United States would not, with 37 percent believing it would and 55 percent uncertain.) Ninety-six percent believed that "the interests of survival of mankind must take precedence over *any* other"; emphasis added. A similar 95 percent said continued buildup of U.S. and Soviet nuclear arsenals "raised the risk of acciden-

Public opinion has also begun openly to express doubts as to the continuing relevance and even compatibility of civil defense with the new thinking. For example, an article in the liberal journal *Twentieth Century and Peace* in 1987 called "Games Adults Play" leveled a devastating criticism at the effectiveness, competence, and even the purpose of civil defense. The author commented further: "A year has passed since Chernobyl. Who needs such nonsense [civil defense exercises] for window dressing?"[47] A physicist, Aleksandr Artemov, set off a lively debate in the mass circulation newspaper for young people the next year, asserting "the incompatibility of existing civil defense concepts with the principles of the new thinking—the impossibility of victory or survival in a nuclear war."[48] Reader reaction seemed to be about equally divided.

The civil defense issue may or may not become a serious one. There is a certain defensiveness by the military leadership. In an interview in 1987, General of the Army Vladimir Govorov, deputy minister of defense and chief of Civil Defense of the USSR, was bluntly asked: "We spend millions on civil defense. But we ourselves are now saying: There can be no survivors in a nuclear war. So what is the point of all this?" The general responded: "A reasonable question, and it does not befit a military man to evade a direct answer. But I would rather put it slightly differently: It is not a question of survival being impossible, rather it is victory that is impossible."[49]

---

tal use," and 93 percent agreed that "a complete liquidation of nuclear weapons was the only path to escape nuclear war." A slightly smaller group, 83 percent, believed a continued nuclear arms race would not give advantages to either side; 10 percent were unsure and 6 percent disagreed. In all, clearly there was near unanimity on a need to work for nuclear disarmament. Yet there was far less confidence that "complete liquidation of nuclear weapons is feasible"—only 71 percent, with 6 percent sure it was not, and 23 percent uncertain. Similarly, only 22 percent were sure the nuclear genie could be put back in the bottle; 48 percent doubted it and 30 percent were undecided. Some 84 percent agreed that nuclear disarmament must be accompanied by reductions of conventional arms (7 percent opposed). Most discrepant was a judgment by 30 percent that "liquidation of nuclear weapons would raise the probability of nonnuclear conflicts between East and West," although 38 percent believed it would not, with 31 percent unsure.

The poll was conducted by the Institute of Sociological Research of the U.S.S.R. Academy of Sciences. See "Muscovites on War and Peace," *Izvestiya*, February 14, 1987, p. 5.

47. Lyudmila Ptitsyna, "Games Adults Play," *XX vek i mir* (Twentieth Century and Peace), no. 10 (October 1987), pp. 7, 47.

48. See Aleksandr Artemov, "Survival! No—Life," *Sovetskaya molodezh* (Soviet Youth), April 28, 1988, and "Let's Debate It!" ibid., September 9, 1988, p. 3.

49. "Never to Be Forgotten," Interview with Gen. Army Vladimir Leonidovich

Civil defense, incidentally, remains a combined military and civilian activity under the overall control of the Ministry of Defense. There were many criticisms of its effectiveness in the aftermath of the Chernobyl nuclear accident and the Armenian earthquake, and it is being more geared to deal with such situations. While it has continued to be described as part of overall Soviet preparation for possible war, the significance of civil defense has greatly declined in Soviet military thinking. It received only one lecture in the General Staff Academy course in the mid-1970s and probably later.[50] One sign of the reduced high-level military attention to civil defense is the fact that the last article devoted to the subject to appear in the General Staff journal *Military Thought* was in 1974.[51]

The most important avenue for *glasnost'* to affect policy is in debate in the Supreme Soviet as it reviews and approves the defense budget. While the first year's review (in 1989) was relatively limited, even then a few significant changes were made; the potential role in the future is great.

New Military Theorizing

Soviet military doctrine includes the development of military *and* political-military, indeed ideological-political-military, theorizing of a kind that has no direct parallel in the West. It is therefore easy to overlook it. But it is in fact important in the Soviet political and military culture.

The development of philosophical analysis led, by the fall of 1987, to published discussion by some Soviet military theorists proposing that because of the inescapable relationship of war to policy, and the utter inability of global nuclear war to serve any rational policy, the very term "nuclear-missile war" should be abandoned and replaced by "nuclear-missile catastrophe."[52] They argued that "the axiom

---

Govorov by I. Morozov, *Komsomol'skaya pravda* (Komsomol Pravda), May 9, 1987, p. 1.

50. See *The Voroshilov Lectures: Materials from the Soviet General Staff Academy*, vol. 2 (forthcoming).

51. See Gen. Army A. Altunin, "On the Theory of Civil Defense," *Voyennaya mysl'*, no. 2 (February 1974), pp. 30–40.

52. [Col.] B. Kanevsky and [Lt. Col.] P. Shabardin, "On the Question of the Correlation of Policy, War and Nuclear-Missile Catastrophe," *Mezhdunarodnaya zhizn'*, no. 10 (October 1987), pp. 120–29. The authors were identified as senior

'war is a continuation of policy' has been so deformed by the realities of the nuclear era that in its essence, content and functional relations it becomes inapplicable for understanding what has come to be called nuclear-missile war." Lenin's authority is cited for the theoretical conclusion that "conflict with nuclear weapons objectively is a contradiction of [the concept of] war and its conversion into global catastrophe."[53]

This distinction, which the authors introduced into theoretical discussion, reflects the continuing development of Soviet policy on the prevention of nuclear war. As the authors note, these new realities have affected the structure of the military forces. In particular, "the strategic nuclear forces of the USSR are called upon, as a weapon of [potential] retribution, to prevent such a catastrophe."[54] They also suggest, without becoming specific, that "the conception of distinguishing war and nuclear-missile catastrophe and the related understanding of the functions of 'conventional' and 'nuclear strategic' forces permits realizing more deeply the objective necessity of optimally ... meeting the tasks of supporting the defense of the country and structuring the armed forces at a level that would permit preventing a nuclear catastrophe and parrying any military attack on the USSR and its allies."[55]

While this theorizing may seem very abstract to most American readers, it could be a very significant step toward substituting a form of minimum deterrence for a deterrent based on war-fighting capabilities.[56] The contingency of *war* may justify hedging preparations for waging it; the contingency of *catastrophe* cannot, it can justify only measures to avert the possibility.

---

members of the Institute of Military History of the Ministry of Defense, but not by rank.

The term "nuclear-missile war" may seem stilted to the Western reader, but it is the standard Soviet term representing what is called in the West "global nuclear war," "all-out nuclear war," or simply "nuclear war," meaning unlimited nuclear hostilities.

53. Ibid., pp. 122, 123.

54. Ibid., p. 128. They also note that, in contrast to the comparable American triad, the Soviet nuclear triad are not called "strategic *offensive* forces."

55. Ibid., p. 129. The phrase I have omitted at the ellipsis to better focus attention first on the underlying point should not be neglected; it is "with account for the aggressive essence of the military policy of imperialism."

56. This point is obscured, no doubt intentionally, by the authors through inclusion of the phrase cited in the preceding note. But they have, nonetheless, chosen to raise the issue.

One of the two authors, Colonel Boris Kanevsky, had in fact a few months earlier made a daring if veiled reference to the gut issue of military requirements for preparations to wage a war. In a review article, he criticized a recent book on military doctrine (General Tyushkevich's *War and the Present Day*) for not making "a more fundamental study" of "such an important problem, particularly for the military reader, as the correlation between the thesis on the impossibility of victory in a nuclear-missile war, and the necessity for raising the combat readiness of the army and navy in order to defeat any aggressor."[57] How, indeed, to "correlate" or reconcile those two propositions! Combat readiness for deterrence, on the other hand, in contradistinction to readiness for waging war to defeat an enemy, can be justified consistently with a belief in no victors in a nuclear war. It is, as the Soviet idiom has it, "no accident" that Tyushkevich and other commentators had theretofore chosen *not* to draw attention to the discrepancy arising between the political and military-technical levels of current Soviet military doctrine.

Finally, this pathbreaking analysis stressed that "an important consequence of this conceptual approach in the spirit of the new thinking to the conception of the essence of nuclear-missile catastrophe is the necessity for a more coordinated approach to the resolution of theoretical and practical problems of foreign and defense policy." The "cardinal tasks" it cited concern "the prevention of nuclear catastrophe, achievement of a nuclear-free world, readiness and capabilities for repulsing aggressive intrigues of the militaristic forces of imperialism," which "now can successfully be reached only by coordinated efforts both in international affairs and in the military sphere."[58]

The article by Colonels Kanevsky and Shabardin provoked a spirited debate in *Mezhdunarodnaya zhizn'*. No one took issue with

57. [Col.] B. Kanevsky, "From the Standpoint of the New Political Thinking," *KVS*, no. 6 (March 1987), p. 88. General Tyushkevich had devoted a whole chapter of his book to the prevention of nuclear war, calling it "the nub question" and saying that "the most important task facing humankind is the prevention of world nuclear war," and that "it is a categorical imperative of the present epoch that nuclear war must not be permitted—not a small one, or great, not limited or total." Maj. Gen. S. A. Tyushkevich, *Voina i sovremennost'* (War and the Present Day) (Moscow: Nauka, 1986), pp. 90, 119, and see pp. 6–9, 90–120. But he had indeed evaded the more difficult question of defining requirements for nuclear capabilities for deterrence, which he substitutes for victory as the aim of Soviet strategy.

58. Kanevsky and Shabardin, *Mezhdunarodnaya zhizn'*, no. 10 (October 1987), p. 129.

the priority requirement to prevent nuclear war, although differing views on the nature of nuclear war or catastrophe did affect thinking on how to further that objective. One supporter of the article criticized the argument that socialism must still seek to defend itself in a nuclear war. "Socialism faces not the problem of its defense in a world nuclear war, as some think, but defending itself and all humanity from such a war or, more precisely, as we have now clarified, from a nuclear catastrophe."[59] Another redefined victory: "In contemporary conditions victory of each and all states consists not in the capability to prevail in a trial of force, but in the ability to avert such a clash."[60] And others conclude that "realities of the nuclear age urgently require that political-military thought be reoriented to the problem of preventing war."[61]

Colonels Kanevsky and Shabardin in a later publication have addressed two related issues. First, they argue that while it would be too much to expect that war in general can yet be excluded from world society, nonetheless its prevention is a pressing current requirement. Second, they argue that the prevention of war must be broader than deterring nuclear attack and "the direct threat of nuclear catastrophe." The term "the prevention of war" must, they argue, "comprehend nuclear war and conventional war of any scale and type between states that possess nuclear and high precision arms."[62] While Soviet official doctrine has not been that precise, it does increasingly stress the need to prevent conventional as well as nuclear war between East and West. These authors, along with others, also stress that prevention of (nuclear) war must extend beyond dissuasion of deliberate and calculated attack to include averting war by accident or miscalculation, beyond political control.[63]

Preventing Unpremeditated War

The danger of war arising from technical malfunction, human error in technical evaluations, political miscalculation of the situa-

59. [Col.] B. Tkachuk and [Col.] V. Tumalar'yan, "Grounds for Reflection," *Mezhdunarodnaya zhizn'*, no. 1 (January 1988), p. 109.
60. [Col.] O. Bel'kov, "Not Victory in War, but Victory over War," ibid., p. 112.
61. [Col.] A. Dyrin and [Lt. Col.] A. Savinkin, "To Take More Fully into Account the Realities of the Nuclear Age," ibid., p. 115. As noted here, most of the discussants in this debate are military men, although the editors have not provided such identification.
62. Kanevsky and Shabardin, *Problemy sovremennoi voyennoi politiki*, pp. 22–23.
63. Ibid., pp. 16–17.

tion, or unauthorized actions has long been recognized by strategic analysts and political leaders in the United States and the Soviet Union. Such dangers have always existed in one or another form, and indeed have led to conflict in many historical cases. In the nuclear age, however, the stakes and dangers are incomparably greater than ever before.[64]

Soviet attention to the danger of war arising from causes other than a deterrable deliberate decision by an enemy can be traced to the late 1950s and early 1960s. It is not a new concern in the Gorbachev period. But it has been given increased weight in political consideration and had a new impact on Soviet military doctrine.

In one of the earliest statements on this subject by a Soviet political leader, Nikita Khrushchev, acknowledging the revolution in weaponry, commented in 1957 that "it is not excluded that war can be unleashed as a result of some kind of fatal error."[65] At the same time, there was a strong stand in Soviet thinking until the mid-1960s to criticize American theorizing about accidental war on the Marxist grounds that wars are caused by basic social (class) conflicts, not by accident.[66] The most important development leading to a more serious Soviet assessment of the possibility of war arising from accident or miscalculation was the Cuban missile crisis of October 1962. There were others as well, including the Sino-Soviet rift and a growing concern over the dangers of nuclear proliferation and the possible "catalytic" generation of war between the superpowers by uncontrollable actions, and even deliberate provocative actions, by third countries.

The first concrete agreement on a measure to reduce the risk of unpremeditated war was the hot line direct communications link between the leaders in Washington and Moscow, concluded in June 1963.[67] The idea had been broached earlier by both sides, but the

64. For a useful discussion of Soviet (and U.S.) command and control postures and risks of accidental war, see Bruce G. Blair, *The Logic of Accidental Nuclear War* (Brookings, forthcoming).

65. "Interview of N. S. Khrushchev with the Chief Editor of the American Newspaper New York Times, Turner Catledge, May 10, 1957," *Izvestiya*, May 14, 1957, p. 2.

66. For a good example, see V. Berezhkov, "Automobile Accident Theory of War," *New Times*, no. 16 (April 18, 1962), pp. 18–19.

67. For a good review of the hot line and its further evolution, see Sally K. Horn, "The Hotline," in John Borawski, ed., *Avoiding War in the Nuclear Age: Confidence-*

experience of the Cuban missile crisis helped spur both to this action. More generally, by the late 1960s Soviet writers distinguished among possible *technical, psychological,* and *political* causes of "accidental war."[68] Unofficial exchanges between Soviets and Americans such as at the Pugwash meetings also reflected the growing Soviet concern about the danger of accidental war and war by miscalculation, and interest in various measures to help alleviate these problems. Andrei Gromyko, in his address to the Supreme Soviet on July 10, 1969, shortly before the Strategic Arms Limitation Talks (SALT) began, gave equal attention to stopping the buildup in strategic arms and to another important aspect of the overall problem that "must not fail to be taken into account in the long-range policies of states," namely, "the fact that systems of command and control are becoming, if one may put it this way, more and more autonomous of the people who create them. . . . Decisions made by man in the final analysis depend upon conclusions provided to him by computers." He concluded that "governments must do everything in their power so as to be able to determine the course of events and not become captive to those events."[69]

While this concern, and a determination to deal with the problem, clearly extended beyond arms control negotiations, they were also regarded as relevant to them. In the diplomatic exchanges in 1968–69 leading to SALT, the Soviet side took the initiative in raising questions of accidental war. In September 1971 an Agreement on Measures to Reduce the Risk of Outbreak of Nuclear War between the United States and the Soviet Union was signed (accompanied by an upgrading of the hot line to use space communications).[70] Soon after, in May 1972, an agreement was concluded on avoiding incidents at sea between the navies of the two powers.[71] In 1973 the

---

Building Measures for Crisis Stability (Boulder, Colo.: Westview Press, 1986), pp. 43–55.

68. For example, see G. Gerasimov, "Accidental War," *International Affairs,* no. 12 (December 1966), pp. 33–38.

69. "Session of the Supreme Soviet of the USSR: Aspects of the International Situation and the Foreign Policy of the Soviet Union, Report by Deputy A. A. Gromyko, USSR Minister of Foreign Affairs," *Pravda,* July 11, 1969, p. 3.

70. For the negotiation of this agreement, see Raymond L. Garthoff, "The Accidents Measures Agreement," in Borawski, ed., *Avoiding War in the Nuclear Age,* pp. 56–71.

71. See Sean M. Lynn-Jones, "Avoiding Incidents at Sea," in Borawski, ed., *Avoiding War in the Nuclear Age,* pp. 72–89.

agreement on Prevention of Nuclear War, discussed earlier, was signed. While the most comprehensive of these agreements, it was in practice almost ignored.

With the decline of détente in the late 1970s and the tensions of the early 1980s, neither country paid much attention to further collaborative measures to reduce the risk of unintended war. Earlier noted was the abortive attempt in 1984 to begin a dialogue on a nuclear "code of conduct"—one of the precursors of a new attention given by the Soviet leadership under Gorbachev. With the revival of American-Soviet dialogue in the latter half of the 1980s, several new agreements were reached, in particular in September 1987 on the establishment of Nuclear Risk Reduction Centers in Washington and Moscow, and in June 1989 on the Prevention of Dangerous Military Activities, an analogue of the naval incidents at sea agreement applicable to all the armed services.

Meanwhile, the earliest multilateral and nonbinding confidence-building measures agreed on as part of the Helsinki accords of the Conference on Security and Cooperation in Europe (CSCE) in 1975 were greatly expanded and made mandatory in a number of confidence- and security-building measures adopted in September 1986 at the Committee on Disarmament in Europe (CDE) established as part of the continuing CSCE process.

These agreements of the late 1980s bore witness to the readiness of the Soviet Union under Gorbachev, and the United States and other Western powers, to contribute to what the Soviets in the 1970s had called "military détente" and what they now refer to as "strengthening strategic stability."[72] While useful for providing greater transparency in military activities, about certain constraints, and in procedures for clarifying uncertainties, perhaps the greatest value of such measures is in contributing to an evolving pattern of common security.

Soviet political and military analyses, and leadership statements, have gone beyond such negotiable arrangements on mutual security interests. The Soviet concept of the objective of preventing war, including deterrence but extending much more widely, has led them also to institute changes in Soviet foreign policy and military doctrine to deal with the threat of the outbreak of unpremeditated war.

72. I. N. Shcherbak, *Mezhdunarodnaya bezopasnost' i problemy doveriya v voyennoi oblasti* (International Security and Problems of Confidence in the Military Sphere), Mezhdunarodnaya series 3 (Moscow: Znaniye, 1987), p. 5.

The Soviets recognize as the principal purposes of confidence- and security-building measures not only reduction of tensions and increased trust, but also specifically "preventing the outbreak of armed conflicts as a consequence of incorrect evaluation of one another's military activities."[73] This recognition has supported the Soviet role in negotiating bilateral and multilateral arms control and confidence-building measures such as those earlier noted.

In foreign policy more broadly, this objective has also contributed to the dynamism of Soviet efforts to expand political détente and dialogue with the United States, Europe, China, and Japan. It has contributed to the decisions to reduce unilaterally Soviet forces in Eastern Europe, in Mongolia, and on the Sino-Soviet border, and overall in the Soviet Union itself. Beyond that, it has undoubtedly contributed to the decision to permit drastic political change in the six once-communist countries of the Warsaw Pact, and a transformation of that pact from a military and political instrument of control to a tenuous political security alliance.

The decisions by Gorbachev and his colleagues to allow, and even to encourage, this change were in part a response to belated recognition of political and economic realities in Eastern Europe (and the Soviet Union). The pace and full extent of the change in 1989 and since were no doubt not fully recognized when the decisions were made. Nonetheless, the change stemmed from a deliberate choice in Moscow to rely on a more conditional but politically and economically viable relationship rather than on enforced control.

The remarkable change in Eastern Europe also stemmed from a decision in Moscow to shift to a significant degree from reliance on military deterrence and defense to reliance on political reassurance of the West. This shift required a revised assessment of the real threat from the United States and NATO, and an appreciation of the importance of reducing Western perceptions of a threat emanating from the Soviet Union and the Warsaw Pact. Gorbachev and other Soviet leaders have on a number of occasions made clear that one of their aims is to dispel unwarranted but not inexplicable Western fears. In particular, Gorbachev has on several occasions said: "We do not build our policy on a desire to infringe on the national interests of the United States. I will say more: we would not, for example,

73. See "Confidence-Building Measures," in A. A. Gromyko and others, eds., *Diplomaticheskii slovar'* (Diplomatic Dictionary), 4th ed. (Moscow: Nauka, 1985), vol. 2, pp. 218–19.

want changes in the strategic balance in our favor. We would not want that because such a situation would strengthen suspicion of the other side and increase instability in our common situation."[74]

Soviet concern over unintended and uncontrolled outbreak of war has risen. As early as 1985 Foreign Minister Eduard Shevardnadze noted in his maiden speech to the UN General Assembly that

> the higher the level of military confrontation in this nuclear-space age, the more shaky and less secure become the foundations of world peace—even if a strategic balance is maintained. In these conditions nuclear war may result not only from a deliberate decision but also from attempts at blackmail or miscalculation by one side as to the intentions or actions of the other, as a consequence of someone's reckless behavior prompted by a sudden aggravation of the situation, or be the result of malfunctions in computers which are increasingly relied upon in the functioning of modern sophisticated weapon systems. This is our understanding of current strategic and political realities. It is based on grim facts that cannot be ignored.[75]

Shevardnadze's statement reiterated in substance the same categories of factors that had been identified years earlier: political (miscalculation and misperception of a threat), psychological (decision-making under crisis and time pressures), and technical (computer malfunction). These have been further elucidated in recent years by Soviet political and military analysts.[76]

Political miscalculation is seen as particularly dangerous in the nuclear age, and above all in times of tension, but also as evident throughout history.[77] One Soviet commentator has observed that "the experience of the first and second world wars demonstrates the presence in the generation of many military conflicts of the element of miscalculation, an inadequate perception of the political and military intentions of one another by the adversaries."[78]

74. "Report of the General Secretary of the CC of the CPSU Deputy M. S. Gorbachev," *Pravda*, November 28, 1985, p. 2.

75. "Address by E. A. Shevardnadze to the 40th Session of the UN General Assembly," *Pravda*, September 25, 1985, p. 4.

76. In addition to other sources referred to in the discussion following, in particular see A. A. Kokoshin and [Maj. Gen. (Ret.)] V. V. Larionov, *Predotvrashcheniye voiny: doktriny, kontseptsii, perspektivy* (Prevention of War: Doctrines, Concepts, Prospects) (Moscow: Progress, 1990), esp. pp. 153–63.

77. Deliberate decision to start a war may of course also involve miscalculation, as Hitler found. In this discussion, I am concerned with political miscalculation contributing or leading to unpremeditated or accidental war.

78. Shcherbak, *Mezhdunarodnaya bezopasnost'*, p. 10.

One important area of political pressures for actions that could lead to a general nuclear war despite lack of intention or desire to have that outcome, not mentioned in this passage by Shevardnadze but often cited by him, Gorbachev, and other political leaders, is the risk of escalation from local regional conflicts involving interests and sometimes the presence of military forces of one or both of the superpowers. "Great attention is given in the Soviet Union," according to Major General Yury Kirshin, "to working out political and strategic measures that could localize regional conflicts and prevent local wars from growing into world nuclear war." He recalled (without specific reference to the Chernenko proposals of 1984) that the Soviet Union has proposed "rules of conduct" for the nuclear powers in relation to regional conflicts, directed to avoiding or reducing their involvement in such conflicts. He also drew attention, in a new element advanced by the Gorbachev leadership, to the role that military contingents of the United Nations can play in "neutralizing local wars and conflicts, preventing their growing into world war."[79]

A central Soviet concern since the mid-1960s, as I have discussed, has been to keep any war, especially in Europe, from becoming nuclear. This of course represents the most direct difference between Soviet and Western conceptions of the requirements for meeting their commonly acknowledged aim of preventing war: the Western conception of nuclear deterrence requires at least a declaratory position and military posture threatening deliberate NATO initiation of use of nuclear weapons to meet a postulated Soviet conventional attack; the Soviet conception postulates a NATO attack and U.S. first use of nuclear weapons whenever judged expedient. But even apart from the conflict of strategic presumptions, there is also a danger of the initiation of use of nuclear weapons *without* deliberate decision by the highest political authorities. This danger is now cautiously recognized in authoritative Soviet discussions. Thus General of the Army Vitaly Shabanov, a deputy minister of defense, has noted that in a conventional conflict there may be "deliberate or accidental attacks on the enemy's nuclear and chemical systems,"

79. Maj. Gen. Yu. Kirshin, "Policy and Military Strategy in the Nuclear Age," *Mirovaya ekonomika i mezhdunarodnyye otnosheniya* (World Economy and International Relations; hereafter *MEiMO*), no. 11 (November 1988), pp. 39–40, quotations from p. 40. See also A. G. Arbatov, *Oboronitel'naya dostatochnost' i bezopasnost'* (Defensive Sufficiency and Security), Mezhdunarodnaya series 4 (Moscow: Znaniye, 1990), pp. 8–9.

and on peaceful nuclear and other power stations, with consequences much greater than Chernobyl and with "unpredictable retaliatory actions" by the other side. And even more directly:

> The speed of combat operations with sharp changes in the tactical and operational situation, pressing advance by the troops of the enemy, the simultaneous compass of vast territories of a number of countries in Europe of combat actions, deliberate destruction of channels of command, conduct of military actions day and night and under all conditions may not permit the political and higher military leadership to authorize [*sanktsionirovat'*] decisions taken, owing to insufficient time and information. In extreme cases this could lead to irreversible escalation of military actions up to and including use of tactical nuclear weapons.[80]

General Kirshin similarly refers to the danger of uncontrolled escalation to nuclear war, addressing a process stemming from the dynamics of the situation rather than being attributed only to the adversary:

> Political leaders and [military] strategists do not exclude war with conventional weapons between the nuclear powers. In such a war a situation can arise when, as a consequence of large manpower losses and the loss of important territories, the political and strategic command will not be in a state to stop the escalation of the armed conflict, and the war may become nuclear—strategy may slip out of the command [*rukovodstvo*] and control of political leaders.[81]

The interacting influences of technical and human error, and especially in the tensions of crisis, is emphasized, again in a politically neutral way as a problem common to both sides.

Soviet analysts recognize and emphasize the increased risk of accidental or unauthorized actions igniting war under conditions of heightened alert. Inasmuch as the natural military reaction to increasing danger of war is to increase combat readiness, there is a dilemma between preventing (or blunting) an attack by high readiness, and unleashing war by those same alerting and readiness measures. As Kokoshin and Larionov remark after reviewing this problem, "High combat readiness—the holy of holies in the operation of the military system—in strategic interpretation in the nuclear age

80. Gen. Army Vitaly Shabanov, "'Conventional' War: New Dangers," *Novoye vremya* (New Times), no. 46 (November 14, 1986), p. 8.

81. Kirshin, *MEiMO*, no. 11 (November 1988), p. 42.

can, as has been shown, play the role of strengthening the danger of accidental outbreak of war."[82]

In this context, launch on warning is seen as a particular danger.[83] So, too, are strategic systems not safeguarded by such technical controls as the "premissive action links" (PALs) on strategic land-based missile systems (U.S. and reportedly Soviet), but not on naval submarine-launched ballistic missile (SLBM) or sea-launched cruise missile (SLCM) systems.[84]

Soviet analysts also stress the relationship of technical error and increased political tension. Colonel Oleg Bel'kov has noted that "at the present time there are weapons systems such that they unavoidably reduce the possibilities for taking political decisions in crises, and increase the risk of an unauthorized clash. . . . On the other hand, the danger that technical error can lead to a world conflict is directly proportional to the degree of tension in international relations."[85] Not all Soviet analysts are content to regard the danger of accidental war as politically neutral. A few argue that "nuclear-missile war and its accidental initiation owing to a technical malfunction is not deprived of political content, because even in that 'accident' the policy of preparation for war is guilty. Even more, the retaliatory measures in such an unintended war will not be accidental; the question of their use will be decided by the political leadership."[86] This is not, however, the view of most military or political analysts, many of whom challenge that assumption of political decision.

One discussion in the restricted circulation *Military Thought* even posed the possibility of a deliberate, provocative use of nuclear weapons by right-wing extremists in the military without authorization—apparently a reference to possible "neo-Nazi" elements in the German military, notwithstanding U.S. custody of nuclear weapons:

> One cannot exclude from calculations even the danger of unauthorized use of nuclear weapons or an accidental detonation of a nuclear munition. Technical malfunction, a mistake in highly complex automated control systems, an accident in transporting can lead to the irreparable. A nuclear incident could also be caused by a provocation

82. Kokoshin and Larionov, *Predotvrashcheniye voiny*, p. 162.
83. Ibid., p. 148.
84. Ibid., p. 157.
85. Bel'kov, *Mezhdunarodnaya zhizn'*, no. 1 (January 1988), p. 111.
86. N. Grachev, "On Nuclear-Missile War and Its Consequences," ibid., p. 103.

124 *Gorbachev's New Thinking*

of right extremist, neo-Nazi groups. Under conditions of unbridled anti-Soviet campaigns in the capitalist world profascist elements, of which there are not a few in bourgeois armies, including even in command positions, can attempt to provoke a global military clash between the Soviet Union and the United States.[87]

Not many Soviet commentators would go that far, but the possibility of an extreme political fringe element provoking a conflict is probably among the worst-case threats seen by the Soviet military. Less extreme cases of political miscalculation are, appropriately, given greater attention.

As for Soviet control over its own nuclear weapons, Marshal Yazov has emphasized the "priority requirement in Soviet military programming, realized in practice in the training of staffs and the troops, and in the organization of strictest control designed to not permit unauthorized use of a nuclear weapon—from tactical to strategic, including at heightened readiness of the troops for repelling aggression."[88] Neither Marshal Yazov nor anyone else has acknowledged any specific past Soviet lapses or concerns over possible unauthorized use of nuclear weapons, but the Soviet Union has provided special security arrangements and to the extent operationally possible has kept nuclear weapons in concentrated storage depots.[89] So-

87. Maj. N. N. Yefimov, "An Urgent Problem of the Present Day (The Socio-Political Aspect of Nuclear Disarmament)," *Voyennaya mysl'*, no. 3 (March 1988), p. 60.

88. Yazov, *Na strazhe sotsializma i mira*, p. 32. The context of his remark was the Soviet pledge not to be first to resort to use of nuclear weapons, and a similar reference had been made by a predecessor at the time the pledge was first made; see Marshal D. F. Ustinov, "To Avert the Threat of Nuclear War," *Pravda*, July 12, 1982, p. 4. Ustinov had said the pledge required "still more strict control" than had existed, but he did not refer to it as a "priority requirement," nor had he referred to the particular need "at heightened readiness." See also Kokoshin and Larionov, *Predotvrashcheniye voiny*, p. 143.

89. The case of greatest potential risk was the short-lived Soviet deployment of medium-range missiles to Cuba in 1962. Only in the last few years has it been learned that some of the nuclear nosecones for these missiles had reached Cuba before the U.S. blockade interdicted further shipment, but under strict orders from Moscow, none of the nosecones were mated to missiles or the missiles erected in firing position, and there was no predelegation to fire them even if attacked. On the other hand, the U.S. U-2 reconnaissance airplane shot down at the peak of the crisis was downed by a Soviet antiaircraft missile fired by authority of local Soviet commanders, not even the overall Soviet military commander in Cuba, and *contrary* to the intent of the instructions to fire only if attacked. The Soviet defense minister, Marshal Rodion Malinovsky, quickly ordered no further antiaircraft firings and reprimanded (but only very mildly) the Soviet military command in Cuba. See Raymond L. Garthoff, *Reflections on the Cuban Missile Crisis*, rev. ed. (Brookings, 1989), pp. 82–85.

viet strategic analysts have often referred to the greater reliability of communications and control as an advantage of land-based strategic nuclear missiles in comparison with sea-based weapons.

Many Soviet analysts stress the increased risks from the trend to automation of information, decision, command, and control processes. This risk is especially great at high alert levels of combat readiness, as in a crisis. In Major General Valentin Larionov's words:

> In general today placing the armed forces at a high alert level of combat readiness presupposes automation of systems for issuance, transmission and receipt of commands for firing, in which the participation of men is extremely limited. For deliberation, consideration and decision the human brain has literally only minutes. And this all greatly increases the risk of accidental outbreak of war. . . . What are the causes that could produce the accidental, unauthorized outbreak of nuclear war? Technical malfunctions or failures of components of weapons systems; errors in early warning systems; deviations from norms of human behavior (alcoholism, drug use, psychic disturbances) in people concerned with military equipment. It is scarcely necessary to prove that the probability of all these deviations significantly increases under conditions of combat readiness alert.[90]

Academician Velikhov of the Academy of Sciences has predicted that a "nuclear catastrophe . . . will inevitably occur, sooner or later, if the level of nuclear confrontation will long remain at such a high level as today." Among the causes he identifies are technical error, false warning alerts, computer malfunction in command and control of nuclear forces, nuclear proliferation, and "a high probability of psychological derangements in facing the necessity of taking responsible decisions in crisis situations."[91]

The question of unauthorized initiation of the use of nuclear weapons, while not raised explicitly in Shevardnadze's or Gorbachev's public statements, has been raised by Soviet military and political analysts, including several references in the passages cited above from Generals Shabanov, Larionov, and Kirshin. Their principal concern is the impingement of new technology on many points of the process of command decision, including political control. As General Kirshin explains:

90. Maj. Gen. Valentin Larionov, "Combat Readiness and Security: Will People Stop Playing at War?" *Novoye vremya*, no. 37 (September 8, 1989), pp. 13–14.
91. Velikhov, *Kommunist*, no. 1 (January 1988), pp. 51–52.

Military strategy has always influenced policy. But in the nuclear age under the impact of military-technical factors this influence has so increased that the relative independence of military strategy has grown by an order of magnitude, and the sphere of political decision can narrow, especially in relation to the unleashing of war. Under contemporary conditions military strategy, always occupying a subordinate position [to policy], may to a great extent slip out from under political control. It seems strange but in the nuclear age war can begin even without the intervention of the political leadership. . . . The independence of strategy can manifest itself in such a way that the accidental initiation of nuclear war is not excluded.[92]

The danger of short-circuiting real political control has been a major concern of the political leadership, even if rarely articulated. Gorbachev did refer to this problem in his report to the Twenty-seventh Party Congress in 1986, in which he advanced the need for moving from unilateral to mutual security. "The appearance of new weapon systems of mass destruction," he noted, "ineluctably reduces the time and narrows the possibilities for taking political decisions on questions of war and peace in case of crises."[93]

One of several reasons for the strong Soviet objection to the U.S. Strategic Defense Initiative (SDI) has been evident concern over further acceleration of the shift of decision on measures unleashing nuclear war from human to computer control.[94]

Clearly, reinforcing deterrence fails to meet this range of concerns. The broader objective of preventing war, in addition to relying on strategic deterrence, requires not merely stable mutual deterrence, but broader strategic stability. Gorbachev had, perhaps for the first time by a Soviet leader, expressly referred to the objective of strategic stability in October 1985.[95]

Soviet military doctrine now also includes increasing attention to measures for preserving strategic stability as a means of preventing war. The very term "strategic stability" (*strategicheskaya stabil'nost'*) made its first appearance in authoritative military guidance in the revised edition of the *Military Encyclopedic Dictionary* in 1986.[96]

92. Kirshin, *MEiMO*, no. 11 (November 1988), pp. 41–42.
93. Gorbachev, *Politcheskii doklad*, p. 82.
94. For one example of many, see Kirshin, *MEiMO*, no. 11 (November 1988), pp. 41–42.
95. See M. S. Gorbachev, *Izbrannyye rechi i stat'i* (Selected Speeches and Articles) (Moscow: Politizdat, 1987), vol. 2, p. 451.
96. "Strategic Stability," *VES*, 1986, p. 703. Such an entry had not been included

While of course the general concept of strategic stability had long been a Soviet objective, and was implied in the acceptance of parity as a goal of force programming in the 1970s, as well as in the strategic arms limitation agreements, it had not been focused on as a specific objective in military doctrine.

The General Staff's *Military Thought,* in one of the first key unsigned editorial guidances on the new thinking, also in 1986 drew particular attention in a criticism of the SDI program to what it would mean for strategic stability: "The 'Star Wars' program is dangerous because its implementation would lead to the disappearance of the very foundation for strategic stability."[97]

Several penetrating analyses of strategic stability also began to be advanced by leading civilian political-military and strategic analysts in 1986–87.[98]

The "new thinking" on security under the Gorbachev leadership, embracing the concept of a shared interest in mutual security, gives a potentially still wider meaning to the concept of strategic stability. So, too, does the new operational attention to the prevention of war as an objective of military doctrine and strategy. Unilateral military policy decisions and negotiated arms agreements, as well as the search for greater use of political means, all provide new opportunities.

New Thinking on Disarmament

The new thinking extends beyond theory and doctrine into concrete actions, exemplified by the Soviet agreement to eliminate all nuclear missile delivery means of 300–3,500 miles (500–5,000 kilometers), and efforts to reduce maximally *all* nuclear weapons, to preclude any weapons in space, to end all nuclear testing, to ban all

in the 1983 edition or in the earlier *Sovetskaya voyennaya entsiklopediya,* vols. 1–8 (Moscow: Voyenizdat, 1976–80).

97. "A Realistic, Multifaceted Weighing of the Program of Communist Creation and Strengthening Peace," *Voyennaya mysl',* no. 3 (March 1986), p. 12.

98. The seminal discussions were V. V. Zhurkin, "On Strategic Stability," *SShA: ekonomika, politika, ideologiya* (USA: Economics, Politics, Ideology), no. 1 (January 1986), pp. 12–25; and A. G. Arbatov, A. A. Vasil'ev, and A. A. Kokoshin, "Nuclear Weapons and Strategic Stability," *SShA,* no. 9 (September 1987), pp. 3–13, and no. 10 (October 1987), pp. 17–24. For a useful, more recent contribution, see S. Kortunov, "Stability in a Nuclear World," *Mezhdunarodnaya zhizn',* no. 2 (February 1990), pp. 3–13.

chemical weapons, to reduce drastically and on a greater scale than the West conventional arms and forces in Europe, and to reach other arms limitation and disarmament agreements.

There was, as noted in the previous chapter, also a history of arms control and arms limitation agreements in the period from 1968 to 1985 directed, among other things, to the prevention of nuclear war.

The more active, imaginative, and forceful push for nuclear arms reductions since 1986 (deep cuts, a comprehensive test ban, elimination of intermediate- and shorter-range missiles) has not been a source of conflict so long as the potential adversary would be taking reciprocal steps. Unilateral tactics (such as the nuclear testing moratorium in 1985–86) have caused some unease. But basically there is a consensus on policy as well as on doctrine. A major reason for the strong Soviet opposition to the American SDI is that it challenges the stability of the defense-offense relationship that the Soviets believed had been resolved in the Antiballistic Missile (ABM) Treaty in 1972. This gives rise to concern over sharp reductions in strategic arms without firmer American reaffirmation of commitment to the ABM Treaty. But there is no doctrinal or basic policy dispute over the desirability of strategic arms reductions, or indeed maximum reciprocal reduction of all nuclear weapons.

Gorbachev's speech of January 15, 1986, was earlier noted as a step in both propaganda and serious efforts to stimulate negotiations and actual reductions of nuclear weapons.[99] There was considerable skepticism in the West over whether the Soviet leader was serious in proposing elimination of nuclear weapons by the end of the century—although little disposition to test his seriousness, either. Since

99. The significance and continuing relevance of this important policy statement, as well as proposal, have not been sufficiently recognized in the West. The important June 1986 editorial in *Military Thought* described it as "a combination of the philosophy of forming a secure world in the nuclear-space age with a platform for concrete actions." *Voyennaya mysl'*, no. 6 (June 1986), p. 5. Deputy Defense Minister Shabanov referred to it in the same General Staff journal as indicating "the central direction of foreign policy in the coming years." Gen. Army V. M. Shabanov, "The Military-Technical Policy of the CPSU in Conditions of Accelerating the Social-Economic Development of the Country," *Voyennaya mysl'*, no. 11 (November 1987), p. 17. Similarly, in the seminar on military doctrines held in Vienna in early 1990, Colonel General Nikolai Chervov referred to the "program" of nuclear disarmament set forth in the January 1986 speech in effect as an alternative to "nuclear deterrence." See *Zayavleniye predstavitel'ya SSSR 25.01.90 g.: O kontseptsii "minimal'nogo yadernogo sderzhivaniya"* (Statement by the Representative of the USSR [Col. Gen. N. F. Chervov]: On the Concept of a "Minimum Nuclear Deterrent"), Vienna, January 25, 1990, official Soviet transcript, pp. 1–2.

Reykjavik, and the complete elimination of medium-range nuclear missiles, there has been far less disposition to believe that it was only a propaganda ploy.

The tragic accident at the nuclear power station at Chernobyl in May 1986 among other things brought home the catastrophic consequences of a nuclear war. Gorbachev and other Soviet spokesmen emphasized that Chernobyl was "a grim warning that the nuclear era necessitates new political thinking and a new policy."[100] While this argument was used to support the January 1986 proposals and other Soviet policy positions, it is clear from later Soviet discourse that the impact on Soviet politico-military thinking was substantial.

Parallel with these developments, General Kozlov, former first deputy chief of the General Staff, wrote in *Military Thought*, not for a public audience, that while both parity and mutual deterrence were necessary for the present, they were not the Soviet preferred state of affairs. The Soviet Union, he stated, "considers military-strategic parity only as a definite frontier beyond which it is necessary to move to achieve a reduction, and ultimately even a complete elimination, of the threat of nuclear war." "Our country," he observed, "is doing everything possible to get out of the situation of 'mutual assured destruction.' The aim of the policy of the USSR is to exclude nuclear weapons from the arsenals of states and in the final account their complete elimination."[101]

Are the Soviet leaders really ready to see the elimination of nuclear weapons? Many Western observers have been skeptical of Soviet readiness to agree to deep reductions or, above all, elimination of nuclear weapons because the claim of the Soviet Union to superpower status rests so much on its military, and especially strategic nuclear, power. Yet there are clear signs that the Soviet leaders have considered the question and decided that preventing war is the cardinal objective. Moreover, Gorbachev and his colleagues express confidence in the ability of the Soviet socialist system to prove itself. Gorbachev has flatly declared that they have faced up to the implications and "the Soviet Union is willing and ready to renounce its status as a nuclear power."[102] Defense Minister Yazov has similarly

100. "M. S. Gorbachev's Address on Soviet Television," *Pravda*, May 15, 1986, p. 1.

101. Kozlov, *Voyennaya mysl'*, no. 12 (December 1986), p. 12.

102. "For a Nuclear-Free World, For Humanism in International Relations, Speech by M. S. Gorbachev," *Pravda*, February 17, 1987, p. 2.

130   *Gorbachev's New Thinking*

drawn attention in the very same words to the readiness of the Soviet Union, along with the other nuclear powers, "to renounce its status as a nuclear power."[103]

Some Soviet analysts have been blunt about *past* Soviet interest in their nuclear status. Dr. Igor Malashenko, writing in early 1989, said, "Unfortunately, during the time of stagnation [the pre-Gorbachev years] for us [in the Soviet Union] too nuclear might became almost the main sign of our status as a 'superpower'—a term that we officially repudiated, although clearly it tickled our vanity." Now, Malashenko added, "we can more soberly see our own participation in the arms race, and approach [arms] negotiations more constructively, recognizing that we will preserve our status as a genuine great power only if we move the socio-economic development of the country off dead center."[104]

In practice, the Soviet Union can reduce reliance on its nuclear status even greatly short of eliminating nuclear weapons. Many Soviet military men and political analysts are doubtful that nuclear weapons will be eliminated.[105] Even in the unlikely case that the United States developed a serious interest, there would be the extremely demanding political and technical tasks in obtaining agreement of all the existing nuclear powers, and undeclared and potential nuclear powers, to accept severely intensive verification monitoring. The prospect of agreement appears beyond the political horizon.

There are, however, a range of more realistic possibilities short of the complete elimination of nuclear weapons. The total number of nuclear weapons has begun a modest decline, the U.S. stockpile having been reduced from a peak of about 32,500 in 1967 to about 23,000 in 1989, while the Soviet stockpile probably peaked at about 33,000 in 1988 and declined to 30,000 in 1990. The more familiar

103. D. Yazov, "The New Model of Security and the Armed Forces," *Kommunist*, no. 18 (December 1989), p. 66.

104. Igor Malashenko, "Hard Parting with the Bomb. . . . Why Does the Conception of Nuclear Deterrence Still Have Adherents?" *Novoye vremya*, no. 13 (March 24, 1989), p. 17. Malashenko was then at the Institute of USA and Canada; soon thereafter he joined the staff of the International Department of the Central Committee.

105. To cite but one rare published example, Lieutenant General Igor Sergeyev, a deputy commander of the Strategic Missile Forces, replied to an interviewer's query about a nuclear free world: "A nuclear-free world? It's hard for me to imagine. Lowering the nuclear threshhold [level]? That's understandable." See "We Have Grown Unaccustomed to Disarming . . . ," an interview with Lt. Gen. Igor Sergeyev by Yury Teplyakov, *Moskovskiye novosti*, no. 8 (February 25, 1990), p. 7.

figure for warheads and bombs in the strategic forces is in 1990 a little over 12,000 in the United States to about 11,000 in the Soviet Union, already declining some in the United States and leveling off in the Soviet Union.[106] There is a balance, but there is a lot of room for reductions.

The strategic arms reduction talks (START) are at this writing working to complete a U.S.-Soviet agreement aimed at nominally 50 percent reductions, to 6,000 warheads. Owing to counting rules and some excluded systems, in practice this would amount to cuts of about 25 percent (a little more for the Soviet Union, and a little less for the United States), bringing the actual levels down to about 8,000–10,000 on each side. This is still about where they were when START began in 1981. Nonetheless, it would revive the process of reciprocal commitments and begin coordinated reductions. While there have been general statements of intent to seek further reductions, there are no agreed guidelines on how far further reductions might be made or on what timetable or conditions (for example, at some point probably all nuclear powers would have to participate).

In this context, it should be noted that the loopholes in "counting rules" and excluded systems that loosened the constraints in the START I treaty and blunted its scope of reduction were *all* introduced by the United States. The Soviet Union was prepared for deeper cuts.

Soviet policy on further nuclear reductions is clearer than that of the United States. Under the long-standing Soviet policy of minimizing the numbers and possible circumstances of use of nuclear weapons, the new military doctrinal guideline of "reasonable sufficiency" has been applied to strategic nuclear forces. The operative guideline is (1) parity, and (2) at the lowest levels on which agreement can be reached, preferably far below remaining levels after START I.

Soviet interest in strategic arms reductions is not only directed to lessening the role of nuclear weapons and reducing the burden of

106. See the useful and careful compilations in the *Bulletin of the Atomic Scientists*, in particular: "Estimated Soviet Nuclear Stockpile (July 1990)," vol. 46 (July–August 1990), p.49; "U.S. Strategic Nuclear Forces, End of 1989," vol. 46 (January–February 1990), p. 49; "Soviet Strategic Nuclear Forces, End of 1989," vol. 46 (March 1990), p. 49; "Estimated Soviet Nuclear Stockpile, July 1989," vol. 45 (July–August 1989), p. 56; "U.S. Nuclear Weapons Stockpile (June 1989)," vol. 45 (June 1989), p. 49; "Estimated Soviet Nuclear Stockpile, July 1988," vol. 44 (July–August 1988), p. 56; and for earlier years, "U.S. and Soviet Strategic Nuclear Forces, 1972–1987," vol. 44 (May 1988), p. 56.

the arms race. Strategic arms limitations and reductions, the Soviets recognize, should be designed to enhance strategic stability. In particular, strategic nuclear reductions should contribute to removing any incentives to preemptive or initial use of nuclear weapons, and any conditions that might lead to unauthorized or accidental use of nuclear weapons.[107]

The situation for other nuclear weapons—constituting most of the respective stockpiles—is less clear.

Negotiations on short-range or tactical nuclear weapons in Europe are on the future agenda, but with the definition of categories and conditions not yet agreed or even addressed. Soviet attempts to open talks on naval nuclear weapons, as with all aspects of naval forces, have so far been rebuffed by the United States, despite a substantial unilateral reduction of tactical nuclear weapons on U.S. naval forces.

Concepts of strategic nuclear deterrence are sufficiently congruent to permit strategic nuclear force negotiations and reductions, at least on the scale now contemplated and probably beyond. The divergent Soviet and Western views on extended deterrence, and the role of tactical nuclear weapons in deterrence, make it more difficult to establish a basis for negotiation: the Soviet Union would prefer to eliminate all tactical nuclear weapons; the United States is not prepared to do so.

Before turning to a new development in Soviet thinking on nuclear weapons that may make finding a basis for further negotiations easier, I wish to note another important aspect of the change under way in Soviet military doctrine. Soviet analysts have defined "reasonable sufficiency" for conventional theater ground, air, and sea forces in a slightly different way than they have for strategic and nuclear systems. The core of the concept is reducing to lower levels, sufficient only for defense. The concept thus includes not only reduction but also restructuring to decrease offensive and to increase defensive capabilities. While this is the direction for military programming, and can in part be effected by unilateral measures, in order to maintain balance with putative adversaries, its full implementation requires at the least reciprocal, and in practice probably negotiated, cuts. Moreover, the reductions should be directed in

107. These points have been made by a number of leading Soviet political-military and strategic analysts; for example, A. A. Kokoshin, "The Reduction of Nuclear Arms and Strategic Stability," *SShA*, no. 2 (February 1988), pp. 4–5.

particular toward sharply cutting back on offensive capabilities while permitting or enhancing defensive force structures.

The substantial unilateral Soviet reductions announced by Gorbachev on December 7, 1988 (and others announced by all the other Warsaw Pact countries) began this process and primed the pump for the Conventional Forces in Europe (CFE) negotiations that began in January 1989. Gorbachev further agreed to accept in CFE significantly greater Soviet reductions in ground force weaponry, such as tanks and artillery, to reach equal levels for both sides below the existing NATO level. These negotiations are, at this writing, moving toward an agreement. He has accepted greatly lower equal troop levels with the United States in central Europe, and lower Soviet levels for Europe as a whole.

Intensified efforts have been made since 1986 to harness both arms control and military doctrine into mutually reinforcing support for Soviet national security policies. This means more than merely coordinating the two—which in the past in the Soviet Union, as in the United States to this day, means above all ensuring that arms control positions do not interfere unduly with one's own military programs.

The enlargement of the scope of Soviet military doctrine, and above all the establishment of the prevention of war as a principal objective of military doctrine, are far more important in this respect than has been recognized in the West. It means, for one thing, carrying further existing involvements of the military in arms control as well as of civilian security analysts and policymakers in military doctrine.[108] The first extensive Soviet military involvement in arms control came in the SALT experience from 1969–79, which has been examined in detail elsewhere.[109] It has continued, and in the 1980s the Treaty and Legal Affairs Directorate of the General Staff, headed by Colonel General Nikolai Chervov, grew both in size and importance as it provided military representation on the several active negotiations and in Moscow in staffing for decisionmaking on arms control policy. In the 1980s General Chervov also contributed five

108. Soviet analysts explicitly note that the increased attention to prevention of war in Soviet military doctrine presupposes a more active role for the military in arms control, disarmament, and confidence-building negotiations and implementation of agreements. See Kokoshin and Larionov, *Predotvrashcheniye voiny*, p. 35.

109. See Raymond L. Garthoff, "The Soviet Military and SALT," in Jiri Valenta and William C. Potter, eds., *Soviet Decisionmaking for National Security* (London: George Allen and Unwin, 1984), pp. 136–61.

articles on arms control policy to the General Staff's theoretical journal *Military Thought.*[110]

Under Gorbachev, a number of military men have been assigned to other parts of the government and Party to bring expertise to consideration there of arms control and security issues. Lieutenant General Viktor Starodubov heads a military-political section in the International Department of the Central Committee; Major General Gely Batenin is in the propaganda sector of the Central Committee; Lieutenant General Konstantin Mikhailov is the deputy head of the Arms Control Administration of the Ministry of Foreign Affairs; other senior officers are assigned to the office of Minister of Foreign Affairs Eduard Shevardnadze himself, and to the Foreign Ministry's Administration of Estimates and Planning. A large number of retired officers have also become staff members or consultants to the leading institutes of the Academy of Sciences involved in foreign affairs and increasingly active in arms control and security issues. At the same time, many civilian analysts are by the same token becoming more directly involved in military matters.

In 1988–89 the first signs appeared in Soviet military circles of the need to integrate arms control into Soviet military sciences, now that the scope of military doctrine has been broadened. A new political-military course, including arms control, has been introduced into the curriculum of the General Staff Academy. Lieutenant General Nikolai Popov, an academy professor, has now acknowledged: "It is very important at the present time for our military science to strengthen its study of the evolution of approaches to problems of disarmament and security, to expose and foresee principles, and to work out recommendations on questions of the limitation, reduction, prohibition and liquidation of arms and of reducing the level of military confrontation."[111]

110. See Col. Gen. N. F. Chervov, "Equality and Equal Security—The Foundation for the Limitation and Reduction of Nuclear Arms," *Voyennaya mysl'*, no. 5 (May 1983), pp. 17–30; Chervov, "Disarmament: Who Is Opposed?" ibid., no. 12 (December 1983), pp. 3–15; Chervov, "The United States: On a Course to Undermine Confidence and Détente," ibid., no. 7 (July 1984), pp. 20–34; Chervov, "Remove the Threat of War," ibid., no. 5 (May 1987), pp. 26–38; and Chervov, "A Treaty Enhancing General Security," ibid., no. 2 (February 1988), pp. 51–58.

111. Lt. Gen. N. G. Popov, "On a New Approach to the Organization of [Military] Scientific Work," *Voyennaya mysl'*, no. 5 (May 1988), p. 50. A theoretical discussion noting military and strategic elements of developing a political-military "mechanism"

Increasingly, arms control and security (in Soviet terms, disarmament and security) have come more into the mainstream of work of the Foreign Ministry, the military, and the institutes of the Academy of Sciences. And the prevention of war is the broadest and also most important focus of this new attention.

Minimum Deterrence and Beyond

One of the central elements of the new political thinking is a call to go beyond mutual deterrence to mutual security. Nuclear weapons should be eliminated, and other arms and armed forces held to a minimum reasonable sufficiency for defense and insufficient for mounting an offensive.

Gorbachev raised this aim soon after coming into office. In 1985 he said: "For the time being, fear of inescapable retribution is one of the obstacles to war and to the use of military forces. Nonetheless, everyone understands that one cannot build a stable peace on fear alone. But the entire question is where to search for an alternative to fear or, to use the military term, deterrence *[ustrasheniye]*?"[112]

Gorbachev gave the first part of the Soviet answer to the question in his very important address of January 15, 1986. "The Soviet Union," he said, "proposes to begin from 1986 to accomplish a program of liberating humankind from fear of a nuclear catastrophe."[113] Too much attention was directed in the West to speculations and debates over whether he really was serious in proposing to eliminate stage by stage all nuclear weapons by the year 2000, and too little to his objective and the underlying conception. He spelled out this conception more fully in his report to the Twenty-seventh Party Congress some weeks later (cited above) when he declared that "security cannot indefinitely be built on ... doctrines of 'deterrence,' " but "more and more becomes a political task," based on recognition that "security can only be mutual."[114]

(or program) to prevent war appeared in Kanevsky, *Voyennaya mysl'*, no. 4 (April 1989), pp. 48–56.

112. "For the Peaceful, Free and Prosperous Future of Europe and All Other Continents, Speech of M. S. Gorbachev," *Pravda*, October 4, 1985, p. 2.

113. "Statement of the General Secretary of the Central Committee of the CPSU M. S. Gorbachev," *Pravda*, January 16, 1986, p. 1.

114. Gorbachev, *Politicheskii doklad*, pp. 15, 81–82.

How do the Soviets envisage mutual security serving as a replacement for mutual deterrence? While various Soviet writers have stressed different aspects of this matter, the overall conception that has been emerging has four elements: strategic stability, respect for national interests of the parties, increased reliance on international institutions, and increased trust. These are mutually reinforcing elements, and movement in each can have a synergistic effect on the others.

The role of strategic arms limitations and reductions in helping to secure parity at even lower levels is obvious. As with other aspects of the changing Soviet military doctrine, some things can be done unilaterally but much can be done only reciprocally.

A military balance and strategic parity in a qualitative deterrent sense retain an important, and at least initially crucial, role. As Colonel Strebkov has put it, "a qualitative approach to parity requires the creation of an integral system of strategic stability on the basis of military equilibrium." As the military factor diminishes in importance, "as parity falls to lower and lower levels, on the basis of a balance of interests and reasonable sufficiency for defense, there will be a corresponding increase in stability in relations between the USSR and the United States and the Warsaw Pact and NATO as a whole. A policy of strength will give way to political and legal means of settling problems that arise."[115]

Stressing reliance on reasonable sufficiency in reducing mutual threat perceptions and thereby in lowering tension, Soviet analysts have begun to emphasize the need to accommodate the national interests of the sides. "Reasonable sufficiency," they note, "presupposes that in order to prevent aggression it is necessary not only to balance forces, and to evaluate the hypothetical capabilities of the other side, but above all to restrain its leadership from unleashing war, by taking into account its real intentions, and most important its interests."[116]

Military analysts as well write that "the search now for ways to prevent war should no longer be carried out in the framework of a strategy of deterrence [sderzhivaniye], but through ensuring strategic

115. Strebkov, *Krasnaya zvezda*, January 3, 1989, p. 3.
116. Vitaly Zhurkin, Sergei Karaganov, and Andrei Kortunov, "Reasonable Sufficiency, or How to Break the Vicious Circle," *Novoye vremya*, no. 40 (October 2, 1987), p. 13.

stability. Precisely here lies the basis for a transition from deterrence and a balance of forces to a balance of interests of the two sides."[117]

The combination of reciprocally reducing and restructuring military forces in accord with reasonable sufficiency, and political measures based on mutual accommodation of national interests, would thus become "the shaping of a new model for ensuring security not by means of mutual deterrence but by the creation of an atmosphere of mutual trust."[118]

Finally, as a concomitant to this diminished military capability and diminished perception of a threat, with increased mutual trust and accommodation, the very role of deterrence will be increasingly assumed by the changing world order and "the role of deterrence in the new world order will no doubt have to be played by political and legal instruments. An important role must be played by international law and international institutions."[119] The increased attention being given by the Soviet Union to international institutions, including in the resolution of regional conflicts, is relevant in this connection.

There is every indication that Gorbachev and the present leadership of the Soviet Union continue to believe that mutual security in a nuclear-free world is both feasible and highly desirable. This conclusion has not to date been shared by the Western governments, although there is agreement in principle and to some extent in practice to seek reductions of arms.

By mid-1989 Gorbachev had decided to seek agreement on an interim objective of "minimum deterrence," with drastic but not complete elimination of nuclear weapons. He advanced this idea in his speech to the European Parliament in Strasbourg. He began by again arguing the case for eliminating all nuclear weapons, asking: "Does the strategy of nuclear deterrence *[sderzhivaniye]* strengthen or undermine stability?" His answer remained that it undermines stability, but in acknowledging differing views on this matter between

117. Col. V. Dmitriyev and Col. V. Strebkov, "From a Strategy of Deterrence to Strategic Stability," *Krasnaya zvezda*, June 5, 1990, p. 3.

118. "Authoritative Opinion: Clear Skies over Europe," interview of Mikhail P. Shelepin by Yury Popov, *Komsomol'skaya pravda*, December 28, 1988, p. 3.

119. Deputy Foreign Minister Vladimir F. Petrovsky, in a roundtable discussion on the "International Program" on *Moscow Television*, March 11, 1989. Petrovsky's career and current responsibilities lead him to stress international institutions, but he was a leading contributor to the new thinking even before the Gorbachev administration and has been promoted under it.

the Warsaw Pact and NATO he said: "But we are dramatizing the divergences. We ourselves are seeking, and we invite our [Western] partners to seek, a way out." He went on to suggest that both sides could "without abandoning their own positions" agree on nuclear reductions, "with the USSR remaining true to its nuclear-free ideals, and the West to its conception of 'minimum deterrence' *[minimal'noye sderzhivaniye]*." And he proposed that experts from the two sides "conduct an in-depth discussion" of such questions as the limit "beyond which a capability for nuclear retribution is converted into a capability for attack."[120]

Although the West does not subscribe to the idea of a minimal deterrent, Gorbachev opened the door for negotiation on how much nuclear weaponry is enough for a deterrent, rather than perpetuating an impasse over the very concept of deterrence. While Gorbachev has not abandoned the goal of completely eliminating nuclear weapons, he is taking into account both American and NATO objections and the reality of numerous difficulties in a world of several nuclear powers in moving by stages toward that ultimate objective.

Gorbachev's invitation to discuss reducing forces to a minimum deterrent has not been pressed as an immediate issue, but it has been reaffirmed by some of his senior foreign policy colleagues. Deputy Foreign Minister Vladimir Petrovsky, a month later, related the idea to the ultimate objective of replacing nuclear deterrence with a mutual security regime. He acknowledged that eliminating nuclear weapons would only occur by stages, and that "of course stability is necessary to a reliable assurance at all stages in the lessening of confrontation." And he reiterated Gorbachev's proposal that the two sides could, without giving up their divergent views on deterrence, "examine quietly what lies behind the concept of minimum deterrence."[121]

Foreign Minister Shevardnadze, in his address to the UN General

120. See "The All-European Process Goes Forward, Speech of M. S. Gorbachev," *Pravda*, July 7, 1989, p. 2.
121. Vladimir Petrovsky, "Renewal and Stability in an Interdependent World," *Za rubezhom* (Abroad), no. 32 (August 4–10, 1989), p. 1. Petrovsky had been one of the first to raise the idea of minimum deterrence in the Soviet new thinking. He and Andrei Kokoshin had introduced it in a chapter on "International Security in the Nuclear-Space Age" in a book edited by soon-to-be Politburo member Aleksandr Yakovlev written in 1986 and published in 1987. See A. N. Yakovlev, ed., *Kapitalizm na iskhode stoletiya* (Capitalism at the Close of the Century) (Moscow: Politizdat, 1987), p. 343.

Assembly on September 26, 1989, also acknowledged that since "advocates of nuclear deterrence do not believe [complete nuclear disarmament] will be possible in the foreseeable future," the Soviet Union proposed as a modest step forward "concepts of so-called minimum nuclear deterrence," again noting that "we must define what we mean by minimum nuclear deterrence and what capabilities are sufficient," but without proposing any specific levels.[122]

As Shevardnadze's formulation makes clear, the new Soviet advocacy of an interim minimum deterrent stems in part from Soviet adoption of a concept of sufficiency. As noted earlier the concept of reasonable sufficiency (later usually termed "defense sufficiency") as elaborated in 1987 calls for eliminating nuclear and other weapons of mass destruction and reducing conventional arms to low levels sufficient for defense but insufficient for an offensive attack. But in the interim, nuclear weapons are to be reduced on a basis of parity to the lowest levels possible. Thus the concept of sufficiency opens the way for a strategic balance at levels reduced to a minimum, that is, to minimum deterrent levels. It does not, and this may be a virtue, prescribe or still less define "minimum deterrence."

The key analyses of possible strategic arms reductions going beyond the START agreement under negotiation since 1985 have been carried out by several institutes and committees under the Academy of Sciences. A working group of the Committee of Soviet Scientists in Defense of Peace and against the Nuclear Threat, cochaired by Academician Roald Sagdeyev and Dr. Andrei Kokoshin, began in 1985 a study that produced in April 1987 an influential report on "Strategic Stability under Conditions of Radical Reductions of Nuclear Arms."[123] Based on extensive strategic modeling analyses, this preliminary report concluded that strategic stability could be retained, and indeed enhanced, by reducing strategic nuclear delivery vehicles of the United States and the Soviet Union by as much as

122. "The Fate of the World Is Inseparable from the Fate of Our Perestroika: Address of the Head of the Soviet Delegation E. A. Shevardnadze to the 44th Session of the UN General Assembly," *Pravda*, September 27, 1989, p. 4.

123. Committee of Soviet Scientists in Defense of Peace and against the Nuclear Threat, *Strategicheskaya stabil'nost' v usloviyakh radikal'nykh sokrashchenii yadernykh vooruzhennii: kratkii otchet ob issledovanii (adaptirovannyi variant)* (Strategic Stability under Conditions of Radical Reductions of Nuclear Arms: A Brief Report on Research [Abridged Version]) (Moscow, April 8, 1987), 48 pp., 500 copies. For a useful discussion based on this analysis, see Kokoshin and Larionov, *Predotvrashcheniye voiny*, pp. 96–106.

95 percent, to about 500–600 single-warhead mobile ICBMs.[124] This does not mean that the Soviet government was considering, or even that the committee of scientists was proposing, that deep a reduction. But the theoretical analysis, also carried out at reduction levels of 50 and 75 percent, indicated that deep reductions were in principle feasible as reciprocal reductions proceeded, if political, verification, third-country, and other factors could be dealt with satisfactorily. Even such a greatly reduced strategic nuclear force on both sides was found to provide both with assured retaliatory capability, thus serving as a minimum deterrent, on a basis of strategic stability, representing reasonable sufficiency.

The assured retaliatory capability was measured in terms of inflicting unacceptable damage on the attacker's population and industry, the classical "deterrence by punishment" rather than "by denial." Although not indicated in the report, the Soviet scientists actually took as a starting point former U.S. Secretary of Defense Robert McNamara's early 1960s guideline of some 400 megatons on target destroying about one-third of the population and three-quarters of industry, as a conservative standard of indisputably unacceptable damage.[125] In choosing mobile ICBMs, they disputed the argument sometimes advanced in the United States that submarine-launched ballistic missiles (SLBMs) are a more secure deterrent. The survivability of land-based ICBMs liable to attack by single-warhead missiles, and all the more if made mobile, was considered to be adequately assured. The stability of the balance would moreover be enhanced by more reliable two-way communications to ICBM forces, as contrasted to SLBM-launching submarines. "This would reduce the possibility of accidental, unpremeditated launches, and of accidental initiation of nuclear war as a result of technical malfunctions, or errors." And in contrast to heavy bombers, ICBMs do not have dual capability for local nonnuclear conflict, thus "not increasing the danger of a local conflict becoming global, and a nonnuclear one becoming nuclear."[126]

124. Ibid., pp. 29–31.

125. Some Soviet authors, in particular Aleksei Arbatov, have referred to the calculations of 400 MT "in the 1960s" and accepted it as more than sufficient. See Arbatov, *Oboronitel'naya dostatochnost'*, pp. 41, 46–47; and Arbatov, *Disarmament and Security, 1987 Yearbook* (Moscow: Novosti Press, USSR Academy of Sciences, Institute of the World Economy and International Relations, 1988), pp. 233–34.

126. Committee of Soviet Scientists, *Strategicheskaya stabil'nost'*, pp. 21–22, 28–29.

Although they did not use the term "minimum deterrent," the scientists presented an analytical case for the feasibility of sufficiency in strategic nuclear arms at greatly reduced levels, with reciprocal and verified reductions.

Some other Soviet analysts, particularly from the Ministry of Foreign Affairs (but writing unofficially), later challenged the choice of ICBMs over SLBMs and introduced the idea of "multipolar," third-country, nuclear threats (in particular from France and Britain).[127] Other variations on requirements for minimum deterrence have also been advanced.[128]

In the United States similar unofficial analyses at strategic think tanks have also been undertaken. Typically, such analyses are somewhat more conservative than the Soviet ones, projecting possible reductions beyond START I of another possible 50 percent cut in START II, for a nominal warhead level of perhaps 2,500–3,000, that is, a 75 percent cut from existing 1989–90 levels.[129] The Soviet analysis with a recommendation of 600 single-warhead missiles would amount to a 95 percent cut from existing pre-START levels of warheads, but the basic concept is the same: deep reductions by agreement, on the basis of parity, with particular attention to ensuring survivability of a force capable of delivering an unacceptable retaliatory strike against the other side if it attacked.

Although the term "reasonable sufficiency" was not used in the United States, and neither side was referring in these studies to a "minimum" deterrent, the two sides have shared conceptions of a stable, survivable strategic nuclear deterrent at greatly reduced levels. Such a force would still be capable of enormous devastation that would be unacceptable to any rational calculation of possible advantage from an attack and thus would be an effective deterrent. It was in this sense that Gorbachev proposed that the two sides move forward from a START agreement by much deeper reciprocal reductions to a "minimum deterrent" force.

127. See, in particular, I. Tyulin and A. Zagorsky, "Contours of a 'Near-Zero' Nuclear Balance," *Mezhdunarodnaya zhizn'*, no. 6 (June 1988), pp. 114–18; and S. Vybornov and V. Leont'yev, "Future Prospects for an Old Weapon," *Mezhdunarodnaya zhizn'*, no. 8 (August 1988), pp. 73–81.

128. For a useful discussion of the above and other Soviet sources on this subject, see Stephen Shenfield, *Minimum Nuclear Deterrence: The Debate among Soviet Civilian Analysts* (Providence, R.I.: Center for Foreign Policy Development, Brown University, 1989).

129. See Michael M. May, George F. Bing, and John D. Steinbruner, *Strategic*

It may also be worth recalling that in the early 1960s the Soviet Union had also proposed an equal minimum deterrent on each side, at that time called the "Gromyko plan" for a "nuclear umbrella." It was presented, then as now, as a compromise from the Soviet preferred position of complete nuclear disarmament, and not as the optimum final solution.[130] The most important difference, from the standpoint of both Soviet and American positions, is that in the 1960s the United States had a massive superiority over the Soviet Union and would have been giving up that advantage, while the Soviets would have retained or even built up their forces to the agreed minimum nuclear umbrella level. Today, from positions of rough equivalence, both would be reducing to lower equal levels.

The idea underlying Gorbachev's adoption of "minimum deterrence" apparently came into current policymaking consideration because of an unprecedented several-day conference in July 1988 sponsored by the Ministry of Foreign Affairs and including a wide range of participants from other official and academic institutions. In reporting on that conference, First Deputy Minister of Foreign Affairs Yuly Vorontsov noted that "proposals were advanced for various alternative strategies over the long term for nuclear disarmament, taking account of the fact of Western commitment to nuclear deterrence *[sderzhivaniye]*, in particular an option for reducing nuclear arms to a minimum level agreed upon with the United States."[131]

Arms Reductions (Brookings, 1988), for a conservative analysis of reductions to 3,000 warheads.

130. Foreign Minister Andrei Gromyko first advanced the nuclear umbrella proposal at the UN General Assembly on September 21, 1962; it was later extended (in 1963) to remain in force until the very end of the process of moving to general and complete disarmament, and presented as an alternative to U.S. proposals for a freeze on strategic nuclear delivery vehicles (in 1964). See *Documents on Disarmament, 1962* (Washington: U.S. Arms Control and Disarmament Agency, 1963), vol. 2, pp. 904–05; *Documents on Disarmament, 1963*, pp. 515–16; *Documents on Disarmament, 1964*, pp. 22–32.

Incidentally, one significantly different element of the 1960s minimum deterrent proposal was that it covered strategic offensive *and defensive* arms, as did Western proposals of that period.

131. First Deputy Minister of Foreign Affairs of the USSR Yu. M. Vorontsov, "The 19th All-Union CPSU Conference: Foreign Policy and Diplomacy," at a Scientific-Practical Conference at the USSR Ministry of Foreign Affairs, *Mezhdunarodnaya zhizn'*, no. 9 (September 1988) p. 42. The conference was held July 25–27, 1988, and the concluding presentations summing up its work were presented in this issue of the ministry's journal.

Some Soviet analysts have, while accepting the principle of strategic parity, argued for some unilateral reductions on the grounds that a band of levels approximating parity would permit such action and that it would stimulate agreement on reciprocal reductions.[132]

This position has, however, been objected to by the military. While it has to date not been officially endorsed or acted upon, some limited measures of this kind might be justified as consistent with maintaining parity. It seems likely that major changes in levels of strategic nuclear forces will come only through negotiated reciprocal reductions.

All these discussions have concerned strategic nuclear forces. The Soviet position since 1986 (and indeed for many years before the current period) has called for the complete elimination at an early stage of all tactical nuclear weapons in Europe. While this remains the official and preferred position, by 1989 Soviet analysts were also considering reductions on a less-than-total basis, to a "minimum nuclear deterrent in Europe."[133] The study offers preliminary findings calling for reducing on both sides (the United States, Britain, and France on the one side; the Soviet Union on the other) to 500–700 delivery vehicles (or warheads). (The question whether to limit

132. In particular, see A. G. Arbatov, "How Much Defense Is Enough?" *Mezhdunarodnaya zhizn'*, no. 3 (March 1989), pp. 33–47. Arbatov's proposals also called for radical cuts in air defense and for abandoning the Moscow ABM defense, as well as for curtailing strategic offensive forces. Military commentators, bridling at his challenge to their role and the general intrusion of civilian analysts into their sphere, raised a number of strong objections. See Maj. Gen. Yu. Lyubimov, "On Sufficiency of Defense and Insufficiency of Competence," *KVS*, no. 16 (August 1989), pp. 21–26; P. O. Cherkasov, Lt. Gen. (Ret.) F. I. Rybintsev, and Lt. Col. A. I. Yur'yev, "On the Article of A. Arbatov 'How Much Defense Is Enough?' " *Mezhdunarodnaya zhizn'*, no. 7 (July 1989), pp. 155–59; and Cols. A. P. Vasil'yev and V. K. Rudyuk, "Is Air Defense Sufficient?" *Voyennaya mysl'*, no. 9 (September 1989), pp. 59–68. Arbatov has replied to the latter article, marking the first "military-civilian" debate on defense issues to appear in the General Staff journal (since April 1989 no longer confidential); see A. G. Arbatov, "On the Question of Sufficiency of Air Defense," *Voyennaya mysl'*, no. 12 (December 1989), pp. 41–45.

133. While the results of this study have not yet been published, a progress report has been prepared, and it is the source of the comments cited in the discussion here. See A. A. Kokoshin and [Maj. Gen. (Ret.)] V. V. Larionov, *Ob urovnye i kharaktere vzaimnogo "minimal'nogo yadernogo sderzhivaniya" v Yevrope (Kratkoye izlozheniye rezul'tatov issledovaniya)* (On Levels and Character of Mutual "Minimum Nuclear Deterrence" in Europe [A Brief Exposition of Research Results]), prepared for the Committee of Soviet Scientists in Defense of Peace and against the Nuclear Threat, and the Institute of the USA and Canada, Academy of Sciences of the USSR (Moscow, November 1989), 6 pp. duplicated.

delivery means or warheads was said still to be under study.) These tactical (or in Soviet terms operational-tactical) nuclear forces should reflect the present choices of the two sides: on the Soviet side principally short-range missiles, on the Western side tactical air and naval air delivery systems. The study also recommends placing these tactical nuclear systems under commands separate from the general purpose forces, and with a ban or maximum constraint on modernization. This study may forecast Soviet positions in future negotiations on tactical nuclear arms reductions in Europe. In any case, it shows Soviet interest in and thinking on reciprocal minimum tactical nuclear deterrent forces in Europe, if a complete ban cannot be agreed upon.

At the CSCE multilateral seminar on military doctrine held in Vienna in early 1990, General Chervov explained that the Soviet concept of "minimum nuclear deterrence" was a response to NATO's lack of support, "at this stage," for the Soviet preference of eliminating tactical nuclear weapons from Europe, and said that under these circumstances "we agree to consider the possibility of an interim stage of reduction of tactical nuclear weapons to quantitative levels lower than those existing for either side," and he proposed talks "without delay."[134]

Glasnost' and the wider scope for initiative in discussion of strategic affairs has led to a debate on a more radically far-reaching idea: *unilateral* minimum deterrence. Gorbachev and other officials have not shown any readiness to adopt such an approach, although the elasticity of the concept of reasonable sufficiency could accommodate it. Indeed, it was from discussion of sufficiency that the accepted idea of reciprocal minimum deterrence, and its radical deviant unilateral minimum deterrence, have sprung.

Discussions of reasonable sufficiency by civilian strategic analysts in 1987 and 1988 laid the groundwork for a challenge to the endorsement of strategic parity so strongly expressed by the military. First, they cited approvingly statements by Defense Minister Yazov and other generals that "the essence of sufficiency is determined by the necessity of not permitting a nuclear attack without retribution" and that parity essentially involved deterrent capability rather than numbers. Moreover, in order to provide such retaliatory capability

134. *Zayavleniye predstavitelya SSSR 25.01.90 g.: O kontseptsii "minimal'nogo yadernogo sderzhivaniya,"* January 25, 1990, p. 3.

for deterrence, "it would be sufficient to use only several percent of the strategic arsenal of the country under attack," in several cases specifically suggesting 10 to 20 percent of the existing Soviet strategic forces.[135] Even though in at least one case in 1987 the authors specifically disavowed a small unilateral "minimum deterrent," the theoretical foundation was being laid.[136]

In December 1988 Dr. Malashenko, then at the Institute of USA and Canada but soon to transfer to the International Department of the Central Committee, went further. He drew approving attention to the example of China, "socialist" and a "great power," which, although it could have built more missiles, deliberately chose to restrict itself to creation of a "minimum potential for deterrence."[137] A few months later Malashenko explicitly endorsed the concept of "minimum nuclear deterrence" as "compatible with reasonable sufficiency for defense." He suggested radical reductions in strategic nuclear arms and said "a transition in practice to minimum deterrence could become an important stage in moving forward a nuclear-free world."[138] He did not, however, explicitly argue that this could be done unilaterally, although his approach implied it.

A bombshell exploded in the debate in June 1989. Radomir Bogdanov, formerly a deputy director of the Institute of USA and Canada and now first deputy chairman of the Soviet Peace Committee, and Andrei Kortunov of the USA Institute, boldly argued for unilateral reduction to a level of minimum deterrence.[139] The unilateral minimum deterrent was set at about the same level as that proposed for negotiated deep cuts: 500 single-warhead missiles, part mobile land-based ICBMs (SS–25s) and part sea-based SLBMs (on Delta IV submarines). Bogdanov and Kortunov sought to anticipate objections

135. The quotations cited are from V. V. Zhurkin, S. A. Karaganov, and A. V. Kortunov, "On Reasonable Sufficiency," *SShA*, no. 12 (December 1987), pp. 14–15; the 10 to 20 percent figure comes in a similar argument advanced by A. G. Arbatov, "On Parity and Reasonable Sufficiency," *Mezhdunarodnaya zhizn'*, no. 9 (September 1988), p. 89, and A. E. Bovin, "Other Variants," *SShA*, no. 12 (December 1988), p. 32. A few months later Aleksei Arbatov suggested 10 to 15 percent; Arbatov, *Mezhdunarodnaya zhizn'*, no. 3 (March 1989), p. 39.

136. Zhurkin and others, *SShA*, no. 12 (December 1987), p. 15.

137. Malashenko, *Mezhdunarodnaya zhizn'*, no. 12 (December 1988), pp. 45–46.

138. Malashenko, *Novoye vremya*, no. 13 (March 24, 1989), p. 17.

139. Radomir Bogdanov and Andrei Kortunov, "'Minimum Deterrence': A Utopia or a Real Prospect," *Moskovskiye novosti*, no. 23 (June 4, 1989), p. 6, expanded version in Bogdanov and Kortunov, "On the Balance of Forces," *Mezhdunarodnaya zhizn'*, no. 7 (July 1989), pp. 3–15.

in their exposition (for example, arguing that any deterrent effective against attack by the United States would also be effective against France or Britain). They bravely, if not recklessly, took really worst-case possibilities into account, arguing that even if 90 percent of the force were destroyed by a U.S. attack, and then 90 percent of the surviving warheads were destroyed by an effective ballistic missile defense, the remaining 1 percent—five warheads—would land on targets. And, they argued, the prospect of even five warheads landing, for example, in the Boston-Washington or San Francisco–San Diego urban corridors would be a sufficient deterrent to dissuade anyone from deliberate decision to attack.[140] In the larger version of their argument, they cite as historical evidence that the United States refrained from launching an attack in the early 1950s when the Soviet Union had a lesser capability than they propose. And they argue that by making warfare with strategic counterforce exchanges clearly impossible, the nuclear threshold is actually raised, and minimum deterrence would serve the strategy of preventing nuclear war.[141]

A strong counterblast was levied by Colonels Vladimir Dvorkin and Valery Torbin three weeks later. They attacked the Bogdanov-Kortunov article as "incompetent," but they also raised and addressed some of the issues. Above all they reaffirmed the need for parity. In addition, they argued that there was a need not only for deterrence of a direct first-strike attack, but also for deterrence of "political pressure and blackmail based on military-strategic superiority." They also argued that rather than encouraging arms reductions by the United States, such a deep unilateral Soviet reduction would only assist in making the SDI more feasible and would encourage third powers such as France and Britain, which already each have nearly 700 warheads.[142]

Other articles followed, mostly by civilians (including Malashenko) who supported Bogdanov and Kortunov.[143] An unexpected

140. Ibid.
141. Bogdanov and Kortunov, *Mezhdunarodnaya zhizn'*, no. 7 (July 1989), pp. 8, 12.
142. Col. Vladimir Dvorkin and Col. Valery Torbin, "On Real Sufficiency for Defense," *Moskovskiye novosti*, no. 26 (June 25, 1989), p. 6.
143. Igor Malashenko, "Parity Yesterday and Today," *Moskovskiye novosti*, no. 31 (July 30, 1989), p. 6; Andrei Nuikin, "On Warheads, Goodwill and Professionalism," ibid., p. 6; Nikita Moiseyev, "Both Calculations and Sound Thinking," ibid.,

entry into the debate was an article solicited from former U.S. Secretary of Defense McNamara. To the great satisfaction of the critics of unilateral Soviet reductions, McNamara expressed his support for negotiated reciprocal reductions gradually leading to a balanced minimum deterrent.[144] A bigger gun from the Soviet military, Lieutenant General Yevgeny Volkov, also carried the debate over to the armed forces newspaper, firmly supporting parity and attacking the idea of unilateral minimum deterrence.[145]

The debate over unilateral reductions to minimum deterrence has abated. Whether it is resumed or not, while the advocates have not prevailed they may have succeeded at least in making pursuit of reciprocal minimum deterrence seem a moderate course. Moreover, the absence of agreement on the precise nature of "parity" leaves leeway for possible unilateral actions more moderate than the drastic cuts proposed by Bogdanov and others. And, as noted earlier, debate on that line continues.

The Soviet Union under Gorbachev is clearly on the move, in all aspects of foreign as well as internal policy, and at their intersection in security policy. Accepting the fact of mutual deterrence based on strategic nuclear parity, and its positive role in contributing to the prevention of war, Gorbachev and his colleagues are nonetheless not satisfied with that status quo. They believe that greater security for the Soviet Union, and for the United States and the world, would be possible and should be pursued by moving on several planes. First, the two powers should seek to move from mutual hostility and suspicion to greater mutual trust and confidence. Second, they should move from a mutual balance of doomsday nuclear deterrence to much lower levels of parity and minimum deterrence. Third, ultimately they should move beyond such reduced, preferably minimum, levels of forces for mutual deterrence based on fear of mutual destruction to mutual security based on the absence of such fear in a nuclear-free world. But in the long meantime, the powers should

no. 28 (July 9, 1989), p. 7; and Yury Bandura, "The Doctrine of Deterrence: Pro and Con," ibid., no. 42 (October 15, 1989), p. 6.

144. Robert S. McNamara, "Minimum Deterrence—A Final Aim," *Moskovskiye novosti*, no. 37 (September 10, 1989), p. 6.

145. Lt. Gen. (Res.) Ye. Volkov, "Not Clarifying, but Beclouding ... On the Discussion on Reduction of Strategic Offensive Arms," *Krasnaya zvezda*, September 28, 1989, p. 3. See also Col. V. Strebkov, "The New Model of Security: The Military Aspect," *KVS*, no. 2 (January 1990), p. 25.

not only reduce levels of arms for deterrence, they should also seek to shift from primary reliance on mutual deterrence to a greater role for mutual assurance. As one Soviet analyst has felicitously put it, there is a need to "transform a situation of mutual deterrence into a situation of mutual restraint."[146]

146. G. K. Lednev, "Is There a Way Out of the Nuclear Blind Alley?" *SShA*, no. 7 (July 1989), p. 8.

The Russian language captures the difference particularly well: from mutual deterrence *[sderzhivaniye]*, meaning mutual constraint of each by the other, to mutual restraint *[sderzhannost']*, meaning reciprocal self-restraint, both words derived from the same root, to hold back *[sderzhivat']*.

Chapter Five

What If Deterrence Fails? Soviet Views on Waging and Ending a War

IN THE SOVIET CONCEPTION, as in that of the United States, war between the two powers could occur only by a failure of deterrence and of policies designed to prevent war. Deliberate choice of war is, in fact as well as declaration, excluded by the leaders of both countries. While ultimately this supreme question of intentions is not susceptible of proof, there is no reason to disbelieve the sanity of the leaders on either side or their awareness of the fatal folly of starting a war in the nuclear age. Whatever suspicions one has as to the motivation of an adversary for aggrandizement, without practical possibilities for avoiding nuclear retribution there is no aggressive impulse that could rationally justify an unprovoked attack. In my judgment, no Soviet or U.S. leadership would decide to launch a war even without the threat of nuclear retaliation, but while that proposition is arguable, the existence of large nuclear arsenals makes it moot. The prospect of nuclear war, and the existence of mutual deterrence, make the *choice* of war incredible and virtually unthinkable.

Yet the *risk* of war, the possibility of war, is not excluded: although improbable, war is not incredible or unthinkable. The most dangerous situation would be an intense crisis in which one or both sides would conclude that the other was about to launch a strike. In addition, military planners on both sides, while not predicting or expecting a deliberate initiation of war by the other side, nonetheless believe it prudent not to exclude even that possibility. So the possibility of enemy attack is a military planning reality, even if not a political-military reality.

American defense policy, as stated by Secretary of Defense Richard Cheney in his 1990 *Report to the President and the Congress*, has as its basic objective "to deter military attack against the United States, U.S. allies, and other U.S. interests; and to defeat such attack should deterrence fail."[1] The Soviet minister of defense, Marshal (then General of the Army) Dmitry Yazov, has similarly stated the Soviet aim is to deter attack or, if that fails, to defeat the attack: "to stop an aggressor, to frustrate his criminal designs, but if aggression nonetheless is unleashed, to give him a crushing rebuff."[2]

Apart from scenarios postulating a deliberate attack by the other side, Soviet and U.S. planners also recognize other ways in which general war could break out, in particular through escalation from limited wars. There is, however, a military planning bias toward the case of deliberate and surprise enemy attack, justified mainly on the grounds that such would be the worst case, and lesser contingencies could presumably be met if the worst case were covered.

There are elements in common, as well as distinguishing features, in Soviet and U.S. military planning and military policy provision to meet the possibility of war. There are also some distinctions between military planning and political-military policy consideration on the three key stages of putative hostilities: the initiation, conduct, and termination of conflict. In military planning, the central focus is on the middle element: waging war. The conditions of the outbreak of a war, including postulating an attacker's objectives, are sometimes "given" assumptions, sometimes "gamed" conditions, but in either case are mainly setting the stage for the real object of attention, successfully waging a war. Similarly, war termination is usually either the outcome of the conflict (A wins and B loses) or an arbitrary cutoff of the exercise. The name of the game has traditionally been simply how to fight and win.

This traditional approach has continued to govern in the age of deterrence. If deterrence fails, one wages war to victory. As a former Soviet minister of defense, Marshal Andrei Grechko, wrote in the mid-1970s, if despite efforts to avert war it occurred, Soviet military doctrine called for "decisive actions with the aim of the complete destruction of any aggressor who attempts to encroach upon the socialist Motherland."[3] As I shall show, this approach has changed in the Soviet Union in recent years. It has not, however, been com-

1. Secretary of Defense Dick Cheney, *Department of Defense Annual Report to the President and the Congress, January 1990* (Washington, 1990), p. 2.

2. Gen. Army D. T. Yazov, *Na strazhe sotsializma i mira* (On Guard over Socialism and Peace) (Moscow: Voyenizdat, 1987), p. 30.

3. Marshal A. A. Grechko, *Vooruzhennyye sily Sovetskogo gosudarstva* (The Armed Forces of the Soviet State) (Moscow: Voyenizdat, 1974), p. 318.

pletely displaced from either Soviet or U.S. military thinking and planning.

The outbreak of a war—conflict initiation—is not merely the opening curtain for waging war. Under a strategy of preventing war, or restoring peace, it is the critical initial element in defining the terms under which a war is fought and terminated.

Outbreak of a War

In the words "outbreak of a war" I have sought a neutral analytical term that would cover a range of ways in which war could arise, including but not limited to deliberate initiation. As discussed earlier, Soviet thinking has come to recognize and give increased attention to the ways in which war could be generated or precipitated without being the product of premeditated choice. At the same time, Soviet analysts and leaders firmly believe that politics basically governs— and should govern—military considerations, including military plans and above all decisions on war. This is partly Russian historical influence, partly Marxism, and partly applied Soviet experience.

The Leninist-Clausewitzian concept of the inherent interrelationship between policy and war causes Soviet military and political leaders to recognize a constant reciprocal interplay before, during, and at the end of a war. In particular, the Soviets recognize a basic interrelationship between reasons for the outbreak of a war, methods of waging war (including possible constraints on the conduct of the war), the nature of war aims, and the terms for conclusion of a war.

In Soviet analysis, foreign policy and diplomacy are coupled with military preparations and military operations in the entire gamut of conflictual relationships. Deterrence, conflict initiation or avoidance, conflict management, arms control, shows of strength, military mobilizations, alliances, and diplomatic consultations are all political-military activities or actions.[4]

4. For a wider discussion, see Raymond L. Garthoff, "Soviet Views on the Interrelation of Diplomacy and Military Strategy," *Political Science Quarterly*, vol. 94 (Fall 1979), pp. 391–405. For useful, if not recent, Soviet military discussions, see V. Dmitriyev, "Diplomacy and Military Strategy," *Voyennaya mysl'* (Military Thought), no. 7 (July 1971), pp. 40–50; and Col. Gen. M. Povaly, "Policy and Military Strategy," ibid., no. 7 (July 1970), pp. 9–20. These articles were part of a series in the confidential General Staff journal in the years 1970–73 developing the new Soviet flexible response doctrine of the post-1965 period. The most interesting recent discussion is

The circumstances and form of the outbreak of a war in many ways predetermines, or at least heavily conditions, options for fighting and ending it. A general nuclear strike, reciprocated, would reduce not only political options but arguably the existential basis for survival, and would certainly confound coherent command and control by leaderships for conflict management and termination. Any more limited war would pose greater possibilities for conflict management, but also constant tensions between limitations and escalatory pressures.

For the case of an enemy surprise all-out nuclear attack, neither the Soviet Union nor the United States has any real response strategy. As complete a retaliatory strike as possible would in theory and probably in fact be the reaction, but if the deterrent function of that retaliation had failed, its execution would not save the victim of the initial attack but only ensure destruction of civilized life in the Northern Hemisphere. War plans in Moscow and Washington, and whatever residual forces and command elements remained, would be essentially irrelevant. The war would terminate through mutual annihilation.

Another way in which general nuclear war could start, other than by deliberate choice, is what might be termed deliberate action in the absence of real choice: preemption. If one side believed the other was initiating nuclear hostilities, it could react by seeking to be faster on the draw, by going first in the last resort. As discussed earlier, the fundamental drawback is that information on an enemy's irrevocable decision to launch an imminent attack may be absent, or may be faulty. A preemptive "prompt retaliation" for a misidentified enemy attack in progress would then amount to starting a war despite the absence of real intention or desire for war by either side. The shift in Soviet military doctrine in the late 1960s from preemption to launch under attack (described in chapter 3) was intended to reduce this risk. It may more recently have been carried further to refrain from launch on warning or under attack and to rely on retaliation to an established attack. Such a shift, if it has been made, may be more in inclination than in firm directive. In any case, it would represent a further step toward reducing any possibility of error and initiation of war by inadvertence through premature and erroneous confirmation that a hostile attack was under way. It would also allow a more

Maj. Gen. Yu. Kirshin, "Policy and Military Strategy in the Nuclear Age," *Mirovaya ekonomika i mezhdunarodnyye otnosheniya* (World Economy and International Relations; hereafter *MEiMO*), no. 11 (November 1988), pp. 35–45.

discriminating response to a limited attack. The purpose would be to reduce still further the risk of initiation of a nuclear war and to maximize control over any ambiguous accidental or limited attack situation. In part, such a tendency toward constraint on prompt retaliation would reflect greater confidence in the survivability of a sufficient retaliatory force, as well as heightened attention to the need for control in uncertain situations.

Soviet leaders may not have made an unequivocal decision. Nonetheless, there are statements strongly suggesting they have rejected preemption. The summary account of a "practical-scientific conference of the General Staff" held in November 1989 and later published in the General Staff journal *Military Thought* cited General of the Army Mikhail Moiseyev, chief of the General Staff, as having emphasized that as a result of the new political thinking "substantial results have been achieved in realization of the requirements of contemporary military doctrine, at the foundation of the conception of which lies the political-military guidance on *employment of the armed forces only in response actions.*"[5] While this would not necessarily rule out preemption as a response, the whole thrust of the statement was that new guidance provides only for retaliatory response.[6] Moreover, at the Vienna seminar on military doctrines in January 1990, Lieutenant General G. A. Burutin reiterated and elaborated on this new directive, saying that "currently operational plans envision the conduct of hostilities in the initial period of a war in the form of response actions. That is, the preparation of the Soviet armed forces at the present time is oriented on the conduct of defensive battles and operations in the air space and in all land and sea theaters of military operations [TVDs] without exception." He further said that "any kind of preventive or preemptive strikes on targets in the territory of the probable enemy is not envisaged in operational plans."[7] Soviet strategic analysts also sometimes ad-

5. Cited by Col. A. I. Alistratov, "The Practical-Scientific Conference of the General Staff," *Voyennaya mysl'*, no. 2 (February 1990), p. 78; emphasis in original.

6. The word I have translated literally as "response" *[otvetnyi]* is in fact often translated in this context as "retaliatory."

7. *Tezisy vystupleniya chlena sovetskoi delegatsii general-leitenanta Burutina G. A. na seminare po voyennym doktrinam; Tema vystupleniya: Voyennaya deyatel'nost' i voyennaya podgotovka Vooruzhennykh Sil SSSR* (Theses of the Statement by Member of the Soviet Delegation Lt. Gen. G. A. Burutin at the Seminar on Military Doctrines; Subject of the Statement: The Military Activity and the Military Training of the Armed Forces of the USSR), Vienna, January 29, 1990, official Soviet transcript, pp. 1–2.

vance conclusions explicitly along this line. Thus Aleksei Arbatov states that "the 'margin of safety' of the military balance is so great and the capability to considerably weaken the forces of the other side by a first strike is so questionable, that for ensuring reliable deterrence there is no need even in a crisis situation to put the strategic forces on the 'launch on warning regime.' "[8]

While it is not certain that the Soviet Union (or the United States) has made a decision to rely on retaliation, it is clear that as the strategic forces of the two sides have become increasingly large and varied, and thus overall less vulnerable despite possible vulnerabilities of components (for example, fixed land-based ICBMs), the disadvantages of precipitous reaction and possibly erroneous action have grown and become more evident. This may have moved the focus of probable reaction along the continuous spectrum of response back from preemption to launch on warning, to launch under attack, and probably under most circumstances to retaliatory launch after confirmed identification of a major enemy attack, that is, after an attack. No firm decision in advance can probably be made: the National Command Authorities (President Bush or President Gorbachev, or a surviving successor) would decide, taking account of all circumstances. But the probability inclination has been shifting in a more conservative direction. Both sides see the current probability of deliberate attack as small, and the incentives for preemption (either great superiority or great inferiority) have declined with the emergence of mature and robust strategic parity in assured retaliatory capability.

If one side did launch a preemptive attack, the other would probably respond with its full surviving forces and the outcome would be the same as in the case of deliberate initiation.

Of somewhat greater interest than general nuclear war are the range of less cataclysmic wars that could occur, possibly with initial limited use of nuclear weapons in a regional theater or more likely with conventional arms alone. While the likelihood of either Soviet or U.S. initiation of such a war remains extremely low, it is possible and warrants at least a brief further look at Soviet thinking on such wars.

8. Alexei Arbatov and Gennadi Lednev, "Strategic Equilibrium and Stability," in *Disarmament and Security, 1987 Yearbook,* USSR Academy of Sciences, Institute of World Economy and International Relations (Moscow: Novosti Press Agency, 1988), p. 257.

The Soviet concept of war (and world politics) envisions a period of rising tension and what is termed in the Soviet military literature "a period of threat" (or, more literally, "a threatening period"). During such a period political and diplomatic, as well as military, actions would occur, for purposes of deterrence and preparation. The late Major General Vladimir Zemskov, some twenty years ago, wrote in *Military Thought* that "under all conditions, a threatening period will evidently be filled with an intricate complex of various measures along diplomatic, political, economic and military lines carried out by both sides. In the diplomatic sphere, for example, there can be various types of diplomatic warnings and declarations, applications of diplomatic pressure on certain states, breaking off relations, and the establishment or confirmation of treaty obligations."[9] More recent discussions in the same General Staff journal continue to address the international political situation in a threatening period.[10]

Besides the threat of premeditated attack in a threatening period, Soviet thinking, as earlier discussed, has become more aware of the danger of political miscalculation, unauthorized military action, or accidental war. There is concern both for situations in which a limited war might break out, with great risk of subsequent escalation, and for general nuclear war. One of the principal Soviet criticisms of Western deterrence theory is precisely that it intensifies these risks of less-than-deliberate war. As one of the Soviet studies that reviewed these possible ways in which war might be generated put it: "Moreover, the indicated particulars of a [possible] genesis of a nuclear catastrophe must not be underestimated, especially because the adherents of a doctrine of 'nuclear deterrence' ('intimidation') do not wish to direct attention to them."[11]

Deterrence, by virtue of its focus on influencing calculation by a punitive attacker, in fact fails to give due attention to miscalculations

9. Maj. Gen. V. Zemskov, "Wars of the Contemporary Era," *Voyennaya mysl'*, no. 5 (May 1969), p. 62. General Zemskov was then editor of the journal.

10. See, in particular, Col. A. G. Khor'kov, "On the Question of the Threatening Period (History and the Present)," *Voyennaya mysl'*, no. 3 (March 1986), pp. 18–25; and Lt. Gen. P. A. Zhilin and Col. V. T. Login, "Lessons on the Unleashing of World Wars (On the 70th Anniversary of the Beginning of the First World War and the 45th Anniversary of the Second World War)," ibid., no. 8 (August 1984), pp. 59–70.

11. [Col.] B. M. Kanevsky and [Lt. Col.] P. M. Shabardin, *Problemy sovremennoi voyennoi politiki* (Problems of Contemporary Military Policy), Mezhdunarodnaya series 5 (Moscow: Znaniye, 1989), pp. 16–18, quotation from p. 17.

or unpremeditated causes of the outbreak of war—including actions taken by the deterrer, in some cases with the aim of enhancing deterrence.

It is very difficult for Soviet, as well as American, strategic analysts to posit ways in which war might be waged if initiated by an accidental or unauthorized action. If the action occurred at a time of tension, force readiness would probably have been increased on both sides. Neither, however, would have put itself in the position of planning beyond an alert for rapid response. Hence both, insofar as any organized military campaign would in fact occur, would be unprepared to carry out further actions in accordance with any meaningful strategy. A Soviet military writer posing the problem commented: "Even if one assumes an unauthorized beginning of a conflict, it would all the same develop on the basis of scenarios worked out and emplaced in the computer memory of machines by man." But he did not draw any conclusions beyond emphasizing the need to prevent war, and that the outcome of a nuclear exchange would no longer be war but a catastrophe.[12]

The new defensive doctrine adopted by the Soviet Union in 1987 is primarily a response strategy in case of attack. It is, however, also intended both to reduce Western perceptions of a Soviet offensive threat, and at the same time to serve as a deterrent. "Defense in the initial period of a war," in the words of an article under the byline of the then commandant of the General Staff Academy, General of the Army Grigory Salmanov, in *Military Thought,* is looked upon not only as an effective military action in stopping an attacker, "but also, and this is very important, to compel an adversary to think long and hard before deciding on an attack."[13]

Military scientists also direct attention under the new thinking to "the need for a new approach to the problem of resolving international contradictions, not permitting general nuclear and conventional war, and ensuring the security of the members of the Warsaw Pact."[14]

12. [Col.] O. Bel'kov, "Victory Not in War, but over War," *Mezhdunarodnaya zhizn'* (International Affairs), no. 1 (January 1988), p. 111.

13. Gen. Army G. I. Salmanov, "Soviet Military Doctrine and Some Views on the Character of War in Defense of Socialism," *Voyennaya mysl',* no. 12 (December 1988), p. 9.

14. Col. Gen. V. V. Korobushin, "On Increasing the Effectiveness of Military-Scientific Research," *Voyennaya mysl',* no. 5 (May 1988), pp. 39–40.

Civilian specialists on political-military affairs spell out more fully ways in which the risk of war can be averted by political means. For example, Vitaly Zhurkin and his colleagues have emphasized the need for adversaries to reconcile differences by compromises that recognize the interests of both sides as a way to avert conflict.[15] This line of reasoning is applied both to "preventive diplomacy," seeking to prevent a war, and to wartime diplomacy, seeking to limit and to terminate a conflict.

The outbreak of a war between the United States and the Soviet Union or between the NATO and Warsaw Pact alliances would by definition represent a failure of the aim and strategy of preventing war, but it would not end the process of seeking to resolve the conflict so long as hostilities being waged were less than general nuclear war; the succeeding stages would involve efforts to control the conflict, prevent its escalation, and end it as soon as possible.

Waging a War

Under traditional thinking in both East and West, "When the cannon speak, the diplomats fall silent." While not without challenge, and almost always an exaggeration, in the nuclear-missile computer age, that aphorism could quickly become irretrievably true. If today's nuclear missiles spoke, virtually *everyone* would fall silent.

Under Soviet military doctrine until 1987, while state policy and the political level of military doctrine were geared to preventing war with the West and hence defensive, at the military-technical level doctrine was directed to waging a war to victory. Soviet military doctrine and strategy continue to focus on the contingencies of major conventional, and possible nuclear, war. Very little is said about general or intercontinental war. To some extent this may be owing to secrecy, but there are strong reasons for believing the subject is given surprisingly little attention. While nuclear war would obviously be of the utmost significance, and the Soviet political and military leadership give the highest priority to possession of strategic nuclear forces for deterrence, they devote virtually no attention to campaigns

15. Vitaly Zhurkin, Sergei Karaganov, and Andrei Kortunov, "Reasonable Sufficiency, or How to Break the Vicious Circle," *Novoye vremya* (New Times), no. 40 (October 2, 1987), p. 13.

for waging such a war. This judgment is based on all available sources of information, but of course cannot take into account unknown materials that may exist and that could modify or even conceivably reverse it. While many Western analysts have argued, or more often assumed, that the Soviets were planning in terms of a cohesive nuclear war-fighting strategy, they have not been able to cite relevant and credible evidence.

Among available sources that can be cited are the full course of General Staff Academy lectures for 1973–75, and a full file of *Military Thought* from the 1950s to the present. Civil defense is one relevant subject. Although civil defense was accorded one lecture at the Academy, no evaluation of its effectiveness was made and the treatment seemed pro forma. The last article on civil defense in the General Staff journal appeared in February 1974.[16] There is no strategic doctrine for waging intercontinental war in the available military strategic literature, open or closed. While strategic nuclear exchanges are computed and programs developed to establish strategic force levels and composition, as discussed earlier, the absence of strategic theory and doctrine for waging intercontinental war is highly significant in a strategic culture that places as much emphasis on those disciplines as the Soviet Union does.

A professor at the General Staff Academy, Major General Mikhail Yasyukov, has noted that Soviet military doctrine on nuclear war lagged badly until very recently. Even when the political leadership concluded in 1956 that a world nuclear war was not inevitable and could be averted, "the need to update the Soviet military doctrine became obvious, but for several reasons, most of them subjective, that process took a very long time. For too long the Soviet armed forces remained unrealistically oriented to [seeking] victory in a nuclear war." He then, in the only acknowledgment I have seen in the open literature to the Soviet discussions of preemption in the mid-1950s, went on to say: "The search for ways to win a nuclear war provoked discussions about the decisive advantage of being the first to strike, the more so since the official U.S. doctrine envisaged the use of nuclear weapons as a means of ensuring survival and victory in a nuclear war."[17]

16. Gen. Army A. Altunin, "On the Theory of Civil Defense," *Voyennaya mysl'*, no. 2 (February 1974), pp. 30–40.

17. Maj. Gen. Mikhail Yasyukov, "Evolution of Soviet Military Doctrine," *Voennyi vestnik* (Military Bulletin), no. 6 (March 1988), p. 2. This is a Novosti

Soviet military statements, in flatly rejecting concepts of limited nuclear war, have reflected the Soviet view that an intercontinental nuclear war cannot be limited, and that an unlimited general nuclear war would simply be a catastrophe. As discussed earlier, limited nuclear war in continental theaters is abjured as extremely dangerous and likely to escalate to general nuclear war, but would be kept limited to the theater if first begun by the United States.[18]

In professional elaboration of military doctrine, the "intercontinental theater of military operations [TVD]" is little more than mentioned (except for allocation to it of most ICBMs, SLBMs, and heavy bombers). Operational and strategic doctrine for the other land and ocean theaters, in contrast, is given detailed analysis and great attention, above all the Western (European) theater of military operations (TVD).[19]

In Europe, the principal theater of engagement in any real war (that is, excluding a general nuclear war of mutual annihilation), the Soviet military strategic concept from the late 1960s to the late 1980s was for a rapid nonnuclear offensive aimed at destroying the NATO forces in the central Western front to the English Channel, optimally in about three weeks.

Since 1985, and especially since the announcement of a new defensive doctrine at the military-technical level in 1987, that whole concept has drastically changed. By 1989 there could be no doubt that the change was real and not rhetorical. Gorbachev's unilateral reduction of forces, in particular the withdrawal of six tank divisions (more than one-third of the tank divisions) from central Europe, coupled with his offer of asymmetrical reductions of many thousands of tanks and artillery in the conventional arms talks (Conventional Forces in Europe, or CFE), bore impressive witness to the fact. Finally, in 1989–90 the Warsaw Pact rapidly collapsed as a military alliance capable of offensive operations, attendant upon the disintegration of communist rule in eastern and central Europe and rapid retraction of Soviet military forces.

While less dramatic and far-reaching than these political develop-

Press Agency publication, not the journal of the ground forces with the same title.

18. See chapter 3, citing in particular the secret Voroshilov General Staff Academy lectures.

19. For a useful analysis of pre-1987 military strategy for these theaters, see Michael MccGwire, *Military Objectives in Soviet Foreign Policy* (Brookings, 1987), pp. 117–210.

ments at the turn of the decade, the Soviet military policy and
doctrinal change from 1985 to 1989 is more important for the present
inquiry. Before these geopolitical changes, at a time when Gorbachev
and the Soviet leadership still had a choice, they chose to reorient
Soviet military strategy away from an offensive concept aimed at
military victory on the continent to a defensive concept aimed at
rebuffing an attack and ending any conflict as quickly as possible.
The conceptual aim was changed from defeat of the enemy to defeat
of enemy attack; from seeking military victory to merely warding off
military defeat.

This radical change has not come easily; indeed, Soviet military
doctrinal and planning experts are still thrashing out some of its
implications and consequences, and the change is still under way.
But the political decision was taken in a series of steps in the latter
half of the 1980s, beginning in 1985.

The clearest and most authoritative statement of the change in
Soviet military doctrine was made under the byline of Marshal
(then General of the Army) Yazov, in the Party theoretical journal
Kommunist at the end of 1989. It is worth citing at some length:

> Our military doctrine earlier as well bore a defensive character. . . .
> [But] in the course of subsequent military development a certain dis-
> junction between the political and the military-technical aspects of
> military doctrine was permitted. While in the political dimension
> [our] military doctrine was always defensive, envisaging rejection of a
> military attack on anyone at all and, with the appearance of nuclear
> weapons, rejection of their first use, on the military-technical plane
> stress was placed on decisive offensive actions in case of the unleashing
> of war against the USSR and its allies. It was assumed that the higher
> the capability of the armed forces for such actions, the more stable the
> defense, the less likely an enemy attack. In other words, in effect the
> defensive thrust of the political aspect of doctrine was in definite
> contradiction with the tenet of its military-technical aspect on offensive
> actions. In the contemporary content of our doctrine, brought into
> effect in 1987, this contradiction is completely eliminated.[20]

Although this may appear to be self-serving, it is not an inaccurate
description of the change in doctrine.

This change in the military-technical level of doctrine, raising the

20. D. Yazov, "The New Model of Security and the Armed Forces," *Kommunist*
(The Communist), no. 18 (December 1989), pp. 65–66. Yazov's identification as
candidate Politburo member as well as defense minister was noted in his byline.

defensive to the dominant form in military strategy, it should be recalled, accompanied the change in the definition of military doctrine to make preventing war the primary objective, along with the traditional objective of preparing the armed forces for the contingency of war. While separate, these important changes were related not only in time (1987), but more importantly in reflecting a further change with respect to the objective in case war occurred and to the very idea of victory in war.

Since the late 1970s Soviet political leaders and commentators have spoken of the futility or impossibility of victory in war in the nuclear age. Military leaders have usually been careful to couch disavowals of victory in terms of the Soviet desire to avert war, and to tie any statements on the impossibility of victory strictly to general nuclear war. Professional military discussions of military science and art, strategy, and operational doctrine continued to posit the aim of victory if war should come, especially for wars less than general nuclear war. There has been and remains a military reluctance to forgo victory as the aim of combat and war. For example, an article in 1988 on the new defensive military doctrine that raised the matter of victory more explicitly than most still hedged. It noted that the Twenty-seventh Party Congress in 1986 had in effect raised "the question of victory in war," and categorically asserted that "in nuclear war there can be no victor." But while acknowledging "the impossibility of gaining victory in nuclear war," it suggested that victory in conventional war was not ruled out, and that "from the military point of view . . . in our opinion the military aspect of victory is not removed at all levels. Therefore it is the duty and obligation of military cadres and the entire personnel of the army and navy to be in the highest readiness to repulse aggression, to defeat the enemy, with the aim of victory in battle."[21] Thus at the tactical and operational level the aim is still to win.

At the strategic level of operations in theaters of war the definition of the aim is less clear-cut. A leading military scientist writing in *Military Thought,* Colonel General V. V. Korobushin, has observed: "The main task of the armed forces in case of the unleashing of war by an aggressor is to repel the attack, to frustrate an invasion, and to ensure not only defeat of the aggressor but also the survivability

---

21. Rear Adm. V. Gulin and Capt. 1st Rank I. Kondyrev, "The Defensive Thrust of Soviet Military Doctrine," *Morskoi sbornik* (Naval Journal), no. 2 (February 1988), pp. 12–13.

of one's own country."[22] That is an interesting formulation, drawing attention to the need in effect to "destroy the enemy" only to an extent that is compatible with limits that preserve the survivability of one's own country—clearly below the threshold of general nuclear war and probably short of even a general nonnuclear war.

More generally, the debate over applying the new defensive doctrine has focused on precisely the objective—if any—beyond defeating an attack. For some, that means defeating "the attacker" in the field; some might construe it to mean destroying "the enemy" and not merely his attacking forces.

The official Warsaw Pact statement on military doctrine in 1987 said that if attacked the Warsaw Pact forces "will give the aggressor a crushing rebuff *[otpor]*."[23] And then? This is the key question the Soviet political-military establishment is still debating. General Yazov, in setting forth the new doctrine in 1987, stated: "Soviet military doctrine considers the defense as the main form of military actions in repulsing aggression. It must be reliable and steadfast, tenacious and active, calculated to stop the enemy's offensive, to bleed him, not to permit the loss of territory, and to defeat the invading hostile field forces." Then, however, he went on to describe a subsequent step: "By defense alone, however, it is not possible to defeat the aggressor. Therefore after repulsing the attack, the troops and naval forces must be capable of conducting a decisive offensive. The transition to it will take the form of a counteroffensive."[24]

Senior Soviet military men have continued to refer to the need for a subsequent counteroffensive, and described the objective variably as defeating or destroying the enemy forces or the aggressor. There has not, however, been a consistent formulation, and there appears to be an unresolved underlying issue.

References to a counteroffensive tended to diminish after 1988. To note but one striking illustration, in late 1987 Marshal Viktor Kulikov, then commander in chief of the Warsaw Pact forces and not known as a "new thinker," wrote in a popular-circulation book that "in the course of strategic defense great attention will be placed on the preparation and conduct of a counteroffensive, because by

22. Korobushin, *Voyennaya mysl'*, no. 5 (May 1988), p. 40. This sentence appeared in boldface type in the original.
23. "On the Military Doctrine of the Member States of the Warsaw Pact," *Pravda*, May 30, 1987, p. 1.
24. Yazov, *Na strazhe sotsializma i mire*, pp. 32–33.

defense alone one cannot secure a crushing repulse of the aggressor."[25] Five months later, in the General Staff journal *Military Thought*, Kulikov addressed the same issue very differently. He wrote: "Special attention needs to be devoted to working out the questions involved in repelling aggression. In doing so it is extremely important to study how to organize and conduct active defense, providing effective fire suppression of the enemy and conducting counterattacks and counterstrikes."[26] There was no reference whatsoever to a counteroffensive, and this omission can only have been deliberate. (Soviet military doctrine clearly distinguishes between counterattacks at the tactical level, counterstrikes at the operational level, and a counteroffensive at the theater strategic level.)[27] The later date, or the confidential nature of the second discussion, or an authoritative editorial change may account for the notable difference.

References to the need for a counteroffensive, however, have continued, with possibly significant variations. General of the Army Vladimir Lobov, chief of staff of the Warsaw Pact forces, in mid-1989 closely paraphrased Yazov's 1987 formulation—indeed, so closely that the differences may be significant. General Lobov's version (with additions in italics and deletions in brackets) described the mission "to stop the enemy's offensive, to bleed him, not to permit the loss *of a significant piece* of territory, and to *create the conditions for the subsequent complete* defeat of the [invading] hostile field forces. By defense alone, however, it is not possible to *achieve that* [defeat the aggressor]. Therefore after repulsing the *enemy* attack, the *Soviet* troops [and naval forces] must be *ready to conduct* [capable of conducting] a decisive [offensive. The transition to it will take the form of a] counteroffensive."[28] In some respects Lobov's formulation is more cautious, for example, by accepting that some

25. Marshal V. G. Kulikov, *Doktrina zashchity mira i sotsializma* (A Doctrine of Defense of Peace and Socialism) (Moscow: Voyenizdat, 1988), p. 79. (Submitted by December 3, 1987, and sent to press January 8, 1988; published in 30,000 copies.)

26. Marshal V. G. Kulikov, "On Military-Strategic Parity and Sufficiency for Defense," *Voyennaya mysl'*, no. 5 (May 1988), p. 10.

27. This distinction, already in loose usage, has been authoritative since 1947. See Lt. Gen. P. Yarchevsky, "Counterattack, Counterstrike, Counteroffensive," *Voyennaya mysl'*, no. 3 (March 1947), pp. 42–51.

28. Gen. Army Vladimir Lobov, "Although the Threat Has Lessened . . . ," *Novoye vremya*, no. 29 (July 14, 1989), p. 9; emphasis added. In both this case and Yazov's, I have translated *vrazheskiye gruppirovki* as "hostile field forces" rather than "hostile groupings" [of forces].

territory may be lost. But while not precisely stated, the objective remains to be "ready" to conduct a decisive counteroffensive to destroy the enemy forces engaged on the battlefield. It is noteworthy that both specify the later stage as merely being "capable" (Yazov) or "ready" (Lobov) for a decisive counteroffensive, rather than taking for granted such a counteroffensive as soon as the hostile invading force had been stopped and repelled. An important reason for this will be discussed later. But it is useful to note at this point that, in keeping with the Warsaw Pact declaration on "repelling aggression," rather than "destroying the enemy," the objective has been narrowed to defeating the enemy's attacking forces, rather than his entire military force.

A discussion by Major General Stepan Tyushkevich in *Military Thought* in May 1989 had also used a variant of the Yazov statement, closer to the original than Lobov's save for one, more drastic, important difference. The aim was focused on "ensuring the decisive defeat of the invading enemy field forces"—but with no reference even to being "ready to conduct" or "capable of" a counteroffensive.[29] As in Marshal Kulikov's statement in the General Staff journal, reference to a counteroffensive was dropped altogether.

The debate among Soviet military and political leaders over the scope of the change to a defensive doctrine, in particular the weight—in forces and capabilities—to be given to a possible counteroffensive in a subsequent phase of a war, continues. For example, the chief of the General Staff, General Moiseyev, in an interview published in January 1990 deliberately left open the possibility of a major counteroffensive. In reaffirming the new defensive strategy, he noted that "undoubtedly counterattacks and counterstrikes will find their place, and also a counteroffensive directed toward destroying the invading foe." This statement put him on the conservative side of the argument, but still clearly in the mainstream on limiting the objective to the defeat of an invading force. He then, however, went much further in explicitly opening up the possibility of a counteroffensive into the territory of the attacker: "As for subsequent actions of the USSR armed forces, including on the territory of an aggressor after rebuffing his invasion, all that would depend on the scale and orientation of the aggression, the character of the military operations, and

29. Maj. Gen. (Ret.) S. A. Tyushkevich, "Reasonable Sufficiency for Defense: Parameters and Criteria," *Voyennaya mysl'*, no. 5 (May 1989), p. 61.

the means and methods of armed conflict." Finally, in what seemed a curious non sequitur, he concluded his discussion of the matter by saying: "I can definitely say one thing: Soviet military doctrine is subordinated to the task of preventing war. And we will devote maximum efforts to its fulfillment."[30] It seems likely that Moiseyev is sincere in wanting to avert war, but still believes some contingencies in wartime could call for large counteroffensive operations.

More recently, in mid-1990, in a much more circumscribed way Marshal Yazov again emphasized that "the main principle" of the use of the Soviet armed forces was "response actions," that "the main form of military operations at the beginning of aggression is defensive operations on strategic and operational scales aimed at repulsing the aggression," and that "counteroffensive actions and operations to rout an *invading* enemy can be conducted *within their framework.*"[31]

Dr. Andrei Kokoshin, deputy director of the Institute of USA and Canada studies, and Major General Valentin Larionov, then a professor at the General Staff Academy, wrote an interesting article in 1988 identifying four possible models or paradigms for the conduct of a war. First would be an attempt by each of the two sides to seize the initiative and mount an offensive to defeat the other. Second, both could abjure the offensive and seek to maintain a strong, deep defense. If one attacked, the other initially would defend, and when able would pass over to a counteroffensive into enemy territory. (The great Soviet defensive battle at Kursk in 1943 was the example.) Third, both would assume a defensive posture, but when one was successful in defeating an attack it would refrain from mounting a subsequent counteroffensive. Fourth would be a reciprocal posture of defense with both sides incapable of mounting an offensive. They implied that the Soviet Union had moved from the first to the second, and they were advocating a move to the third, and eventually if the West agreed on deep arms reductions to the fourth.[32]

30. "What Kind of Army?" An Interview with Gen. Army Mikhail A. Moiseyev, *Voyennyi vestnik* (Military Herald), no. 1 (January 1990), p. 6.

31. Marshal D. T. Yazov, "Military Reform," *Krasnaya zvezda* (Red Star), June 3, 1990, p. 2; emphasis added.

32. A. Kokoshin and V. Larionov, "A Counterposition of General Purpose Forces in the Context of Securing Strategic Stability," *MEiMO*, no. 6 (June 1988), pp. 23–31. These authors elaborated their outline of four strategic models in a later book; see Kokoshin and Larionov, *Predotvrashcheniye voiny: doktriny, kontseptsii, perspektivy* (Prevention of War: Doctrines, Concepts, Prospects) (Moscow: Progress, 1990), pp.

While Soviet doctrine seems to be in transition from the second to the third variant, as indicated in the earlier discrepant references on the counteroffensive, since mid-1987 all Soviet military leaders repeat that the new doctrine calls for designing forces capable only of defense.[33] The policy issue is over how far the Soviet Union should go unilaterally, or whether it should wait for negotiated arms reductions that result in such a posture on both sides.

Shifting military doctrine at the military technical level to give primacy to the defense is not an easy transition.[34] Nonetheless, it has been occurring, especially since 1988. The unilateral reduction of the Soviet armed forces by half a million men, with the withdrawal from central Europe of six tank divisions and more than 5,000 tanks, announced by Gorbachev in December 1988 was one concrete sign of this shift. The restructuring of the forces that remain in Eastern Europe, and of others in the Far East, also reflects this shift to a defensive strategic concept. No less significant is the Soviet readiness in the CFE negotiations to make drastic asymmetrical reductions giving up their superiority in numbers of tanks, artillery, and aircraft.

128–47. They had earlier written an article on the Kursk battle; see Kokoshin and Larionov, "The Kursk Battle in the Light of Contemporary Defense Doctrine," *MEiMO*, no. 8 (August 1987), pp. 32–40. See also Maj. Gen. V. V. Larionov, "A Triumph of Premeditated Defense (On the 45th Anniversary of the Battle of Kursk)," *Voyennaya mysl'*, no. 7 (July 1988), pp. 12–21. This kind of collaboration between civilian and military experts has been unusual. Larionov retired in 1989.

33. For example, see the press conference statement by deputy chief of the General Staff of the USSR Armed Forces, Col. Gen. M. A. Gareyev, in "A Doctrine for Preventing War," *Krasnaya zvezda*, June 23, 1987, p. 3; Gen. Army D. T. Yazov, "The Military Doctrine of the Warsaw Pact—A Doctrine of the Defense of Peace and Socialism," *Pravda*, July 27, 1987, p. 5; Marshal Sergei Akhromeyev, "A Doctrine of Prevention of War and Defense of Peace and Socialism," *Problemy mira i sotsializma* (Problems of Peace and Socialism), no. 12 (December 1987), p. 26; and Akhromeyev, "On Guard over Peace and Security," *Trud* (Labor), February 21, 1988, p. 2. See also M. S. Gorbachev, "Reality and Guarantees for a Secure World," *Pravda*, September 17, 1987, p. 1.

34. The new role of defense in Soviet military doctrine, adopted in 1987, is entirely different from a revision of the nature of the defense undertaken in the first half of the 1980s by the military. This professional military reevaluation of defense in operational doctrine was based on both military technological developments and on Soviet evaluation of evolving U.S. and NATO strategic concepts using the emerging new high technologies. While the revision in the early 1980s gave more attention to defense (and meeting engagements) than theretofore, it addressed a growing "convergence" of defense and offense, with defense becoming more active and with greater maneuver—more "offensive defense," in a way, rather than the new post-1987 stress on more "defensive defense" less capable of offensive action. See Raymond L.

Since 1988 a number of Soviet military leaders have said that a firm decision to shift to a defensive doctrine had been taken and was being carried out. Most authoritatively among references that can be publicly cited is a statement by Chief of the General Staff General Moiseyev in early 1990 to the seminar on military doctrines sponsored by the Conference on Security and Cooperation in Europe (CSCE):

> At the present time we have reviewed our strategy. In case of aggression, the main form of operations by the Soviet armed forces will be defensive operations. Defense on the strategic, operational and tactical levels has been advanced to the forefront in training of the army and navy. On this basis, operational-strategic plans have been reworked, and all underlying documents including regulations and combat manuals, which have been brought into strict conformity with the theses of defensive doctrine and which guide our armed forces.[35]

Other military leaders have said that the curricula of the General Staff Academy and other military schools were all being revised.[36] The shift to a defensive strategic concept has been authoritatively corroborated by a review of the confidential General Staff journal *Military Thought*, which shows a growing serious attention to actually working out how to implement the new defensive doctrine. Several editorial and other key articles in 1987–88 stressed the change clearly but without spelling out the implications. The lead editorial on the 1988 training year stressed that the new strictures on defense and prevention of war were meant as operational guidance: "The defensive character of Soviet military doctrine will exert great influence on the orientation of the operational and combat preparation of all arms of the armed forces, including air defense, the air force, and the navy."[37] And, indeed, exercises in

---

Garthoff, "Continuity and Change in Soviet Military Doctrine," in Bruce Parrott, ed., *The Dynamics of Soviet Defense Policy* (Wilson Center Press, forthcoming).

35. *Tezisy vystupleniya M. A. Moiseyeva o voyennoi doktrine Sovetskogo Soyuza* (Theses of the Statement by M. A. Moiseyev on the Military Doctrine of the Soviet Union), Vienna, January 16, 1990, official Soviet transcript, pp. 14–15.

36. Personal interview with Col. Gen. Nikolai Chervov of the General Staff in the Ministry of Defense, Moscow, February 2, 1989. This was also stated on the occasion of then Secretary of Defense Frank Carlucci's visit to the General Staff Academy in August 1988.

37. "The Defensive Character of Soviet Military Doctrine and Preparation of the Troops (Forces)," *Voyennaya mysl'*, no. 1 (January 1988), p. 10. This sentence appeared in boldface type in the original.

168   *What If Deterrence Fails?*

1988 and the years following have given greater attention to the defense.[38]

A review of the development of Soviet military doctrine under the byline of the then commandant of the General Staff Academy, General Salmanov, in February 1988 laid a baseline for evaluating changes in Soviet doctrine at the military-technical level—and acknowledged that in the postwar period until recently it had been offensive. Now, however, the article emphasized it would be defensive.[39] By December 1988 another key article on current Soviet military doctrine under General Salmanov's byline emphasized not only the new defensive orientation of Soviet military doctrine but also the need to reconsider the initial period of a war from the standpoint of the new role of defense as the basic form of strategic operations. The article made clear that this change in military doctrine was the result of the new political thinking.[40] Many other articles dealt with various aspects of defensive doctrine, and by the January 1989 issue of *Military Thought* all four articles on strategy, operations, and tactics dealt with aspects of defense, complemented by an article on doctrine for offensive operations of the U.S. Army. This trend continues.

The underlying element in this change in military doctrine to a defensive strategy was the redefinition of victory. As Colonel Oleg Bel'kov has put it, "Under contemporary conditions [of the nuclear-missile age] victory of each and all states consists not in the capability to prevail in armed confrontation, but in the ability to prevent conflict."[41] There is also increasing awareness of the need for a change in the objective of military operations. The traditional objective of all armies has been victory, and the most common strategic concept has relied upon defeating the armed forces of the enemy. Even with

38. In the major "Fall 88" exercise, the Red side tested Soviet defensive operational concepts against a Blue attack, reportedly under the direct supervision of the minister of defense and the High Command. An earlier exercise in March 1988 also tested defense against a NATO invasion force.

39. Gen. Army G. I. Salmanov, "The Soviet Military Art over 70 Years," *Voyennaya mysl'*, no. 2 (February 1988), pp. 26–37, esp. pp. 30–32.

40. Salmanov, *Voyennaya mysl'*, no. 12 (December 1988), pp. 9–10. I have used the term "under the byline" because, while ghostwritten articles are common, there is particular reason to believe both of these articles were in fact written by others. General Salmanov, more noted as a field commander than a military thinker, was relieved of this post in 1989, reportedly for being insufficiently in tune with the new defensive doctrine.

41. Bel'kov, *Mezhdunarodnaya zhizn'*, no. 1 (January 1988), p. 112.

the important overlay of a primary deterrent role for military power, the first wave of a revolutionary change in military thinking in the period after 1945, the traditional doctrine in the Western armies as well as in the Soviet Union has been that if deterrence fails and war comes, the role of military forces is to prevail or win by defeating and destroying the armed forces of the other side.

Now members of the Soviet establishment are urging an objective not of winning, but of preventing the other side from winning; not defeating and destroying the enemy's forces, but only defeating the accomplishment of his offensive aims. As expressed by Zhurkin and colleagues, "the level of reasonable sufficiency for conventional armed forces must thus be defined not by the capability to win victory in the course of a large-scale local conflict, but by ensuring sufficient defensive potential so that an aggressor could not count on a 'local blitzkrieg.' "[42] Or, as these analysts put it in another discussion, "Formerly the level of sufficiency for the military power of the USSR in the European theater was determined by the requirement to repel any aggression, to destroy any possible coalition of hostile states. Now the mission has been established in principle in a different way: to deter, to prevent war itself. That task, in turn, requires a reconsideration of many traditional postulates of military strategy and the operational art, beginning with a reevaluation of the quantitative demands for various arms (for example, tanks), the character of maneuver, and the like."[43]

Clearly, for many years before they acknowledged the fact publicly, the Soviet leaders and senior political and military men realized full well that "victory" in a nuclear war in any meaningful sense was unattainable by anyone.[44] With "new thinking" the Soviet leaders have become more aware of the political and other costs of blindly preparing for the contingency, if deterrence failed, of waging war with the aim of "winning." Vadim Zagladin, long the first deputy chief of the International Department of the Central Committee,

42. Zhurkin and others, *Novoye vremya*, no. 40 (October 2, 1987), p. 15; this entire passage appeared in boldface type in the original. See also Andrei Kokoshin, "The Best Defense Is Defense Only," *Novoye vremya*, no. 33 (August 12, 1988), p. 19.

43. V. Zhurkin, S. Karaganov, and A. Kortunov, "The Challenges of Security—Old and New," *Kommunist*, no. 1 (January 1988), p. 46.

44. See chapter 3 above, and Robert L. Arnett, "Soviet Attitudes towards Nuclear War: Do They Really Think They Can Win?" *Journal of Strategic Studies*, vol. 2 (September 1979), pp. 172–91.

and since 1988 an adviser to Gorbachev, has acknowledged that
while waging a determined struggle against nuclear war for decades,
"we were not, however, always logical in this. On the one hand we
spoke of the deadly threat of nuclear catastrophe, while on the other
we proceeded for a long time, too long, from the possibility of winning a nuclear war" and were drawn into an arms race.[45] He clearly
did not mean that the Soviet leaders had seen a prospect for winning
a nuclear war; rather, they had continued military programs on the
assumption that if deterrence failed and war came, the military
would fight and seek to prevail. Zagladin's main conclusion was that
as a consequence they had missed opportunities for averting an arms
race, thus contributing to a confrontational cycle. Others, too, have
emphasized the reciprocal stimulation of political tension as well as
an arms race for pursuit of security through military means.

In addition, Soviet political leaders have become increasingly
sensitive that their pursuit of military capabilities for a contingent
offensive, or now even a counteroffensive, has the unintended effect
of stimulating Western perceptions of a threat. Thus at an important
Ministry of Foreign Affairs conference in mid-1988, First Deputy
Minister Yuly Vorontsov noted in his summation on military-political
aspects of security that a "deep, critical analysis of the problems of
military doctrines was undertaken. All speakers unanimously expressed the need for a serious study of the question of the defensive
character of Soviet doctrine and for reinforcing the corresponding
political declarations with concrete changes in military planning,
structure of the forces, military training, and so on. . . . The need
was noted to take into account critical views regarding the thesis
about a 'crushing rebuff,' which is often perceived in the West as
implying offensive actions . . . that are in actual fact not contained
in our defensive doctrine."[46]

45. V. Zagladin, "Following a Course of Reason and Humanism," *Pravda*, June
13, 1988, p. 6. He paraphrased the same idea in a Moscow television roundtable two
weeks later: "While rejecting nuclear war and waging a struggle to avert it, we
nonetheless proceeded from the possibility of winning it." Moscow Television, June
25, 1988, in Foreign Broadcast Information Service, *Daily Report: Soviet Union*, no.
123, June 27, 1988, p. 2. Zagladin's comments were seized upon and distorted by
some Western commentators seeking to prove "admission" of a previous Soviet
interest in fighting and winning a nuclear war.
46. First Deputy Minister of Foreign Affairs of the USSR Yu. M. Vorontsov, "The
19th All-Union CPSU Conference: Foreign Policy and Diplomacy," at a Scientific-
Practical Conference at the USSR Ministry of Foreign Affairs, *Mezhdunarodnaya
zhizn'*, no. 9 (September 1988), p. 43.

One important subject, to which the Soviets have given serious attention in the past, apparently did not figure in the post-1987 revision of doctrine. I put this reference in the past tense, because events since 1989 have already greatly changed its application. Nonetheless, if in a new form yet to be devised, the consideration remains important. The Soviets are well aware that during a war "the role of diplomacy will increase sharply. The point of diplomatic conflict will obviously be directed toward weakening the hostile coalition in every way possible, by means of separating individual states from it and depriving the main enemy of his international ties and support from allies and dependent and neutral states."[47] Historical cases are cited and examined.[48] Strategists give particular weight to the gearing together of military and political-diplomatic efforts: "It is sometimes important for military strategy to assure the neutrality of a number of states or of particular states, and this is also an obligation of diplomacy."[49] And, in turn, military successes in a war may assist diplomacy to ensure neutrality, or lead members of the enemy coalition to become neutral or even switch alliance. Thus, for example, military analysts credit the Soviet success at Stalingrad with helping convince Turkey and Japan to remain neutral toward the USSR during World War II.[50] Moreover, these diplomatic actions can in turn "influence the course and even the character of military operations."[51]

More specifically, Colonel General Nikolai Lomov has stated frankly in the confidential pages of *Military Thought* that "it is clear that in the course of a war one of the main political tasks of the socialist coalition will remain attracting on to its side the peoples

47. Zemskov, *Voyennaya mysl'*, no. 5 (May 1969), p. 53. On the importance accorded to political-diplomatic aspects of the initial period of a war, see also [Lt. Gen.] M. M. Kir'yan, *Problemy voyennoi teorii v sovetskikh nauchno-spravochnykh izdaniyakh* (Problems of Military Theory in Soviet Scientific-Reference Publications) (Moscow: Nauka, 1985), p. 114.

48. See the discussion and references in Raymond L. Garthoff, "Soviet Views on the Interrelation of Diplomacy and Military Strategy," *Political Science Quarterly*, vol. 94 (Fall 1979), pp. 397–400.

49. Marshal V. D. Sokolovsky, ed., *Voyennaya strategiya* (Military Strategy), 3d ed. (Moscow: Voyenizdat, 1968), p. 30.

50. See in particular, Dmitriyev, *Voyennaya mysl'*, no. 7 (July 1971), pp. 47–48. These historical cases have been frequently cited; for example, Sokolovsky, ed., *Voyennaya strategiya*, p. 30; Povaly, *Voyennaya mysl'*, no. 7 (July 1970), p. 16; and Col. Gen. N. Lomov, "Some Problems of Command in Contemporary Warfare," *Voyennaya mysl'*, no. 1 (January 1966), p. 4.

51. Dmitriyev, *Voyennaya mysl'*, no. 7 (July 1971), p. 48.

of nonsocialist countries."[52] Again, historical examples are noted, including the Soviet success in "turning" Hitler's Balkan allies against Germany, after military successes made it feasible (Romania, Bulgaria, and Hungary in 1944–45).[53]

At least equally prominent in Soviet thinking, though rarely articulated, has been concern over *Western* ability to do the same to them: the imperialists have been expected to "attempt to break up the socialist community and to wrest individual countries from its ranks."[54]

One would assume that the Soviet Union (like the United States after 1961) would build preplanned "withholds" or flexible war plans to permit, for example, excluding attacks on countries of the hostile coalition that might opt out at the start of a war. One finds confirmation in the secret General Staff Academy course materials of the mid-1970s that nuclear war plans must be "constantly reviewed, readjusted, and modified as needed, according to changes in the military and political situation," and more specifically that "political reasons may affect the selection of areas of the TSMAs [theaters of operations; TVDs] for actions, the selection of countries to be hit by nuclear strikes, or nations not to be attacked or temporarily not to be attacked by nuclear weapons."[55]

While the Soviet military establishment was still adjusting to the revision of its operational-strategic doctrine for waging a defensive strategy, the sudden and drastic collapse of communist rule in Eastern Europe in late 1989 imposed still greater changes on future military planning. Until then the circumstances of a possible counteroffensive once the general NATO–Warsaw Pact central front was stabilized could be debated, and the force posture as well. The Soviet military would not be given the forces that had been provided there-

52. Lomov, *Voyennaya mysl'*, no. 1 (January 1966), p. 10.

53. Povaly, *Voyennaya mysl'*, no. 7 (July 1970), p. 17.

54. Zemskov, *Voyennaya mysl'*, no. 5 (May 1969), p. 55. It has only recently been revealed that in 1963 Romania secretly conveyed to the United States that it would not participate in a war touched off by Soviet actions undertaken without consultation with Romania, for example the Soviet deployment of missiles in Cuba that had caused the Cuban missile crisis. This remarkable secret declaration of contingent neutrality by a member of the Warsaw Pact represented a serious breach of alliance obligations. See Raymond L. Garthoff, "The Warsaw Pact Today—and Tomorrow?" *Brookings Review*, vol. 8 (Summer 1990), pp. 38–39.

55. *The Voroshilov Lectures: Materials from the Soviet General Staff Academy*, vol. 1: *Issues of Soviet Military Strategy*, comp. by Ghulam Dastagir Wardak (Washington: National Defense University Press, 1989), pp. 271, 266.

tofore for assuming the offensive if war came, or even optimal forces for a counteroffensive. But the CFE negotiations would at least stabilize equal force levels on the two sides along the NATO-Pact border. Soviet forces in East Germany, Czechoslovakia, Poland, and Hungary were being shaved, but remained as four "Groups of Forces" or nuclei for wartime fronts.

After the Revolution of '89, all this changed. While the Warsaw Pact remained, at least for a time, it was radically transformed.[56] Five of its seven members soon had noncommunist governments, and the Pact summits were no longer conclaves of Communist leaderships. It became necessary to agree on withdrawal of all Soviet forces from Czechoslovakia and Hungary by mid-1991, and an end to Soviet military presence in what had been the German Democratic Republic and in Poland became only a question of time. All the Eastern European armies were also substantially and unilaterally reduced, and sharply reoriented to serve national interests. Not only was the Pact evidently no longer a potential offensive force, it was only marginally and conditionally a defensive one. Even the intermediate-term survival of the alliance was in doubt. For most practical purposes, the Soviet defense line was now again for the first time since 1944 along the western Soviet border. And even that was questionable, with the likely effective secession of Lithuania, and probably Latvia and Estonia.

NATO, meanwhile, while undergoing some force reductions, remained not only intact but prospectively enlarged by the addition of eastern Germany.

A defensive strategy became a necessity, with the territories of Poland, Czechoslovakia, Hungary, Romania, and Bulgaria likely at best to constitute a neutral buffer belt, and eastern Germany not even that. Thus the voluntary change of Soviet *intention*, from a contingent offensive westward if deterrence of a Western-initiated war failed, to a counteroffensive (1987–88), and later to defensive counteractions (1988–89), was by the events of late 1989 decisively reinforced by a drastic decline in *capabilities* to do anything more than defend. This situation would be further consolidated by the CFE agreement.

Internal economic, political, and social developments in the Soviet Union required not only a retrenchment of the Soviet armed

56. Garthoff, *Brookings Review*, vol. 8 (Summer 1990), pp. 35–40.

forces, but also adding unpleasant and difficult internal security tasks, distracting forces from maintaining their full potential for external defense.

While the probability of a war with NATO remained very low, the Soviet military leadership still faced its professional responsibilities to provide military capabilities for defense of the country, and to fashion a new doctrine and strategy under an extremely adverse combination of conditions.

Controlling and Terminating a War

The inescapable imperative for both the Soviet Union and the United States if a war between them were to break out would be to end it as soon as possible. It is likely, but by no means certain, that that imperative would be recognized and promptly acted upon.

If either country's leadership had deliberately initiated a war against the other, there would of course be a powerful competing objective—whatever it was that had led to the decision to accept the costs and risks inherent in launching a war between nuclear superpowers. The great difficulty in imagining what could constitute such an objective reflects the compelling judgment that premeditated war is extremely unlikely.

Under American deterrence theory, however, a clear shot at a truly disarming strike against the other side, either through a successful first strike alone, or better still in combination with even partially effective strategic defenses to soak up any surviving enemy intercontinental strike forces, is assumed to be a possible objective warranting an adversary's decision to attack. For such a scenario, there is no need to consider limits on waging war, and none for terminating it except through annihilation of resistance and imposition of one's terms.

But under *any* other scenario for the outbreak and conduct of a war, it is necessary to consider how to wage such a war so as to end it expeditiously. There may, however, be competing considerations and even objectives in deciding how to wage the war. Beyond the classical aim to win, some may argue that the best basis for terminating a war remains to wage it successfully so as to prevail within limits that permit its termination before it escalates into catastrophe. Even in this case, it would be incumbent to articulate less than total war aims as a basis for negotiating the terms of the vanquished adversary's cessation of hostilities.

It is highly unlikely that national leaders of the Soviet Union or the United States have ever seriously addressed "war aims" for the successful termination of a nuclear war.[57]

In the event of a Soviet attack in Europe, according to Defense Secretary Cheney, "The United States' aim is to be clearly able to defeat such an attack quickly and decisively, preferably without resort to nuclear weapons and without extending the conflict to other theaters." The objective is "to convince the enemy leadership that it has gravely miscalculated our resolve, that we possess substantial military capability to inflict further harm, and that it is in the enemy's interest to halt its aggression and withdraw."[58] Former Secretary of Defense Caspar Weinberger, in his last annual report in 1987, had also said that "U.S. strategy seeks to limit the scope and intensity of any war, and confine it to conventional means. Our goal is to end hostilities on favorable terms to us by employing conventional forces that do not engender or risk escalation." He continued, however, by expressing determination if necessary to provide for escalation, and avowed maximalist war aims: "We would seek to terminate any war at the earliest practical time and restore peace on terms favorable to the United States that secure all our aims and those of our allies and friends" and "deny the aggressor any of his war aims."[59]

Soviet analysts see such statements of U.S. war aims as aggressive, or at the least as implying in case of war continuing "efforts of the American leadership to create the conditions for victory in any conflict—nonnuclear or nuclear, local or global."[60]

The Soviets have been quite conscious of the interrelation of

57. The National Security Council attempted in 1948 to outline basic U.S. objectives in the event of war with the Soviet Union (NSC *20/4, 1948*). At the urging of the Joint Chiefs of Staff, efforts to specify "war aims" more precisely were renewed several times from 1950 through 1954, without real success (NSC *79, 1950*; annexes to NSC *153/1, 1952*, NSC *162/2, 1953*, and NSC *5410/1, 1954*). see *Foreign Relations of the United States 1948*, vol. 1: *General; The United Nations* (Washington, 1976), pp. 662–66; *FRUS 1950*, vol. 1: *National Security Affairs, Foreign Economic Policy* (1977), pp. 390–93; *FRUS 1952–1954*, vol. 2: *National Security Affairs* (1984), pp. 197–201, 386, 596–97, 644–46.

58. *Report of the Secretary of Defense, 1990*, pp. 3, 32.

59. Secretary of Defense Caspar W. Weinberger, *Department of Defense Annual Report to the Congress, Fiscal Year 1988* (Washington, 1987), pp. 47, 46.

60. A. Savel'yev, "The Prevention of War and Deterrence: Warsaw Pact and NATO Approaches," *MEiMO*, no. 6 (June 1989), p. 21.

limiting war aims and limiting and controlling the conduct of war. Perhaps the most frank and authoritative statement remains one made in the confidential General Staff journal in 1970 by Colonel General Mikhail Povaly, then recently deputy chief of the General Staff and chief of the Main Operations Directorate—the chief Soviet war planner. General Povaly emphasized that "in studying the problem of the interrelationship of policy and military strategy Soviet military science takes as its foundation the *real* political aims of a war." In stunning contrast to the standard Soviet military and political pronouncements of the 1960s tying any clash of the capitalist and communist world social-political systems to all-out general nuclear war, Povaly (citing the late Marshal Boris Shaposhnikov) stated: "The strategic leadership works out a concrete war plan against certain and probable enemies. Under conditions when a fierce struggle is waged between the two social systems, *the war plan must be flexible and correspond to different political combinations.*" Povaly noted that "the interrelation of policy and military strategy exists continuously," and that "the political aim of a war" must correspond to "strategic capabilities," and if that has not been properly calculated it may require "limiting or changing the political objective." Accordingly, "Strategic concepts and strategic planning *before and during a war* must always be brought into correspondence with the interests of policy."[61]

Nonetheless, though Soviet military and political leaders have at least until recently assumed that while local—even major—nonnuclear wars might be limited, any war between the United States and NATO and the Soviet Union and Warsaw Pact would probably be unlimited, primarily because they have conceived of direct war between the two great coalitions as possible only if the United States had decided to launch such a war, and that it would not do so for less-than-unlimited aims. The only exception was a war initiated by the United States under its own ground rules for controlled, limited nuclear war to defeat the Soviet Union without a full nuclear exchange. This, however, has always been seen by the Soviets as unacceptable as well as unlikely to be kept limited. Nor would it be practical to control and terminate a nuclear war. Thus, as an influential consultant to the Central Committee put it in *Kommunist:*

61. Povaly, *Voyennaya mysl'*, no. 7 (July 1970), pp. 10–11; emphasis added.

The concepts and doctrines of controlled scale, duration and intensity of nuclear war developed by the Pentagon are completely devoid of foundation. By its very nature nuclear war is such that its duration and intensity cannot be subjected to regulation. Even concluding wars in the past was not all that simple to plan consciously. A nuclear war may be extremely fast-moving, and may begin and end without the taking of political decisions. A conflict situation can be settled under conditions of general peace, but settling a nuclear conflict once it has broken out has doubtful chances of success.[62]

The Soviets have seriously misjudged American interest in "limited nuclear options" and limited nuclear war, attributing to such U.S. thinking and strategy an interest in finding an acceptable way to use the power of nuclear weapons while avoiding nuclear devastation of the United States. Their own rejection of resort to any use of nuclear weapons, and firm determination never to start a war, engenders deep suspicion of U.S. insistence on possible first use, and limited use, of nuclear weapons. They have failed to recognize that the United States has been interested in limited nuclear use not as a possible option and choice over nonuse, but only as a better alternative than unlimited use in general nuclear war, if vital interests required resort to such weapons to defeat a major conventional attack.

The American concept of deterrence does, however, require carrying over into the conduct of war the idea of escalation to convince an attacking enemy to back down. The new Soviet thinking on the prevention of war, in contrast, carries over into the conduct of war the idea of de-escalation to seek its early termination. Thus instead of controlled application of force, it calls for controlled restraint on the use of force and for corresponding limits on aims.

In practice, the distinctions at present may not be so great. Neither Soviet nor U.S. operational doctrine adequately meets criteria for a war termination strategy. A Soviet strategic analyst at one of the leading academic institutes has noted that despite statements of the new defensive doctrine, "nonetheless the USSR is compelled to preserve its nuclear arms as a deterrent force against possible U.S. attack or attempts at nuclear blackmail. Thus, one can state that today on the purely military plane the strategic arms of the USSR

62. Yu. Zhilin, "The Factor of Time in the Nuclear Age," *Kommunist*, no. 11 (July 1986), p. 120.

are called upon to perform approximately the same missions as those of the United States, with the one substantial difference that the leadership of the Soviet Union in distinction to the American considers future reliance on nuclear weapons as a [deterrent] means of preventing war to be without prospect and extremely dangerous."[63]

One important respect in which new thinking in both the Soviet Union and the United States has almost certainly failed to affect actual war plans is the need to spare the enemy's leadership and command and control so that authorities can reach political agreement and military control to terminate the conflict. To the contrary, military doctrine on both sides has long specified the enemy command and control system at all levels, and above all at the central national and military level, as a priority target. The aim is clear and militarily sound: to disorganize and weaken the enemy's ability to strike (or to strike back) with its forces, optimally to "decapitate" the enemy.

In contrast, the new political thinking on security in both countries emphasizes the need to spare central command and control authorities and communications. Andrei Kokoshin, one of the leading civilian strategic analysts, has thus described as one of the key elements of strategic stability:

> Not only the structure and means of the sides, but also the systems of observation (intelligence), command, control, and communications must be such that in case of the outbreak of armed conflict they would give the highest state leadership and military command of both sides the possibility to receive in real time the necessary and sufficient information on the state of the conflict in order to terminate it at the lowest possible level.[64]

The Soviets are also well aware of the importance of developing and ensuring one's own command, control, and communications (C^3) systems so as to allow the control necessary for management and termination of conflict. One argument they see for land-based ICBMs in contrast to sea-based SLBMs, notwithstanding possible greater vulnerability, is the much greater constant communications

63. Savel'yev, *MEiMO*, no. 6 (June 1989), p. 24.

64. Kokoshin, *Novoye vremya*, no. 33 (August 12, 1988), p. 19. For a more extended analysis, see A. Arbatov and A. Savel'yev, "The System of Command, Control, and Communications as a Factor in Strategic Stability," *MEiMO*, no. 12 (December 1987), pp. 12–23.

and control over land-based systems, not only better ensuring against unsanctioned firing, but also providing greater flexibility for central wartime control.

Soviet analysts have also identified other aspects of traditional war waging that contradict criteria for moving toward war termination. "In case of the outbreak of a global nuclear conflict . . . precisely the striving for damage limitation can even carry the war to that global level, having completely blocked the possibility for de-escalation of the conflict."[65] De-escalation is particularly important to prevent crossing the nuclear threshhold. Soviet analysts stress the need for "an effective mechanism for the 'de-escalation' of conflicts, that is, preventing their growing into nuclear war."[66]

These considerations also apply to some extent to possible nuclear or nonnuclear military engagements and campaigns in Europe and other continental theaters of military operations.

Soviet proposals for new East-West European security arrangements are intended to launch a process that ultimately can supersede confrontation of the NATO and Warsaw Pact alliances. This aim serves a range of political and military purposes, including in particular an effort to substitute a new basis for their own security to compensate for the sharp decline that has already occurred in the role of the Warsaw Pact, as well as to reduce the role of NATO. Among these purposes, however, is also creation of a security regime in Europe that would make war less likely, and if it arose, more amenable to control and termination. Thus since mid-1988 the Soviet Union has been urging creation of a multilateral risk reduction center in Europe, both to provide a mechanism that can help clarify uncertainties that could contribute to crises, and to help build a pattern of East-West cooperation in the security realm. For the same reasons they have supported the development of confidence-building and security-building measures, and discussions of military doctrine.

The traditional Soviet view, unchallenged until the late 1980s, was authoritatively and well stated in the General Staff Academy lectures of the mid-1970s: "If aggressors attempt to invade our Socialist homeland and attack the national interests of the Soviet Union, decisive military action will be conducted for the complete destruction of the enemy by using the full military power of the

65. Savel'yev, *MEiMO*, no. 6 (June 1989), p. 28.
66. S. Kortunov, "Stability in a Nuclear World," *Mezhdunarodnaya zhizn'*, no. 2 (February 1990), p. 9.

country and all forces and means at the disposal of our State. The Soviet Army and Navy will rapidly initiate dynamic offensive actions when the enemy invades our borders."[67]

As discussed earlier, this view was sharply changed in 1987 to an initial defensive strategy, with a debate over the role of a subsequent counteroffensive. Among the main arguments of the new thinkers was precisely the need to control escalation and move toward termination of the war. This, in turn, requires abandoning the aim of complete defeat and destruction of the adversary's armed forces and substituting the much more limited aim of preventing the success of the enemy attack. A particularly clear statement is worth citing at length:

> The objective of defeat of the armed forces of the enemy also, in our view, requires serious reexamination in light of the declared defensive thrust of the military doctrine of the USSR and the Warsaw Pact. This conclusion is related in particular to the fact that such a defeat is not possible without a strong counteroffensive potential and, as the experience of the Great Fatherland War bears out, without a significant quantitative superiority in the armed forces. In that connection it is necessary to take into consideration that from the political and, what is more, the military point of view as well, that mission is insufficient to existing realities. From the political standpoint, in that connection we do not see such contradictions between the countries of East and West as would require placing on the line the very existence of these countries; from a military standpoint, "success" in defeating the armed forces of the enemy [that is, NATO forces in Europe] would inevitably lead to escalation to the nuclear level with all the consequences that would flow from that.
>
> Hence the transformation of the mission indicated to a mission of repelling the attack on the level of conventional arms, and refraining from prompt counteroffensive actions . . . would best correspond to the proclaimed defensive principles of the construction of the armed forces. In this connection, special attention must be placed on the question of localizing the conflict and not permitting its horizontal escalation (for example, from land to sea theaters). All this would give time and possibility for political settlement [of the war].[68]

Dr. Aleksandr Savel'yev is a civilian strategic analyst, and it is clear from this discussion that he believes some further change was

67. *Voroshilov Lectures*, vol. 1, p. 263.
68. Savel'yev, *MEiMO*, no. 6 (June 1989), pp. 28–29.

probably necessary in Soviet operational military doctrine and strategy, at least at the time he wrote. The fact that changes were occurring in the statements of military leaders suggested that the kind of change Savel'yev was arguing for was under way.

Some more recent military discussions have dealt more directly with this issue, and specifically in the context of war termination. Most explicit and detailed have been several articles by Lieutenant General Vladimir Serebryannikov, a professor at the Lenin Military-Political Academy and writer on military doctrine. In discussing the role of the army in prevention of war, he has noted that it has become more difficult "at the operational level to combine steady resolve and active combat in defeating an invading enemy with preparedness to stop the conflict if the aggressor gives up his intentions and aims [of aggression]." He noted that the task of "terminating a conflict that has broken out has become exceptionally complex in connection with the diversity of ways in which events can develop," and "of course specific actions will be determined by the situation. But it is clear," he emphasized, "that no matter how the other side were to conduct itself in these conditions, the defensive doctrine requires of us maximum activeness both in the struggle with the aggressor and in measures to terminate the conflict."[69] And in another discussion, General Serebryannikov has also emphasized that under the new Soviet military doctrine it is essential "even in the course of combat to be prepared for even the slightest opportunity to terminate the war (conflict) on the sole condition of not violating the territorial integrity and sovereignty of the country and its allies."[70]

A Soviet war aim of ending any war as soon as possible on the basis of preserving or restoring the status quo ante is of course entirely consonant with the identical Western aim. Such an approach is legitimated by the Soviet shift to a defensive strategic concept, as well as being implicit in the conclusion that there can be no winner in a nuclear war. Nonetheless, its application to the military-technical level of military doctrine is a major and important step. The process is undoubtedly not complete. As General Serebryannikov

69. Lt. Gen. Avn. V. Serebryannikov, "The Prevention of War: The Army's Contribution," *Kommunist vooruzhennykh sil* (Communist of the Armed Forces; hereafter *KVS*), no. 17 (September 1989), pp. 26–27.

70. Lt. Gen. [Avn.] Vladimir Serebryannikov, "Dilemmas and Priorities . . . ," *Novoye vremya*, no. 12 (March 17, 1989), p. 17.

put it, to "strengthen the role and importance of the defense factor in preventing war means ... to teach methods of preventing and terminating military conflicts."[71]

General Serebryannikov has acknowledged:

A scientific elaboration of the theory of preventing war must be realized in the framework of teachings on war and peace, military science, military doctrine, and the military art. In essence, the theory and practical means of action of an army to prevent war are not yet worked out, inasmuch as in the past all attention was concentrated on working out means of conducting military operations. There are only weak suggestions in the history of military-theoretical thought on the potential by means of a strong defense and skillful use of the army for preventing, delaying, or terminating a war.[72]

General Larionov has suggested one novel approach. Noting the extensive use by both sides of military exercises and military games to assist in learning how best to wage war, he suggests "alternative security games," the aim of which would be to "work out procedures for climbing down a ladder of de-escalation from the most explosive situation" to prevent wars from breaking out, or to terminate them. He has further advanced the interesting idea that such games might be played by retired NATO and Warsaw Pact military personnel and security analysts.[73]

How has this new thinking on controlling and terminating a war affected actual Soviet military strategy and planning? That is the most important and most difficult question for each side to answer as it observes the other.

Marshal Sergei Akhromeyev has disclosed on several occasions since mid-1988 a very important application of this thinking to current Soviet strategic planning. While obviously Soviet contingent war plans are not available to confirm what he has said, everything that the Soviet Union has been doing is consistent. According to Akhromeyev, under the new Soviet doctrine the defensive stage of a war arising in Europe would last about three weeks. That should, in his view, provide enough time for political leaders to end the conflict. If the war continued, he said on one occasion in mid-1988,

71. Ibid.
72. Serebryannikov, *KVS*, no. 17 (September 1989), p. 25.
73. Maj. Gen. Valentin Larionov, "Combat Readiness and Security: Will People Stop Playing at War?" *Novoye vremya*, no. 37 (September 8, 1989), p. 14. As noted earlier, Larionov himself has recently retired.

a counteroffensive to expel hostile invading forces would follow. On another occasion later in 1988 when a General Staff Academy professor referred to this same concept and spoke as though a counteroffensive would come after about twenty days, Akhromeyev reportedly interrupted to reemphasize the need and expectation that the conflict could be ended during that period.[74] In an interview for a Soviet military readership in late 1989, Akhromeyev made similar statements, referring to the defensive stage as one that "might go on for several weeks." He then stated: "During that time the political leaders of the Warsaw Pact will, we expect, take measures to confine the emerging conflict and to prevent the expansion of the war. If political efforts are unable to terminate the conflict, then it is in effect impossible to predict now what direction events might follow from then on. The sides would deploy their military forces according to wartime plans."[75]

This development in Soviet military planning guidance represents an important step in Soviet efforts to prevent the continuation or escalation of a war if one should break out. As an indication that the Soviet political and military leadership is thinking in such precise operational terms about active diplomacy for war termination in the event of hostilities, it is unique (with respect to Soviet *or* Western strategic wartime planning), although quite in keeping with a long-standing Soviet recognition of the interrelationship between military strategy and diplomacy.

Although Marshal Akhromeyev did not spell out the terms for a political resolution of the conflict, quite properly given the range of unknown circumstances involved in any outbreak of war, his reference to expelling invading forces is consonant with General Serebryannikov's specific reference to maintaining "the territorial integrity and sovereignty" of the Soviet Union and its allies, and with the avowed defensive purpose of Soviet military doctrine.

A military planning guidance to prepare for a three-week defen-

74. Marshal Akhromeyev made this statement during his visit to the United States in July 1988, on an occasion when I was present. He also made such a statement during Defense Secretary Frank Carlucci's visit to the General Staff Academy in Moscow in August 1988 (information from a participant present). Colonel General Nikolai Chervov of the General Staff also told me in 1988 that this was current Soviet doctrine and guidance.

75. "Our Military Doctrine," An Interview with Marshal S. F. Akhromeyev by Novosti Military Commentator V. Pogrebenkov, *Agitator armii i flota* (Army and Navy Agitator [Political Propagandist]), no. 24 (December 1989), p. 3.

sive stage in order to permit political termination of any conflict that might arise leaves open the possibility of either a very geographically limited counterstrike or a more far-reaching counteroffensive if the war were to continue. Nonetheless, the Soviet decision in 1988 to offer far greater reductions in Soviet and Warsaw Pact arms and forces than those in the West, including the whole of the European part of the Soviet Union, in order to reduce forces to a balance between the two alliances in Europe, could only reflect a readiness to abandon serious plans for an offensive or even a counteroffensive to the English Channel.

One gain in stability of the Soviet defensive strategy, not to my knowledge noted in any Soviet source, would be the reduced likelihood in such a circumstance of Western escalation to use of nuclear weapons. If Soviet and Pact forces were not advancing deep into NATO territory, but remained on the defensive essentially in their own territory, any perceived need for, or realistic possibility of decision for, NATO resort to nuclear weapons would be greatly reduced—it would in fact probably be nil. That would facilitate controlling and terminating any conflict that arose.

The Revolution of '89 in Eastern Europe marks the collapse of the Warsaw Pact both as a putative military threat to the West and as the instrument of a Soviet or Pact offensive or prompt counteroffensive in the event of war. If war were to break out during the transitional early 1990s, the Soviet Union would have no alternative but to assume the defensive. By the mid-1990s there will no doubt be a large semi-neutral zone in central Europe east of Germany, with greatly reduced Soviet forces—if any—in the eastern part of Germany and Poland, more for political than military reasons, and none elsewhere beyond Soviet borders. The Warsaw Pact may or may not survive for some time, perhaps with reduced membership, but it will constitute only a weak forward defensive space for the Soviet Union at best. Even the Soviet borders may have moved eastward from one or more of the Baltic states.

So long as a Gorbachev-line leadership remains in power in Moscow, and East-West relations continue to develop normally, Soviet defense policy is unlikely to change. If a hard-line conservative leadership came to power in the Soviet Union, it might seek to build its military forces back up, but still only on Soviet territory. In that case a contingent offensive strategic concept for a war of defense might be resuscitated, this time directed not at wiping American and

German military power from the continent, but at restoring a Soviet defensive line at the center of Europe rather than on the Byelorussian and Ukrainian borders of the USSR. For the foreseeable future, however, the Soviet Union is essentially compelled to rely on the defensive strategy that it had adopted by choice before the Revolution of '89.

Looking to the more favorable, and I hope more likely, future, the new Soviet thinking on security gradually implemented since 1985 calls for increasing movement toward a mutual security relationship with the rest of the world. This conception is based on further development of the concepts of disarmament, war prevention, and control and termination of any conflict. As Gorbachev's adviser Aleksandr Yakovlev noted several years ago: "The formation of a universal system of international security presupposes the development of *preventive diplomacy*, called upon to prevent the [outbreak and] escalation of conflicts. These questions demand close scientific research."[76] They do indeed, and although he was addressing a Soviet audience, the problem and contribution to the solution are also ours.

76. A. N. Yakovlev, "Achievement of a Qualitatively New State of Soviet Society and the Social Sciences," *Vestnik Akademii Nauk SSSR* (Herald of the Academy of Sciences of the USSR), no. 6 (June 1987), p. 76. Emphasis in original.

Chapter Six

Implications for U.S. Policy
and Strategy

THE TRANSFORMATION OF world politics, including in particular the political situation in the Soviet Union and Europe, cannot fail to have major implications for U.S. policy and strategy. Deterrence of nuclear war and of possible aggressive Soviet moves remains an American policy objective. In no way, however, can it in the 1990s and beyond compare with the centrality and sometimes urgent priority attributed to this objective in the last four decades. Containment of Soviet expansionistic impulses—real and imagined—was the cornerstone of American policy during the cold war. It is no longer because that threat is manifestly less real, and other problems clearly present more actual challenges. To some extent, the Soviet threat, the communist threat, and the threat of war have in fact declined; to some extent, it is our overexcited past perceptions of such threats that have now been brought into line with realities that were never as threatening as they seemed.

In the present study, I have examined Soviet concepts of deterrence and the prevention of war and their similarities and differences with American thinking. The new Soviet thinking of the Gorbachev period and the remarkable recasting of the Soviet concept of security, and hence of the role of military power, commands special attention. Important processes of this change in Soviet political and military thinking, and in the military and political situation, are still under way. Nonetheless, it is not too early to address the questions of their implications for U.S. policy.

U.S.-Soviet Relations

The most immediate impact of changes in Soviet, and American, concepts and perceptions of the central security issue—the prevention of war—is naturally on the state of relations between the two countries. Ever since the waning of the alliance in the closing phases of World War II, security concerns about each other have been uppermost in the thinking of both countries. Since the escalation in 1945–50 of political conflict into cold war, dealings between the two countries have been dominated by an adversarial political-military relationship, ranging from uneasy stalemate through occasional sharp confrontations to periods of lessened tension. This adversarial relationship was based on real conflicts of interest; it was not imagined. But it was exacerbated and sustained by perceived threats that were greater than the underlying realities.

Today for the first time there is progress not only in dealing with particular problems, but in dismantling the sources of the conflictual relationship, both the exaggerated fears and the real clashes of interests of the two sides. While some Americans remain wary of, and others are eager to welcome, this momentous change, there is general recognition that it is occurring.

One explanation is that the U.S. policies of deterrence and containment have succeeded, and the new Soviet leadership today finally recognizes the futility of attempts to seek world domination. We have waged well and won the cold war. Not only is this explanation the easiest to square with our past conceptions; it is also satisfying because it justifies our policies of peace through strength and requires the least revision of our perceptions of Soviet aims. The change is attributed to Soviet recognition of the inadequacy of their capabilities, and thus does not place in question our traditional view of their ambitions. Evident Soviet economic difficulties, overextension in the third world, and presumed efficacy of our policies of "staying the course" in modernizing our military deterrent are regarded as having led the Soviets to agree to strategic arms reductions, to reduce their armed forces in Europe, to withdraw from Afghanistan, to contribute to resolving regional conflicts in Central America, Africa, and Southeast Asia, to seek normal political and economic relations, and to concentrate on domestic economic reform. Under this view they may (or will) again rebuild their military power once their economic strength has been restored. A strong U.S. military deterrent remains the key.

Another explanation holds that the new Soviet leadership has reassessed the world, now recognizes economic and political strengths in the West and weaknesses at home, and sees security as depending more on mutual reduction of perceived threats than on constant competitive building of military deterrents. Under this view, the Soviet changes are owing not only to recognition of inadequacy of means, but to a new setting of goals as well as priorities. Withdrawal from Afghanistan is in recognition not only of futility, but also of error in having gone in. Eliminating twice as many intermediate-range nuclear missiles as the United States is recognition not of a surplus, but of an error in building a force in the first place that increased Western fears and military countermeasures. Asymmetrical, and unilateral, reductions in conventional forces in Europe (and in Asia, and in general) are made in recognition that building forces for fighting wars that must not be permitted to occur is both economically unsound and politically and even militarily unsound as well. While not necessarily making wars more likely, the concept of preparing to wage a range of possible wars did preserve tensions and fuel a continuing arms competition that kept alive the possibility of war escalating from uncontrollable conditions and that fed the political confrontation.

The second explanation is far more persuasive. For one thing, it reflects what the Soviets are saying to one another, and more openly than ever. More important, it reflects more fully and accurately what they are doing. The first explanation can answer why Soviet leaders have ventured upon economic reform, but not why they have embarked on far-reaching political democratization, or why they have permitted and even encouraged the deposing of communist rule in Eastern Europe and retraction of the Soviet military security frontier from the former iron curtain to the borders of the Soviet Union—even, in the Baltic states, possibly accepting a retraction of the Soviet frontier.

What should the United States do? President Bush, with wide consensus support, has responded (after initial hesitation) by moving to normalize relations with the Soviet Union. This includes expanding political consultation, recognizing that the Soviet Union as well as the United States has legitimate security interests in Europe, ending economic warfare with the Soviet Union and taking steps toward restoration of nondiscriminatory economic and trade relations, and engaging in arms reduction negotiations.

Normalization of relations may sound like very little. Yet against the history of the forty-odd years of the cold war, it is an important and due step. "Normal" relations by definition does not mean a complete absence of competitive interests and frictions. But it does mean that relations are based on mutual respect for what the Soviets now call "a balance of interests," and on the need to compromise differences. While trust is not automatically extended, it is also not automatically excluded. And trust can grow under normal relations.

Preventing war should be based primarily on eliminating the sources of a possible war, rather than merely controlling the symptoms of a permanent ailment. Nuclear deterrence will no doubt remain a bedrock element of the U.S.-Soviet relationship for the foreseeable future. More specific implications for U.S. military, alliance, and arms control policies will be discussed presently. But while mutual deterrence will remain an element in the relationship, even an essential element, it need not and should not be in the forefront. Indeed, the military relationship as a whole should recede in prominence.

As the bipolar, cold-war-driven, militarily mobilized world of the past several decades is replaced by a multipolar, economically driven, less-militarized world, the United States and the Soviet Union may find new challenges not only in their bilateral relations but in their respective responses to other situations and other countries. In some cases the governments may have common interests and even engage in joint action. Both may see new virtues in contributing to the role of international organizations.

Elements of cooperation and competition have always coexisted in U.S.-Soviet relations, in confrontation and détente. Even in the depths of the cold war, there was a common interest in averting war. And in the vaunted détente of the 1970s each side "waged détente" against the other to the ultimate disadvantage of the process as well as to the interests of both powers. Today, not only have cooperative elements again come to the fore, but in the long run the relationship can even develop into a predominantly cooperative one. Détente (already restored in fact, if not in name) can even develop into entente.

The NATO and Warsaw Pact Alliances

The cold war engendered the confrontation not only of the United States and the Soviet Union, but of the two alliance coalitions that they headed. That situation was new for both sides. While alliances are almost as old as history, neither the United States nor the Soviet Union had anticipated or even previously belonged to a permanent (that is, long-term) peacetime alliance. But of course, despite the absence of war it was not really a peacetime situation; it was the cold war.

The NATO alliance, it is sufficient to recall, came into being in 1949 chiefly as a reassurance of American commitment to European defense, in the wake of the communist subversion of Czechoslovakia and Stalin's effort to strangle West Berlin. After the outbreak of the Korean War in 1950, it developed as a functioning military alliance for deterrence and defense, ultimately reliant on American nuclear deterrence.

In 1967 NATO (with some European qualms) bowed to American pressure to adopt the strategy of flexible response, calling for graduated deterrents based on initial conventional defense in case of attack, resort to a limited nuclear response if and as necessary, and finally escalation to general nuclear war if necessary. To support this doctrine and strategy, efforts were made to ensure a mounting range of strengthened conventional, tactical nuclear, and long-range nuclear capabilities for selective or extensive employment if required.

Soviet military doctrine and strategy also evolved from the mid-1960s into the 1970s, in important part in response to the Western adoption of flexible response (as well as to the underlying cause of both, the evolution of strategic nuclear parity). The Western reaction to the Soviet acquisition of modern conventional as well as nuclear forces was not, however, to see a new balance of deterrents, but new threats.

Thus the elaboration of an array of nuclear and conventional military forces on each side was seen by the other as steps taken in active pursuit of new "options" for compellence, that is, intimidation and possibly even military action, rather than for strengthening deterrence. Each side at the same time not only regarded its own actions as defensive, but assumed the other side would recognize this benign purpose.

As recently as mid-1989, although before the "Revolution of '89" in Eastern Europe, NATO reaffirmed graduated deterrence as its "strategy for the prevention of war": "For the foreseeable future, there is no alternative to the Alliance strategy for the prevention of war. This is a strategy of deterrence based upon an appropriate mix of adequate and effective nuclear and conventional forces."[1] While that policy still stands, "the foreseeable future" has been unusually short.[2] The possibility of building European security arrangements that do not rely so heavily on military deterrents may grow, and the appropriate mix of military forces is already changing rapidly.

NATO has a viability not entirely dependent on its military deterrent strategy. It can play a continuing important security role on other bases, and it will clearly be under challenge in the 1990s to develop these other roles.

The Warsaw Pact, established in 1955 (six years after NATO), was extended in April 1985 for a further thirty years. Today, some five years later, most analysts doubt that it will last even to the tenth anniversary of its renewal. While its strategic rationale is not quite so explicitly stated in terms of deterrence as is that of NATO, the similarity is substantial: "Proceeding from the level of the threat of war, the Warsaw Pact member states will continue to take the necessary measure to maintain their collective defense capability at the requisite level."[3] The one significant divergence is that in contrast NATO's rationale is not tied to the existence of the opposing alliance. In practice, by the spring of 1990 the Warsaw Pact members were no longer maintaining "their collective defense capability at the requisitē level." As a cohesive military alliance, the Warsaw Pact had collapsed. Its future as a political alliance is uncertain.[4]

The rapid disintegration of the Warsaw Pact was due to the inter-

1. "Declaration of the Heads of State and Government Participating in the Meeting of the North Atlantic Council in Brussels, 29th–30th May 1989," in *NATO Review*, vol. 37 (June 1989), p. 28.

2. The United States in particular has not begun to reexamine its long-standing assumptions about a basic requirement for deterrence, and equating deterrence with military strategy. Thus even in 1990 General Colin Powell, chairman of the Joint Chiefs of Staff, referred to deterrence as "the cornerstone of our military strategy." Gen. Colin Powell, USA, Statement to the Military Doctrine Seminar of the Talks on Confidence- and Security-Building Measures, Vienna, January 16, 1990, p. 1. And President George Bush, in his first annual statement on U.S. national security strategy, identified as the first point in U.S. strategy to "deter any aggression that could threaten its security and, should deterrence fail, repel or defeat military attack and end conflict on terms favorable to the United States, its interests and allies." *National Security Strategy of the United States*, White House (March 1990), p. 2.

3. "Communiqué on the Meeting of Top Party and State Figures of the Warsaw Pact Member States," *Pravda*, April 27, 1985, p. 1.

4. See Raymond L. Garthoff, "The Warsaw Pact Today—And Tomorrow?" *Brookings Review*, vol. 8 (Summer 1990), pp. 35–40.

nal political transformation of its member states—including, less dramatic only by comparison with the others, the Soviet Union. The new Soviet view of military requirements in Europe had permitted the Soviet political reevaluation that in turn spurred the revolutionary political changes in Eastern Europe.

In a very real sense, Gorbachev has concluded, and acted decisively on the basis, that military deterrence of NATO attack was no longer necessary. NATO councils have not yet reached such a conclusion, but the evaporation of the Warsaw Pact military threat could not escape notice, and rhetorical reaffirmations of the need to maintain NATO's military deterrent posture are less and less convincing. Increasingly, the rationales of "stabilization" and "insurance" are replacing deterrence, and the underlying purpose of the American military presence is increasingly an amalgam of American reassurance of those Europeans who may still seek it, and perhaps unconscious reassurance of ourselves that we are still wanted and needed by the Europeans.

The NATO decision in July 1990 to underline that any first use of nuclear weapons would be only as a "last resort" was politically helpful. Revision of the forward defense strategy was a due and welcome move. So, too, are steps to eliminate short-range ground-based nuclear delivery systems. Real debate over the role of nuclear deterrence has, however, not even begun.

There is a risk that the United States will try *too* hard to keep NATO alive and in a central role in Europe. If this is perceived by some Europeans as erecting an obstacle to pan-European normalization and to the development of European security institutions, it could be unnecessarily divisive and could work to the disadvantage both of the United States and of NATO. In addition, if the United States invests its efforts too singlemindedly to buttressing NATO, it may retard the development of the Conference on Security and Cooperation in Europe (CSCE) and other European processes and institutions that can and should play an increasing role in furtherance of European security. NATO has been a mainstay of U.S. and Western European security for the last forty years; it will not be for the next forty. We should look forward, and we should move forward.

NATO has a good chance of survival to the end of the decade and perhaps beyond *if* it accepts a new mission and a new conception of security. The Warsaw Pact has little chance of lasting out the decade, but if it has a future it also lies in a transitional role of reassurance to the Soviet Union (especially military and other conservatives), and conceivably a transitional role (along with NATO) in buttressing CSCE and Conventional Forces in Europe (CFE) confidence-building and security-building and arms verification activities. But new European institutions that include the United States and the Soviet Union in their membership as well as all European states should come increasingly to the fore.

U.S. Military Policy

At least until recently, an American secretary of defense could say: "In a word, our basic defense strategy is deterrence."[5] To be sure, in more than a word, Secretary of Defense Caspar Weinberger made perfectly clear that he meant more than prevention of war: "We seek not only to deter actual aggression but also to prevent *coercion* of the United States, its allies, and friends through the *threat* of aggression."[6] Secretary Richard Cheney has reiterated the standing U.S. objective: "to deter military attack against the United States, U.S. allies, and other U.S. interests; and to defeat such attack should deterrence fail."[7]

There remains a very cautious and reluctant strain in the judgments of successive secretaries of defense on changes in Soviet military doctrine and national policy. As Secretary Frank Carlucci put it in 1988: "Regardless of Gorbachev's stated intentions, Soviet military capability continues to grow, and U.S. policy decisions must be made in light of these growing capabilities. Intentions can change overnight. . . . We must ensure that we continue fielding forces capable of deterring aggression at all levels."[8]

While the basic objective of deterrence remains, however, no

5. Secretary of Defense Caspar W. Weinberger, *Department of Defense Annual Report to the Congress, Fiscal Year 1987* (Washington, 1986), p. 32.

6. Secretary of Defense Caspar W. Weinberger, *Department of Defense Annual Report to the Congress, Fiscal Year 1988* (Washington, 1987), pp. 42–43; emphasis in original. The unconvincing example he cites is that "the Soviets seek to dominate Western Europe and Japan without having to fire a shot" to have "the fruits of war without actual conflict" (p. 43).

7. Secretary of Defense Dick Cheney, *Department of Defense Annual Report to the President and the Congress, January 1990* (Washington, 1990), p. 2.

8. Secretary of Defense Frank C. Carlucci, *Department of Defense Annual Report to the Congress, Fiscal Year 1989* (Washington, 1988), p. 24.

longer can it be equated with our overall defense strategy. It may be necessary, but it is certainly not sufficient.

In reevaluating U.S. defense policy and posture for the years ahead, planners must clearly prepare for, and seek to deter, contingencies that may never occur. They must also recognize that preventing war is a much broader objective than military preparedness and deterrence. Precisely because intentions are the crux of deterrence, and because intentions are affected by both political and military interactions and perceptions, deterrence and war prevention are too important to be left to these who produce and consume estimates of relative military capabilities.

The United States and NATO must take into account such developments as the massive retraction of Soviet military power from central and eastern Europe. Not only have all sixty non-Soviet Warsaw Pact divisions in effect been subtracted from the total available to Soviet command (and up to half are being disbanded), but by 1995 all of the thirty Soviet divisions previously deployed west of the Soviet frontier will no longer be there. All Soviet nuclear weapons will be back on Soviet territory. Even within the European USSR Soviet forces and major weapons will be reduced, in part by significant unilateral decisions, probably further by agreement in the CFE negotiations.

Strategic force reductions under the strategic arms reduction talks (START) agreement will be a modest, but useful, beginning that can lead to much larger prospective reductions. Public attention has only gradually begun to focus on the fact that although Ronald Reagan and Mikhail Gorbachev agreed in 1985 to conclude a START agreement reducing strategic warheads by 50 percent, the actual net reductions under the draft treaty will be much less— probably about 25 percent by the United States and 30 percent by the Soviet Union. The reason is that some warheads, such as those carried by sea-launched cruise missiles, are excluded altogether from the ceilings, or are counted only nominally (for example, a heavy bomber carrying twenty bombs and short-range attack missiles counts as only one warhead; a bomber carrying twenty air-launched cruise missiles counts as only ten warheads). These changes *all* favor U.S. systems; the Soviet Union would clearly prefer lower actual ceilings. The generous discounting of these systems does not bode well for future larger reductions, and is even being used to argue for additional buildups (for example, one argument advanced for the

B-2 stealth bomber is that it would permit larger forces given the generous START counting rules).

The most serious dissonance between U.S. military policy and the requirements of strategic stability is not, however, in numbers of strategic forces or even their growing counterforce capabilities. Nor is it the subject of arms negotiation. It is a disturbing trend in U.S. war planning to target the Soviet leadership.

Ever since the Carter administration's Presidential Directive 59 (PD–59) in 1980, but especially under the Reagan and Bush administrations since 1983, the strategic nuclear war plan, the Single Integrated Operations Plan (SIOP), has given greater emphasis and priority than before to targeting the Soviet leadership, in the name of enhancing deterrence. The current plan, SIOP 6F, which went into effect on October 1, 1989, under the Bush administration, carries this tendency to its greatest extreme.[9]

Although in theory targeting leadership can enhance deterrence, it is very doubtful that such action is either needed or effective in calculations that could potentially lead to a Soviet decision to attack. Leadership targeting is at least as likely to help pressure an enemy into preemption in order to avoid having his command and control decapitated. While that risk of preemption may be low, knowledge of such an American war plan would probably lead the Soviets to retaliate fully and promptly to any use by NATO of strategic nuclear weapons. Moreover, even in peacetime it could lead Soviet officials to predelegate authority to fire under certain conditions, thus weakening assurance of full control in a crisis. It would surely reduce possibilities for de-escalation in case of a conflict and thus reduce possibilities for early termination of the conflict before it got out of control.

There is no better illustration of the unappreciated risks of giving priority to deterrence over considerations of crisis control, conflict de-escalation, and war termination. The issue is not, and should not be seen as, one of choosing between deterrence and other means of prevention of war. The need is to have a balanced perception of risks and a balance between preventing deliberate recourse to war and preventing or terminating an unpremeditated conflict.

Capabilities as well as intentions are changing. There are opportunities for significant cuts in U.S. forces even apart from any man-

9. For a detailed, informed, and thoughtful account, see Desmond Ball and Robert C. Toth, "Revising the SIOP: Taking War-Fighting to Dangerous Extremes," *International Security*, vol. 14 (Spring 1990), pp. 65–92.

dated in reciprocal negotiated reductions. Policymakers and others are already actively reevaluating force requirements.[10] There clearly should be, but is not yet, reconsideration of war planning to give greater recognition to war prevention and termination. The Soviet concepts of security, defense, deterrence, and prevention of war discussed in this study are a highly relevant but to date essentially unused additional input to such reevaluation.

In the past, characterizations of Soviet military doctrine introduced into the U.S. defense requirements debate have ranged from cautious discounting to caricature and outright misrepresentation.

The President's Commission on Strategic Forces (the Scowcroft Commission) in 1983 advanced the eminently sound observation that "deterrence is the set of beliefs in the minds of the Soviet leaders, given their own values and attitudes, about our capabilities and our will. It requires us to determine, as best we can, what would deter them from considering aggression, even in a crisis—not to determine what would deter us."[11] The commission report, though, failed to note that the Soviet Union also had a policy of deterrence and saw a parallel need to estimate what would be seen as an effective Soviet deterrent in Washington. Nor did the report examine the problem that forces procured to demonstrate a credible and assured *deterrent* capability also have a credible and assured *strike* capability. But at least it posed the need to try to put ourselves in the Soviet position in evaluating the U.S. deterrent. Efforts to do so, however, misfired badly.

Secretary Weinberger was very taken with the Scowcroft Commission observation. He quoted it in his next three annual reports to the Congress. But his understanding, or at least his presentation, of the Soviet view was that "we face an adversary whose leaders have, through their writings, force deployments, and exercises, given clear indications they believe that, under certain circumstances, war with the United States—even nuclear war—may be fought and won."[12]

10. For two thoughtful unofficial but expert analyses of feasible major reductions in U.S. defense programs and expenditures, see William W. Kaufmann, *Glasnost, Perestroika, and U.S. Defense Spending* (Brookings, 1990); and Defense Budget Task Force, *Restructuring the U.S. Military: Defense Needs in the 21st Century* (Washington: Committee for National Security and the Defense Budget Project, 1990).

11. *Report of the President's Commission on Strategic Forces*, Washington (April 1983), p. 3.

12. Secretary of Defense Caspar W. Weinberger, *Department of Defense Annual Report to the Congress, Fiscal Year 1985* (Washington, 1984), p. 27.

This judgment could be sustained only by very selective and distorted use of the record.

The Weinberger effort to develop a military policy providing "effective deterrence" led to justification of war-waging capabilities. By the next annual report, Weinberger was arguing for U.S. strategic strike capabilities that would persuade the Soviet leaders that "a nuclear conflict could lead to the destruction of those military, political, and economic assets they value most highly."[13] By 1986 Weinberger was saying that "incorporation of this insight [on the adversary's perception of deterrence] in operational defense planning for deterrence presents formidable intellectual and institutional problems we have not yet fully resolved," but he was not fazed. "But all the evidence we have suggests that preparing to deter an attack only by assembling forces adequate to deter us under similar conditions could provide too little to deter the Soviets."[14] The attempt to gauge a Soviet perspective on deterrence had become a blind alley.

I have reviewed this recent attempt to introduce recognition of the Soviet perspective into evaluating deterrence requirements to illustrate the difficulty in doing so, and the depth of the gap that has developed. Serious analysis of Soviet thinking, policy, and action in the security field, and of the deficiencies in reciprocal perceptions of the intentions and motivations of the other side, should at least prevent us from making the situation worse by such facile misunderstandings or misrepresentations as those advanced by Weinberger. One can even hope that enhanced understanding would permit actions that reduce mutual threat perceptions and permit reciprocal building-down of military forces that do not really contribute to mutual deterrence, by parallel unilateral actions as well as under negotiated arms agreements.

Arms Control and Disarmament

Negotiations on arms limitations and reductions are complex and difficult, even when there is serious interest and goodwill on both sides. But the process of negotiated arms reduction has several im-

13. Secretary of Defense Caspar W. Weinberger, *Department of Defense Annual Report to the Congress, Fiscal Year 1986* (Washington, 1985), p. 46.
14. Secretary of Defense Caspar W. Weinberger, *Department of Defense Annual Report to the Congress, Fiscal Year 1987* (Washington, 1986), p. 38.

portant advantages: commitment, verification, predictability, and the opportunity for step-by-step actions.

The present juncture is by far the most propitious ever for arms control. There is a rough equivalence or balance in military forces, permitting equivalent reductions. There are economic incentives, even pressures, on both sides to reduce military expenditures and resource outlays. There is political dialogue and momentum for further agreements. And there is unprecedented readiness to accept monitoring for verification, and an ongoing process of inspection. Confidence in compliance, shaken by some evasions and violations, and also by unwarranted accusations, is gradually being restored. Above all there is the Soviet acceptance of a new concept of security and a desire to reduce the role of military power, as well as levels of military forces.

The Soviet policy preference for minimal nuclear deterrence over an indefinite interim period should be engaged; it would also be in the American interest to reduce greatly the strategic nuclear arsenals of the two powers. Multilateral nuclear arms control and reductions will become necessary at a later stage. The far more difficult questions of whether eliminating nuclear weapons is feasible and would serve the interests of world security can be considered in the future.

The Reagan and Bush administrations have argued that continued nuclear weapons development and testing is a requirement imposed by nuclear deterrence. So far there has not been even a willingness to consider lowering the threshhold for underground nuclear tests below 150 kilotons. A reevaluation might well conclude that no further nuclear testing was really necessary. At the least, a threshhold reduced to 10 or 20 kilotons would permit continued proof testing and moderate modernization at verifiable levels.

There is an opportunity for agreement on effective constraints against antisatellite (ASAT) weapons and all weapons in space. Even some forms of strategic ballistic missile defense, if desired, would not be ruled out by barring the stationing of weapons in space.

Conventional arms reductions in Europe are proceeding apace on the Eastern side even before agreement on a CFE treaty. Nonetheless a CFE agreement remains important to assure predictability, future commitments, balance among countries, and verification. Also it can be built on for further reductions that may not otherwise occur in a balanced way.

Arms control and disarmament have far better prospects than ever before for success in reducing arms, curbing the arms competition, and contributing to strategic stability and security. This is true both with respect to the U.S.-Soviet arms balance and with respect to Europe. There are two principal reasons. First is the general (though not universal) realization in both East and West of the changed security relationship between NATO and the Soviet Union (and, to the extent still relevant, the Warsaw Pact). Second, and underlying the first, is the shift in Soviet outlook and policy under Gorbachev since the late 1980s. The Soviet Union, and the United States, have been serious about strategic arms limitation ever since parity was achieved in the late 1960s and early 1970s, as the ABM Treaty and SALT I Interim Agreement demonstrate. On the other hand, this interest has been cautious and conservative, as the Interim Agreement, SALT II Treaty, and START agreement show. Both sides have preferred to protect their own military programs and limit them only minimally, while seeking to limit maximally the forces of the other side. The result has been long periods of negotiation without agreements, and lowest-common-denominator accords. The Soviet Union has now begun to take much more resolute and far-reaching steps, as their positions in the Intermediate Nuclear Forces (INF) Treaty and Conventional Forces in Europe (CFE) negotiations demonstrate. There has not yet been comparable American readiness to constrain and reduce its forces, as the terms of the START agreement show (far less than the advertised goal of 50 percent reductions, owing to loopholes and arbitrary counting rules lopsidedly favoring the United States).

Apart from reductions in existing and planned forces, arms control can and should also be more responsive to other measures increasing stability. One prime example is the opportunity to ban antisatellite weapons. In the most recent negotiations, 1977–79, both sides— particularly the Soviets—were still protective of existing programs. In the 1980s the United States was unwilling to accept the Soviet proposals even to resume negotiation. Yet development and deployment of ASAT weapons would have a clearly destabilizing effect in times of crisis.

Other bilateral, multilateral, and even unilateral arms control measures can also contribute to stability. To cite but one important example, the single most effective additional measure to guard against the potentially disastrous consequences of accidental or unauthorized strategic missile launchings would be the installation of "command-destruct" mechanisms permitting the destruction or disabling of any missile or its warheads launched without authorization. At present, if one or more U.S. ICBM missiles were so launched, the president would have no recourse except to try to contact the Soviet authorities and say that he was sorry but some missiles were heading toward, say, Leningrad. Nor could the Soviets then do anything about it. Theoretically, antiballistic missile (ABM) deployments could provide a final recourse (at present, only around Moscow). Such a system has been suggested, an Accidental Launch Protection System (ALPS). But the most sensible, economical, and stabilizing measure would be the installation in operational missiles of command-destruct mechanisms permitting the destruction of missiles by the country from which they had been launched. Test missiles have such devices, which are used when a missile flies off course or otherwise malfunctions.

The United States has not deployed a command-destruct system. There are tenuous indications that the Soviet Union may have done so. Most intriguing was an unofficial statement attributed to Deputy Foreign Minister Viktor Karpov, who reportedly stated in 1989 that the Soviet Union had installed command-destruct devices in accordance with Article 2 of the Accident Measures Agreement of 1971. Under that provision, the parties have undertaken in case of, for example, an accidental nuclear missile launching to "immediately make every effort to take necessary measures to render harmless or destroy such weapon without its causing damage."[15] The United States has not considered that obligation to require us to install a command-destruct system. Whether or not the Soviet Union has done so, it would be highly desirable for both countries to do so. This could be achieved without degrading operational readiness of the missile forces, and it would add significant protection against accidental or unauthorized missile launchings.[16]

15. See Raymond L. Garthoff, "The Accidents Measures Agreement," in John Borawski, ed., *Avoiding War in the Nuclear Age: Confidence-Building Measures for Crisis Stability* (Boulder, Colo.: Westview Press, 1986), p. 63.

16. This proposal has been advanced by a number of analysts; for further discussion and a similar recommendation, see Bruce G. Blair, *The Logic of Accidental Nuclear War* (Brookings, forthcoming). For a less explicit Soviet recommendation for joint attention to this problem, see the remarks of Andrei Kokoshin in testimony before the House Armed Services Committee on March 10, 1989, *Gorbachev's Force Reductions and the Restructuring of Soviet Forces*, Hearings before the Defense Policy Panel of the House Committee on Armed Services, 101 Cong. 1 sess. (Government Printing Office, 1989), p. 35.

Global Order and Security

The most significant prospect, if also the most ambitious and difficult to realize, is the vision of an emerging new global security order. A new understanding of the very concept of security has been evident ever since Gorbachev's address to the Twenty-seventh Party Congress in early 1986. This remarkable change in thinking by the new leadership of the Soviet Union cannot alone bring about the kinds of change envisaged. But such changes could not develop without it. "New thinking" is also needed in the United States. And there are increasingly many other relevant actors on the world stage who must come to participate. Most important of course are the underlying realities on which Soviet, American, and other concepts of security must be based. Growing global interdependence in many spheres—economic, ecological, cultural, and political, as well as military—reflects new interrelationships and requires new arrangements.

Gorbachev's vision of a "comprehensive system of international security" appears utopian, but if it is seen as a goal and the realization as a long process of building on existing foundations, it may not be unrealistic. Indeed, it may be more realistic than attempts to reshuffle long-familiar concepts and institutions designed to provide security in a world now passed.

We can have no objection to the effort to develop political, economic, and humanitarian as well as military dimensions of security. Indeed, Gorbachev has now articulated and advocated many ideas long championed in the West. To the extent we believe they should be modified or supplemented, we should advance our own ideas.

It is not the purpose of this discussion to attempt to elaborate the shape or scope of a global security order, but to note the unparalleled opportunity for collaboration in working toward one.

Preventing war remains a bedrock objective of all sane people. We also need ways of strengthening peace. Nuclear deterrence is likely to remain an element in efforts to prevent war, and should be made more stable. But it should not be confused with the objective. Deterrence is a means of preventing war; it is not a means of regulating political disputes. Even as a means of preventing war, it is clearly not fail-safe. It therefore cannot be the solution for the indefinite future. The Soviets recognize that truth, and so should we.

Index